TREACHERY AND DIPLOMACY

TREACHERY AND DIPLOMACY

THE SHADOW POLITICS OF US–AFRICA RELATIONS

SOBUKWE ODINGA

Columbia University Press
New York

Columbia University Press
Publishers Since 1893
New York   Chichester, West Sussex
cup.columbia.edu

Cataloging-in-Publication data is available from the Library of Congress
ISBN 9780231202688 (hardback)
ISBN 9780231202695 (trade paperback)
ISBN 9780231554664 (epub)
ISBN 9780231566391 (web PDF)

LCCN 2025051006

Cover design: Elliott S. Cairns
Cover image: US Ambassador to Liberia W. Beverly Carter Jr. and President of Liberia William Tolbert Jr. (center), "Commissioning New Coast Guard Vessels," July 22, 1976 (Box 4, Liberia, Photographs 1976–1979, W. Beverly Carter Papers, Manuscript Division, Library of Congress, Washington, DC).

GPSR Authorized Representative: Easy Access System Europe, Mustamäe tee 50, 10621 Tallinn, Estonia, gpsr.requests@easproject.com

FOR ELIZABETH B. MOYE
I PROMISED AN ADVENTURE

CONTENTS

ACKNOWLEDGMENTS

I would like to express my immense appreciation and admiration for my mentors: Irving Leonard Markovitz, the late Kwame Akonor, Edmond Keller, Donald Robotham, Robert Vitalis, Manthia Diawara, Leonard N. Moore, and Harry Mokeba. If I were to detail their myriad acts of kindness and words of wisdom, these acknowledgments would be longer than the text itself. Likewise, I am indebted to Peter James Hudson, Seth Markle, Anthony Johnson, Alden Young, and Paul Mangura, who read countless drafts of this monograph. My gratitude for their insights and friendship is boundless. Those who have encountered the works of this group of scholars surely recognize how fortunate I was to benefit from their guidance. Their ethics, political convictions, and good humor have been just as inspiring. Any flaws in this text are the result of my shortcomings rather than their assistance.

Many thanks as well to the staff and archivists who granted me access to the African Union Archives in Addis Ababa, Ethiopia; the Republic of Uganda Ministry of Foreign Affairs in Kampala, Uganda; the W. Beverly Carter Papers at the Library of Congress Manuscript Division in Washington, DC, the CIA Records Search Tool (CREST) at NARA II in College Park, Maryland; the Ronald V. Dellums Congressional Papers at the African American Museum and Library in Oakland, California; the Donald M. Payne Papers at Seton Hall University; the Ralph J. Bunche

Papers at the Charles E. Young Research Library at UCLA; and the New York Public Library's Schomburg Center for Research in Black Culture. I am also grateful to the numerous diplomats, security officials, journalists, politicians, and political activists who agreed to sit for interviews as I conducted my research.

Invaluable funding for this project came from the University of Pennsylvania Provost's Postdoctoral Fellowship, the UCLA Society of Hellman Fellows, UCLA's Ralph J. Bunche Center for African American Studies, UCLA's African Studies Center, The City University of New York (CUNY) Graduate Center's Ralph Bunche Institute for International Studies, and the CUNY Graduate Center's Institute for Research on the African Diaspora in the Americas and the Caribbean.

During my graduate studies I was also fortunate to have the support of remarkable professors from whom I learned so very much about the ideals and practices of great educators. Special thanks to Alyson Cole, Herman Bennett, Susan Woodward, Ruth O'Brien, John Harbeson, Quincy Troupe, Tricia Rose, Anthony Browne, George Andreopoulos, the late Jerry Watts, and the late Ngũgĩ wa Thiong'o. I would also like to express my immense gratitude to Christina Greer, Lorrie Frasure, Zachariah Mampilly, and Jemima Pierre, near-peer mentors whose intellect and ethics are incomparable.

My colleagues at UCLA have been incredibly warm, welcoming, and thoughtful. It has been a rare privilege to work with Ugo Edu, Scot Brown, Justin Dunnavant, Bryonn Bain, Kyle Mays, Terence Keel, Celia Lacayo, Marcus Hunter, Robin Kelley, Cheryl Keyes, Walter Allen, Dominic Taylor, Brenda Stevenson, Eboni Shaw, Shamara Wyllie Alhassan, Keston Perry, Arturo Díaz, Ellen Scott, Harold Torrence, Hannah Appel, Andrew Apter, Michael Lofchie, and Claudia Mitchell-Kernan. I also owe a debt of gratitude to Samar Al-Bulushi, Brittany Meché, Miles Tendi, and Damien Van Puyvelde, with whom I collaborated and exchanged ideas at conferences.

I simply cannot overstate my appreciation for Stephen Wesley, my editor at Columbia University Press, whose support for this project was unwavering and whose interest in my well-being was genuine and unfailing. I acknowledge Taylor & Francis for granting permission to use sections of my article in *Diplomacy & Statecraft*, "The Privileged Friendship: Reassessing the Central Intelligence Agency Operation at Zaire's Kamina Airbase" (2018), which appear in chapter 3 of this book.

On a personal note, I would like to extend my eternal gratitude to my parents, Kamau Odinga and Dr. Tamanika Odinga. Everything that is principled, compassionate, and intellectually rigorous about me is a testament to your love, guidance, and endless patience. To call you the best parents in the world would be an understatement. It is truly an honor to be your son, and this book would have been impossible to complete without you. To my sisters, Thea Fields, Aisha Sanford, and Nneka Odinga, who protected me and championed my dreams with vigor beyond belief, I love you more than words can express.

To my grandmothers, Carmen Leshmore Fortune and Sadie Bell Fields, for whom no sacrifice was too great—models of dignity and eloquence despite life's daily perils—I will forever cherish every memory, prayer, meal, and insight that you shared along the way.

To my aunts, Karen Manning, Lavenia McGee, Gertrude Belt, Claudette Rowe, the late, great Marion Neely, and cousin Betty Parker; elder cousins, Mary Ellen Hebron, Shirley Blackston, Delores Randall, Catherine Willett, Maureen Woods, Annette Tyson, Patsy Munroe, and Lena Augustus—thanks for accepting me just as I am and embracing me with warmth and empathy that know no bounds. The same is true for my great aunts, Emma Louise Blackston, Bessie G. Hall, Catherine Mai Robinson, Majorie Bascombe, Merle Henry, Pearl "Tantie Minnie" Roberts, and Rosalind "Aunt Rose" Wilkinson, whom I cannot thank enough.

Thanks to my nephews, Nassir Holden, Robert Davis, and Christopher Fields, and nieces Anthea Fields and Eboni Fields. I am sure greatness lies ahead for you all. Likewise, this project would never have gotten off the ground without the support of my cousins, Cross Robinson, Walter Belt Jr., Kenney Manning Jr., Kevin Manning, Kimo Manning, Rhonda Shabazz, La'Kesha Manning, La'Shelle Manning, Tahnee Fields, Trista Fields, and Arlin Willet.

I also owe a huge debt of gratitude to my St. Charles Parish family. To my godmother Janice Guss, my "big brother" Michel (Mike) Bolden, my first teachers Alfred and Katie Green, Elder Albert and Mrs. Mable

Charles, Eulice and Carolyn Garrett, Percy and Barbara Wilson, Herbert and Audrey Taylor, and to Ida Martin, Leola White, Charles and Eula Robinson, Katherine Robinson, Sandra Morris, Karen Tejada, Donnie and MaryAnn Hills, and Rhonda LeBeauf—thanks for embracing my family with boundless generosity and for teaching me so many formative lessons.

I am also extraordinarily grateful to have had a remarkable group of friends that kept me hopeful and grounded and never failed to offer counsel and shelter when storms loomed. Infinite thanks to Brandon Garrett, Carlos Dupaty, Courtney Smalley, Ted Sammons, Michael Meyers, Javon Tate, Brandon Cooley, Jamal Johnson, Dan Rousseve, Erik Blackwell, Michael Thomas, Ishua Credit, Komi Hassan, Naimah Jabali-Nash, Naadu Blankson Seck, George Morris, Dr. Lester Efebo Wilkinson, Khary Polk, Hillina Seife, Christopher Winks, Mike Miller, Larissa Laskowski, Lillian Marsh, Walker Lee, Lorraine T. Dean, Christina Walker, Aaron Shapiro, Joshua Sperber, Elizabeth Nelson, Elizabeth Eisenberg, Chris Michael, Alan Koenig, Jonathan Keller, Erika Iverson, Rafael and Ina Martinez, Jawn Anthony Bramble, Margaret Turner, Suzanna Reiss, Njoroge Njoroge, Keenan Davis, and Thomas Davis.

Finally, I could not have made it down this path without my wife, Dr. Elizabeth Moye. You are a true humanitarian, my best friend, and the love of my life. You've invested just as much into this project as I have, and I will never forget it. To our son and daughter, Nia and Kam, I will always love you. I hope that one day you both will read this and it will make you proud.

TREACHERY AND DIPLOMACY

INTRODUCTION

This book pierces the veil of diplomacy shrouding US–Africa security partnerships. It is a history of discord and contentious bargaining between the United States and its African allies. Across the twentieth and twenty-first centuries, I document the considerable influence African governments often wield in their security relations with Washington. From the Horn of Africa to the Gulf of Guinea, governments have granted the United States military access to their territories and dispatched their troops to advance US strategic objectives. I illustrate the ways that Ethiopia, Liberia, Zaire (now D.R.C.), and Uganda reaped the rewards of these initiatives and pressured the United States into supporting their domestic and regional ambitions. The aim is to reveal the overlooked agency and guile of African leaders as they spurred Washington to back them in regional disputes, increase aid to their governments, and downplay criticisms of their domestic policies.

This is not, however, simply a story of competing interests among allies around the rewards and burdens of coalition operations and military basing agreements. I argue that the African security partners of the United States have confronted American policymakers who are often convinced not only of these partners' political subordinance but also of their racial inferiority. As such, *Treachery and Diplomacy* accounts for the workings of American racial thought in US security policy toward

Africa. More important, it lays bare the ways that Pan-Africanism and Black transnationalism have shaped the responses of African and African American leaders to US alliances in Africa. This international nexus of racial allegiances has both bolstered and threatened US–Africa security partnerships.

When I took to the field to research this project, I had little choice but to notice the salience of racial politics. In dozens of interviews, African and American diplomats, politicians, and defense officials spoke candidly about questions of race in the context of US-Africa security relations. Race loomed large at the African Union when a senior official in the Peace and Security Department dropped his technocratic pose to whisper condemnations of Western racism and laud the "Pan-Africanism of W.E.B. Du Bois, George Padmore, and Kwame Nkrumah."[1] It was there when a white US diplomat, who held posts throughout Africa, told me I would be "naïve" to believe that race was not a powerful force in US policy toward the continent.[2] This idea was roundly echoed in Kampala by Ugandan officials who did not hesitate to denounce Western narratives of white supremacy. One Ugandan general who worked closely with US forces was unsparing: "The US never learns. They didn't learn in Vietnam. They didn't learn in Iraq. They didn't learn in Afghanistan. And they haven't learned in Africa."[3] Racial politics even surfaced when a retired Black CIA agent spoke of Washington sending him to Pretoria as an intelligence liaison, in the immediate wake of apartheid, with hopes that his race would make him more palatable to South Africa's newly appointed Black intelligence personnel.[4]

Put plainly, what I encountered, time and time again, were shifting currents of racial difference and racial solidarity shaping interactions between US and African officials. Taking a cue from the pioneering works of Rayford Logan and Merze Tate, *Treachery and Diplomacy* does not argue that these currents supersede the dictates of realpolitik as they influence US-Africa security relations. But it does contend that ideas around racial difference and racial solidarity serve as an accelerant, an intensifying force, for key trends and tensions within these relations.

Despite the persistence of security partnerships as defining features of US–Africa relations, scant attention has been paid to the gambits

African governments have relied on to take advantage of them. Instead, the African allies of the United States have been framed largely as clients, pawns, or desperate recipients of the hegemon's largesse. It is often acknowledged that their security cooperation comes at some cost to Washington, but the details of how African governments go about extracting this cost are widely overlooked. By contrast, this book chronicles a range of disputes within US–Africa security partnerships. Along the way, it traces a variegated landscape of African influence, from the courtly protests of early US security allies such as Ethiopia and Liberia to the more confrontational bargaining of later allies such as Zaire and Uganda.

Similarly, *Treachery and Diplomacy* documents the consequences for US–Africa security partnerships of moments of accord, apathy, and antipathy between African leaders aligned with Washington and African Americans officials, activists, and intellectuals. In doing so, it illustrates the ways that African and African American leaders put to work ideas around Pan-Africanism and Black transnationalism in the context of US–Africa security politics. It is worth cautioning at the outset that the priorities of the authoritarian African governments in question are not to be confused with those of the citizens whom they claim to represent. Nor should it be assumed that the foreign policy stances of paternalistic African American political elites align neatly with those of their constituents. The resulting tensions, in both instances, form an undercurrent throughout the text and prompt us to look beneath the lofty aims that African and American officials often publicly assign to security partnerships. Only then can we discern the consequences of these partnerships for peace and democracy in Africa.

PLAN OF THE BOOK

The first chapter lays out the book's analytical framework. I argue for a view of US–Africa security partnerships as bargaining processes rather than hierarchical institutions. I then offer a historical and ideological profile of statist Pan-Africanism, the progenitors of which were Liberia and Ethiopia. Later, Zaire's Mobutu Sese Seko and Uganda's Yoweri Museveni would also oversee statist Pan-African regimes. This vein of Pan-Africanism often aimed to mask the authoritarianism and expansionism of African governments with the emancipatory ideals of Black solidarity. It was also a means for African leaders to publicly assert their autonomy from the West while maintaining intimate and profitable security partnerships with Washington. Leaders who managed to thread this needle, such as Ethiopia's Haile Selassie and Liberia's William Tubman, often benefited from the support of the African American foreign policy elite.

During the late nineteenth and twentieth centuries, African American activists, intellectuals, and government officials who championed US security partnerships with states such as Ethiopia and Liberia were guided by what I deem Black moderate transnationalism. Pioneers of this political tradition include the jurist D. Augustus Straker, a young W.E.B. Du Bois, newspaper publisher Carl Murphy, and Congressmen William L. Dawson and Adam Clayton Powell Jr. Black moderates often fiercely opposed racism in US foreign policy while defending the sovereignty of African governments and encouraging them to adopt liberal economic policies. In the course of doing so, many moderates supported US economic and military aid to Liberia and Ethiopia. To keep this aid flowing, they called attention to the ways that US access to military bases in both states served American interests. This vein of advocacy often led Black moderate elites to endorse the militarization of US policy toward Africa and champion authoritarian African governments. Chapter 1 concludes with an account of the ways that American racism, Black moderate transnationalism, and statist Pan-Africanism shaped US–Ethiopia security relations in the wake of World War II.

Chapter 2 offers an extended treatment of similar dynamics in the context of US relations with Liberia throughout the twentieth century. It traces the efforts of successive Liberian administrations to capitalize on their country's security partnership with Washington. The Tubman and Tolbert administrations benefited primarily from a US desire to maintain access to Liberia's airfield, port, and, later, communication facilities. This is largely a story of cautious Liberian diplomacy that powerfully served the interest of Liberia's often abusive, ruling elite. African American moderates ranging from Executive Secretary Walter White of the NAACP to Ambassador W. Beverly Carter Jr. often strongly backed Monrovia's efforts to leverage its security cooperation with Washington.

The historical ties between Liberians and African Americans allow for a stark portrait of the dilemmas of Black moderate transnationalism. An amalgam of sentimentality, class allegiances, and global race-consciousness often led luminaries such as W.E.B. Du Bois and Mary McLeod Bethune to support the Liberian government at the expense of democratic reforms that may have served the Liberian people. This was a dilemma that would dog African American leaders who championed the African security partners of the United States during the twentieth century. There were moments, however, when the African American foreign policy elite was repulsed by the abuses of Washington's African security partners and their opportunistic ties to white reactionaries in America and Africa. Such was the case in the 1980s when African American leaders began to criticize the Reagan administration's security cooperation with the Samuel Doe regime in Liberia and the Mobutu Sese Seko government in Zaire.

Chapter 3 turns to contentious bargaining between the United States and Zaire over CIA access to southern Zaire's Kamina air base. During the Reagan and George H. W. Bush administrations, the CIA used Kamina as a transshipment point for weapons that were being funneled to Jonas Savimbi's National Union for the Total Independence of Angola insurgents. Zaire's president, Mobutu Sese Seko, routinely reminded US officials of Kamina's strategic importance and the risks Zaire incurred because of his covert assistance to the CIA. American officials took seriously Mobutu's periodic threats to deny the CIA access to Kamina and responded promptly with aid increases when he did so in 1990.

In the context of this diplomatic wrangling, I underscore a tide of support for the Kamina operation that strengthened Mobutu's hand. This tide was fueled by American conservatives whose apologias for white minority rule in Southern Africa resonated with their nostalgia for an earlier era of American segregation. Confronting these forces was a cadre of Black congressional officials who opposed Reagan and Bush's ties with Mobutu, Jonas Savimbi, and the South African government. The determined efforts of members of Congress such as Ron Dellums and John Conyers served as a powerful check against Mobutu's influence in Washington and helped to bring an end to the CIA operation at Kamina.

Chapter 4 traverses the 1990s and charts the emergence of the Clinton administration's counterterrorism agenda in Africa. In the middle of the decade, the administration turned to Uganda and Ethiopia for military support in confronting Islamist extremism in Sudan and Somalia. However, the United States was loathe to admit that security objectives, rather than economic or humanitarian initiatives, were guiding its agenda in Africa. As such, the Clinton administration obscured its expanding strategic ties with Uganda and Ethiopia by crafting and popularizing a discourse around a "new breed" of African leaders.[5] According to Clinton officials, the most promising members of the new breed were Uganda's Yoweri Museveni and Ethiopia's Meles Zenawi. The United States insisted that these new breed leaders were poised to usher in an "African renaissance," despite their bellicosity and halting democratic reforms.[6]

Clinton's allies and appointees among the African American foreign policy elite played a pivotal role in advancing the new breed discourse. Some, such as Congressman Donald Payne and Reverend Jesse Jackson, appeared to genuinely hope that Museveni and Meles were harbingers of a new era of enlightened African leadership. Others, such as Assistant Secretary of State for African Affairs Susan Rice, would later admit that the new breed discourse was promoted primarily to serve US strategic interests.[7] Peace and democracy were, in fact, often tangential to Museveni's and Meles's domestic and regional agendas. Nevertheless, these leaders were adept bargainers, and they routinely cornered Clinton into supporting their policies in exchange for their contributions to security partnerships with the United States. This dynamic would intensify after the declaration of the US War on Terror in 2001.

It is in the context of the War on Terror that chapter 5 assesses Uganda's waxing and waning influence. Using Uganda's intervention in

Somalia as a vector of analysis, it documents Museveni's record of compelling successive US administrations to back his often militaristic agenda. As one of Washington's key security allies in Africa, Uganda's intervention in Somalia was launched with the full support of the United States. The intervention was primarily a Ugandan and US coalition operation to neutralize insurgents in Somalia, despite being billed as an African Union peacekeeping mission. Chapter 5 underscores the centrality of Museveni's statist Pan-Africanism in this endeavor, his calculated invocations of Black solidarity, and the consequences of US support for the Ugandan president's ambitions.

1

THE MAKING OF US-AFRICA SECURITY RELATIONS

American Racial Thought and the African Quest for Influence

When it came to Africa, US Secretary of State Henry Kissinger was appalled by the paucity of criminal ingenuity among his colleagues.[1] In early 1976 Congress cut the funding for the Ford administration's covert military aid program for "anticommunist" fighters in Angola amid fears that the United States was poised to enter another costly conflict less than a year after the Vietnam War.[2] Under this constraint, administration officials labored to get the remainder of the clandestine program's authorized aid into the hands of Jonas Savimbi's National Union for the Total Independence of Angola (UNITA). No less important, in nearby Zaire, President Mobutu Sese Seko needed to be compensated for allowing his country to serve as a transshipment point for the US operation and forwarding American arms to the Angolan fighters since the prior summer.

In March 1976 Secretary Kissinger, Director of Intelligence George H. W. Bush, and Secretary of Defense Donald Rumsfeld met with US National Security Council (NSC) officials to devise a plan. Kissinger was warned that if a commercial aircraft were chartered to quietly make the final weapons shipments, it might first have to land in Liberia and submit a bill of lading that revealed its cargo and destination. The Liberians, in turn, might block the shipments. "I know that we are most moral—to a degree not rivaled by anyone in history," the secretary of state scoffed, "but to tell me that the US would declare in a bill of lading that we were delivering arms to Zaire! Now really!"[3]

Liberia's Tolbert administration might have refused to release the last of the US weapons because it had recently recognized the Popular Movement for the Liberation of Angola (MPLA) as the legitimate government of Angola. It had done so, against the protests of US diplomats, in deference to the Organization of African Unity's consensus.[4] Aiding in the American scheme to arm Angolan combatants who were fighting the MPLA would be an act of duplicity. Were it publicly revealed, this would deal a blow to Tolbert's attempts to bill himself as a champion of African peace and solidarity.

It was also apparent by the mid-1970s that the Liberians would be backing a moribund cause. The MPLA, with the help of Cuban troops, had largely routed Savimbi's UNITA and Roberto Holden's National Liberation Front of Angola (FNLA).[5] Liberia's foreign minister made it clear to his American counterparts that his government had to "face the realities" on the ground in Angola or "look foolish" in the eyes of other African leaders.[6] Though Savimbi and Holden were in retreat, Kissinger remained determined to reward Mobutu, if no one else, for funneling US weapons to Angola. The prospect of Liberia refusing to help—refusing to bend to Washington's will—could be a "monumental problem." For Kissinger, smuggling the final arms shipments through Liberia's Roberts Field Airport with a bogus bill of lading was an option that had to remain on the table. The Secretary was emphatic: "I just can't accept that we are cowed by a small African nation like Liberia."[7]

Kissinger's bombast aside, the United States chose not to test Liberia's resolve. American weapons did not transit Roberts Field as the Ford administration scrambled to end its foray into Angola's civil conflict. Much of the US matériel that was already on the ground in Africa was ultimately transferred to Mobutu, rather than Savimbi, to allay the Zairian leader's mounting discontent with Washington.[8] The decision to appease Mobutu while avoiding Roberts Field offers a glimpse of just how lightly the United States had to tread, at times, in relations with even its closest African allies. This tentativeness belies common portrayals of the United States as a Cold War patron, brandishing foreign aid and doling out orders to reliably loyal African clients.

Guided by this insight, this chapter establishes *Treachery and Diplomacy*'s historical and theoretical footing in the context of US relations with its oldest African security allies. The cautious, early to mid-twentieth-century diplomacy of Liberia and Ethiopia serves as a point of departure and a contrast to the more assertive bargaining of states such as Zaire and Uganda that would later gain standing as US security partners. Both cautious and assertive strategies offered avenues of influence in Washington and intersected closely with America's racial politics. To cast light on this dynamic, I begin by underscoring the ways that Ethiopia and Liberia navigated currents of racism in US foreign policy that accommodated not only the persistence of white-minority rule in Africa but also a host of European threats to their sovereignty. It was in this context that many liberal African American leaders sought to shore up Ethiopia and Liberia by highlighting the importance of US security partnerships with these states, despite the often repressive practices of their governments. The goal was to challenge Western racism in the interest of African progress, but in practice this often meant supporting the militarization of US policy toward the continent.[9]

THEORIZING AFRICAN INFLUENCE: US-AFRICA SECURITY PARTNERSHIPS AS BARGAINING PROCESSES

The scope of US strategic interests in Liberia during the mid-twentieth century was unrivaled anywhere else in Africa. During World War II the United States built and garrisoned Roberts Field air base in the small African state while breaking ground on a port facility, both of which the US military maintained the right to access during the Cold War. By the mid-1970s, Liberia also hosted the largest US Embassy in Africa, a Voice of America radio relay station, a US diplomatic and intelligence communications facility, and a Coast Guard OMEGA navigation station.[10] A Central Intelligence Agency (CIA) memo was succinct: These assets offered "considerable strategic value."[11] The same could be said for Kagnew Station, a telecommunications and intelligence listening base that the United States maintained in Ethiopia from the 1940s to the 1970s.

These facilities were at the heart of US security partnerships with Liberia and Ethiopia. While the term "security partnerships" gained prominence in the 1990s, the outlines of these relationships have been discernable in US–Africa relations since the Cold War's earliest days. Security partnerships often lack explicit security guarantees and are rarely governed by comprehensive, bilateral defense agreements. Instead, they are institutionalized through sustained security cooperation, stable channels of communication, and the rapport and institutional memory of allied officials. Memoranda of understanding and improvised agreements often set the terms for arms transfers, intelligence sharing, coalition military operations, military training assistance programs, and access to shared military facilities. These partnerships, despite their grounding in ostensibly shared security interests such as anticommunism or counterterrorism, have been more informal, in practice, than traditional military alliances.[12]

During the Cold War, military basing agreements were at the center of the most important security partnerships that the United States had with independent African states. Toward the end of the conflict and into the twenty-first century, intelligence liaisons and coalition operations began to figure more heavily in these relationships. Fourteen Sub-Saharan African states, ranging from Somalia to Burkina Faso, established security partnerships with the United States throughout the twentieth and twenty-first centuries.[13] This process began in the early 1950s when the Liberian and Ethiopian governments signed defense agreements with Washington.[14] At the time, they were the only Sub-Saharan African states beyond the European colonial ambit. Despite the ballast of these formal agreements, the broader terms of US security relations with Liberia and Ethiopia were often fluid. Washington placed far greater value on defense pacts with its Western allies, while Africa held a shifting, often marginal status in the eyes of US strategic planners.

Playing host to Washington's African outposts was rarely as rewarding as the Liberians and Ethiopians hoped. Beneath the surface, relations between the United States and these allies were often tense. The Barclay, Tubman, and Tolbert administrations in Liberia and Selassie's monarchy in Ethiopia—regimes that protected US access rights to African facilities—were often dissatisfied with the foreign aid that they received from Washington. In fact, the regimes that overthrew Tolbert and Selassie were rewarded with sharp, if short-lived, increases in US aid.[15] When Ethiopia's Coordinating Committee of the Armed Forces, Police, and Territorial Army seized power from Selassie in 1974 and Master Sergeant Samuel Doe unseated Tolbert in 1980, Washington feared that the new governments might threaten US access to long-held strategic assets. These fears were realized in Ethiopia when the Marxist military government forced the United States to abandon Kagnew Station in 1977.

US facilities in Liberia and Ethiopia clearly held "asset specificity."[16] Kagnew Station and Liberia's port, airfield, and communication stations offered the United States unique strategic benefits. It would be costly to find viable, alternative sites for these facilities. But asset specificity is both temporally and geographically contextual, and a facility's value is often determined by the extent to which it can serve US interests at specific moments in conflicts. The value of the strategic assets that African states possessed rose and fell with shifts in US military priorities and US technological advancements throughout the Cold War and the War on Terror. Hence, as the twentieth century progressed, US access to airfields in Zaire and Uganda, for example, came to be more prized than access to Roberts Field. Tellingly, in the late-1990s, when the United States began to intensify its counterterrorism initiatives on the continent, it was only a modest exaggeration for one French official to call Uganda "the aircraft carrier of central Africa."[17]

The vagaries of mid-twentieth-century US military planning reinforced Liberia and Ethiopia's general aversion to hard bargaining with US administrations. Throughout his reign, Emperor Selassie maintained a largely pro-American bent and sought US help to face threats from neighboring states and irredentist movements in the Horn of Africa. The Liberians often took a "congenial" and "technocratic" approach to negotiations with Washington, emphasizing their unique historical ties with the United States and haggling over the minutiae of security and economic agreements.[18] Only occasionally did Ethiopian and Liberian diplomats question the broader terms of their government's security relations with Washington. By contrast, President Mobutu of Zaire and President Museveni of Uganda would show far less restraint. In the early 1980s, when Liberia's Tolbert administration criticized the amount of aid it was receiving from Washington, an internal US National Security Council memo conceded: "We are getting a pretty good deal." The memo noted that "for virtually no rent (and with $7/8 million or so in aid)," the United States maintained access to Roberts Field and its other strategic assets in Liberia—assets that it would be "hard pressed" to replicate elsewhere in Africa.[19]

While their partnerships with the United States rarely lived up to expectations, Liberia and Ethiopia were by no means bereft of influence in these relationships, a reality made apparent in Kissinger's still-born designs to smuggle weapons through Roberts Field airport. Taken as a whole, influence is not only a matter of what African governments do, but also a matter of what US officials anticipate they may do. It is discernable when US officials pursue or forgo initiatives because of their perceptions of the goals and potential responses of African allies. In this sense, as one recent definition suggests, influence is "the achievement of (a part of) an actor's goal in political decision-making, which is either caused by one's own intervention or by the decision maker's anticipation."[20]

For states like Liberia and Ethiopia, with strategic assets of fluctuating value in Washington, this type of influence helped to get the United States "more in line" with their domestic and regional aims.[21] It has been salient when US officials have improvised policy initiatives in Africa under sharp time constraints while assessing the willingness of African allies to cooperate with these plans. Such moments of hasty policy improvisation are not anomalous. They are instead a recurring indication of the traditionally marginal interests of the United States in Africa and an associated dearth of long-term policy planning. Especially after the Cold War, this improvisational approach to US policymaking opened the door to a host of more direct and confrontational interventions by African governments in search of influence in their security relations with Washington. Such interventions include instances in which African governments have broken the terms of their agreements with Washington and suddenly pulled their troops from coalition operations with the United States or denied US forces access to their airspace or military facilities.

With these historical realities in mind, I contend that US–Africa security partnerships are best appraised as bargaining processes rather than rigidly hierarchal institutions. It is through this lens that the influence of those that the United States once deemed its "black-African moderate" allies can be assessed.[22] It should go without saying that for the purposes of this analysis, "moderate" does not carry a normative charge. Washington's assessments of moderation among African governments were colored by the extent to which these governments supported US goals rather than, for example, their approaches to electoral politics or freedom of expression. It can hardly be argued that during the Cold War states such as Liberia, Ethiopia, and Zaire maintained moderate commitments to broad political participation.

My assessment of African influence builds on political scientist Moses Tesi's theorizing around the "art of negotiating or bargaining" among states.[23] Tesi's scholarship documents the ways that postindependence Cameroon stood up to France during political disputes, undeterred by economic dependence on its former colonizer. Tesi notes that "the literature has tended to emphasize bargaining output, i.e., the 'what' and 'why' questions and not the 'how' question. But output is just as dependent upon what takes place in the bargaining process as it is on the major country's power."[24] He directs our attention to *how* governments bargain as well as the asymmetries between them.

Treachery and Diplomacy applies this logic to the diplomatic ploys and gambits, the sanctions and comprises, the pleasantries and tough talk that characterize US–Africa security partnerships. It also takes in the political networks, at home and abroad, that African governments rely on to derive influence from their security partnerships with Washington. Such influence can lead to immediate rewards, such as US military aid, but it is more than simply a fulcrum for extracting short-term concessions. Influence is also a means for African governments to shape the broader terms and direction of relations with the United States while pursuing their own domestic and regional goals.

Tesi's ideas correspond with more recent theorizing around compliance or postagreement bargaining. Most contemporary studies within this paradigm focus on disputes between governments over the terms and obligations of signed, carefully negotiated economic accords. Signatories share a commitment to maintaining these accords but often disagree about the details of compliance, execution, and costs. I contend that postagreement bargaining analysis has purchase in the bloodier, more informal context of US–Africa security partnerships. In this regard, Jönsson and Tallberg's framework is instructive.[25] It accounts for bargaining as a process characterized by both enforcement and management and shaped by contingency and human agency. This is well suited to US–Africa security partnerships, a world where direct sanctions among allies are rare and diplomatic jousting abounds. In this milieu, historical and geopolitical context weigh heavily, as does the timing and judgment of diplomats and security officials.

Jönsson and Tallberg note that the "international compliance game rests not only on rational calculations but typically involves intercultural aspects as well."[26] Fittingly, racial politics form a rarely noted undercurrent in the research on US policy implementation that serves as a referent for Jönsson and Tallberg's framework. Pressman and Wildavsky's *Implementation*, for example, is an analysis of struggles among US federal bureaucrats, corporate interests, municipal officials, and citizens that doomed a 1960–1970s economic development program in Oakland, California. The authors admit that they "load the dice" by assuming that all of these players want the program to succeed to varying degrees. Even with loaded dice, Pressman and Wildavsky cannot help but note the racist lens through which corporate interests viewed the Oakland community, the belief among US officials that Black bureaucrats would fare better in Oakland, the vigor of organized Black political networks, and a broader history of American racism and Black rebellion. I take seriously the authors' suggestion that the fraught bargaining processes inherent in the implementation of US domestic programs find parallels in US foreign policy initiatives.[27] In doing so, I bring to light a similar set of racial dynamics in US–Africa security relations.

RACE AND GLOBAL SOUTH DIPLOMACY

As early as the 1940s Howard University historian Rayford Logan began to call explicit attention to the salience of racial politics in diplomacy and bargaining between Black-governed states and Western powers.[28] Logan hewed closely to the classical realist line and resisted an impulse to grant racism undue influence in relations between Western powers and states throughout Africa and the Caribbean.[29] Racism was present and persistent but not always central. Racial politics served more as an accelerant for trends in relations between the West and the Global South than a pervasive catalyst. Logan saw the "the nexus between race relations in the United States and America's African policies" as more "taut" in some historical moments than in others.[30] This nexus nonetheless always bore a potential to influence US officials and to shape the foreign policies that they pursued. However, as a careful scholar of diplomacy, Logan also documented the efforts of Global South states to exceed their standing within international hierarchies.

This dynamic is rendered clearly in his account of the Harrison administration's failed effort to establish a US coaling and naval station at Haiti's Mole Saint Nicolas in 1891. "Haiti Thwarts the United States" was Logan's distillation of the contentious bargaining between the Black republic and the soon-to-be superpower.[31] Logan's tableau is familiar to any student of African politics. The historian noted Haiti's debt burden, border tensions, and internal political cleavages, as well as the meddling, coercion, and strategic designs of Germany, France, and the United States.

Though the brutal US occupation of Haiti lay just beyond the twentieth century's horizon, Logan underscored the "consummate skill" of the Haitian government as it bargained with the United States over the fate of the strategically valuable Mole St. Nicolas.[32] Not only did he trace Haiti's attempts to "be meticulously correct in its negotiations," Logan highlighted the influence of America's racial politics in its geostrategic diplomacy.[33] According to the historian, the Harrison administration's aversion to direct aggression in pursuit of the naval base was colored by the president's racial paternalism toward African Americans. Harrison's restraint was also grounded in a more practical desire to win Black votes at home—a desire that likely played a role in his decision to appoint Frederick Douglass as US minister to Haiti during the doomed negotiations.[34]

Logan drew parallels between the dilemmas and diplomatic strategies of the leaders of independent Haiti and those of Africa states.[35] Much like the Haitian leaders that he studied so closely, African leaders could be buffeted by domestic power struggles while also displaying perspicacity as they bargained with foreign powers.[36] I appraise African executives through a similar lens—not as pawns, but as political actors with discernable if circumscribed autonomy. A similar perspective is notable in Brenda Gayle Plummer's magisterial account of Haiti's early twentieth-century diplomacy.[37] Plummer, who interviewed Logan for her study, builds on and transcends his insights, enriching her analysis with Black Marxist theory and a focus on Haiti's multilateral foreign policy.

Plummer notes Haiti's vulnerability within an international hierarchy underpinned by racism, imperialism, and gunboat diplomacy. But she also underscores, the "artful dodging and feinting" of Haitian diplomacy, Haitian officials' "skillful and subtle orchestration" of hostility to foreigners and at the same time "their effusive official professions of amity and cooperation." This "talent for dissimulation" bewildered great powers and made it difficult for them to discern the true substance of threats emerging from the island.[38] In the coming pages, I document the resonance between this repertoire of government action and the bargaining tactics that African governments have mobilized in their security "cooperation" with Western powers.

As a bargaining process, security cooperation offers a forum for weaker states to amass influence, but we overlook the resourcefulness and diplomatic acumen of these states' officials at our peril. Though various factors in the relations between states—such as Zaire offering the CIA an airfield—can be identified as potential sources of bargaining influence, the ways that these factors are put to use in negotiations are pivotal. Charles Lockhart aptly notes, "What makes these factors sources of bargaining influence is resourcefulness that sees and develops a connection between a source of influence and a problem and applies the one to the other."[39] Resourcefulness, then, is a matter of "ingenuity" in policymaking, which is no mean feat for African states whose potential sources of influence are often circumscribed and whose militaries often stand to benefit from external aid.[40] Lockhart also argues that resourcefulness can require policymakers to appeal to constituencies that can help them to achieve their ends. As he puts it, "resourcefulness includes a practical political component that in some instances reduces to salesmanship."[41]

To keep their bargaining chips on the table—to keep airfields functional or maintain reliable streams of covert intelligence—African leaders have had to placate constituencies within their own polities, quite often cadres of security officials. But African leaders have also sought the support of American constituencies, within and beyond the US administrations in power. During and after World War II, for example, President Edwin Barclay of Liberia and Emperor Haile Selassie of Ethiopia sought allies within the US State and Defense Departments in an effort to ensure that their government's benefited from US military operations at facilities in their countries. At the same time, the Liberian and Ethiopian governments sought the backing of African American political elites, including Minister to Liberia Lester Walton, Representatives Adam Clayton Powell Jr. and William Dawson, President Mordecai Johnson of Howard University, and a host of journalists and intellectuals. Looking back on this moment, a State Department memo highlighted an African American interest in Liberia on which the West African state "used to count heavily."[42] This stands to reason. Liberia was settled in the 1820s by formerly enslaved African Americans and their patrons in American Colonization Society. Ethiopian efforts to woo African Americans began in earnest on the eve of World War II when the country was invaded by Italy.[43]

It is in such relationships between African leaders and the African American foreign policy elite that we begin to see the significance of Black transnationalism for US–Africa security politics. My efforts to throw this dynamic into relief owe a debt to Pearl T. Robinson's "Afrocentric" analytical framework, which assesses the international alignments and solidarities that African leaders cultivate in pursuit of regime security.[44] Conceptualized in 1984, Robinson's Afrocentric framework predates more widely heralded theories of omni-balancing and extraversion.[45] The Afrocentric approach was developed to examine fraught security ties between "black African" states and states often considered members of the Arab world, such as Libya and Morocco.[46] Central to Robinson's analysis is a history of tenuous, opportunistic Afro-Arab solidarity among governing elites.

In her assessments of the alignments that governments in Niger and Chad established with Arab states, Robinson foregrounds internal threats to their rule or regime security that motivated their foreign policy decisions. She then accounts for the fragmented nature of foreign policymaking across issue areas and elite coalitions. In this often disjointed context, the Afrocentric framework never loses sight of the historical and cultural dynamics that both buttressed and disrupted security alignments between African governments interested in maintaining power and Arab states pursuing their own interests. For these African governments, Robinson writes: "The ideological, political, and economic facets of Afro-Arab solidarity are integral to a broadly defined notion of regime security; but they are made operational as discrete spheres of activity with narrowly conceived policy objectives—often with contradictory implications."[47]

The Afrocentric approach accounts for both interests and ideology, the competing priorities of African leaders in the face of internal and external threats, and processes of "conflict and accommodation" between African leaders and elite coalitions among their allies. This approach has helped to hone the focus of this book on the ways that African leaders turn to Pan-African ideas and networks as they "plot alliance strategies and cast about for resources."[48]

STATIST PAN-AFRICANISM AND AMERICAN STRATEGIC INTERESTS

Since Pan-Africanism's early twentieth-century theorization by figures such as Henry Sylvester Williams and W.E.B Du Bois, it has been marked by a host of varied, often competing intellectual and cultural tendencies. Its most persistent, if pluralistically conceived, foci have been anti-imperialism, antiracism, the unification of Africa and its diasporas, and affective solidarity among people of African descent.[49] These concerns have animated a panoply of everyday artistic expression as well as movements for civil and human rights, but the heads of African governments have been highly selective in embracing these precepts.

This became apparent in the second half of the twentieth century as African nationalist movements gave rise to newly independent African states and Pan-Africanism's center of gravity shifted from the African diaspora to the African continent.[50] African leaders with disparate governing philosophies and geopolitical allegiances faced unique domestic challenges and were called on to negotiate the concrete political and economic stakes of Pan-Africanism. This period is associated with the emergence of a statist Pan-Africanism among African governments that was often marked by elitism, pragmatism, and an authoritarianism that existed in tension with the humanist and liberatory ideals of cultural and social movement Pan-Africanism.[51]

In particular, the second wave of postindependence African leaders, ranging from Uganda's Idi Amin to Kenya's Daniel arap Moi, sought to harness the cultural appeal of Pan-Africanism to advance their narrow interests, whether remaining in power, pushing through economic reforms, or expanding their regional influence.[52] Single-party governments often aimed to dictate the domestic and global priorities of the African masses. Though this was largely a top-down project, it was not everywhere a matter of elite opportunism. Pan-African leaders such as Tanzania's Julius Nyerere expressed genuine revulsion to "racialism" across the globe and made tangible sacrifices in support of numerous African liberation movements.[53]

Statist Pan-Africanism ranged from President Kwame Nkrumah's vision in Ghana for the full unification of Africa to President William Tubman's commitment in Liberia to economic liberalism and trim multilateral institutions that preserved state sovereignty.[54] Liberia and Ethiopia were standard-bearers of a moderate, statist Pan-Africanism in the era of African decolonization as well as its progenitors throughout the early twentieth century. In this sense, they laid a template for US security allies in Africa that later would gain standing, including Zaire and Uganda. Governments that embraced this Pan-African paradigm often welcomed security partnerships with the United States that served their initiatives at home and regional agendas. In return, they negotiated for US aid, silence, or political backing.

To strengthen these partnerships, statist Pan-African leaders often established ties with the African American political elite. When executives such as President Tubman of Liberia and, later, President Yoweri Museveni of Uganda courted African American officials, intellectuals, and activists, their central objective was regime security. They were determined to use political networks, at home and abroad, to drum up the economic and political backing they needed to keep their governments in power. They also looked to these networks to cultivate their images as influential actors on the world stage. These priorities often fostered a fluid and transactional approach to antiracism and international Black solidarity on the part of statist Pan-Africanists. This became clear in the latter half of the twentieth century as close US allies such as Zaire's Mobutu and Uganda's Museveni enlisted the support of both African American politicians and white conservative interests.[55]

On the other side of the ledger, Washington's efforts to harness Pan-Africanism in support of its geopolitical aims have a long history. This history is marked primarily by public celebrations of African multilateralism and behind-the-scenes skepticism toward the "mystical" ideas and "ideological illusion" US policymakers often attributed to Pan-Africanism.[56] As the handwritten notes of the US government's first deputy assistant secretary of state for African affairs reveal, the aim has largely been to "ride African unity."[57]

In the run-up to the 1963 founding of the Organization of African Unity, many US officials believed that Pan-Africanism across the continent "could be impeded or even reversed by US intervention." When this proved unsuccessful, the Kennedy and Johnson administrations applauded the OAU's potential while quietly encouraging moderate allies in the Monrovia Group, particularly President Tubman and Emperor Selassie, to "push responsible and realistic points of view." These leaders were meant to serve as a check against the vocally anti-imperialist, leftist leaders of Casablanca Group states such as Ghana, Guinea, and Egypt. Throughout the Cold War, the "responsible and realistic points of view" that Washington supported largely aimed to guide Pan-Africanism toward a focus on collaborations in liberal economic development while guiding it away from communism and racial solidarity that might stoke opposition to US domestic and foreign policies.[58]

In this context, most "moderate" African leaders who were aligned with the United States saw their ties with African American elites as currency that fluctuated in value and had to be amassed cautiously for it to properly serve their domestic interests and international agendas. This was, of course, a matter of call and response. Many African American leaders were also cautious, and well aware that among US security allies in Africa, the pursuit of regime security was often brutally at odds with democratic policies and human rights. At the same time, they perceived enduring currents of racism in American and European policies toward Africa. For many, this perception justified their support for moderate African leaders with suspect commitments to peace and democracy.

Due to this book's interest in the relationships between statist Pan-African leaders and the African American foreign policy elite, it does not examine US security relations with European colonial governments or white-minority-ruled regimes that held power in Africa. In fact, African Americans often perceived relations between the United States and these governments as the hallmark of a shared commitment to white supremacy. In this regard and many others, they assessed the landscape of US–Africa relations through the prism of racial politics. This perspective likewise influenced their support for or skepticism toward the leaders of independent African states as well as their views on governance and development across the continent. The ways that this perspective influenced African American foreign policy elites as they intervened in the politics of US–Africa security relations, guided by their own class and ideological commitments, have largely escaped scrutiny.

AFRICAN AMERICAN POLITICAL ELITES AND US-AFRICA POLICY

The "moderate" African leaders at the heart of this study are the heads of African governments. The thornier question is who can be deemed a member of the African American foreign policy elite. Sizing up this cadre is a matter of some complexity. There is, after all, scant consensus on the composition and defining attributes of the broader, multiracial US foreign policy elite.[59] There should be little dispute, however, that African American intellectuals and social movement leaders ought to be accorded prominence alongside a more recent wave of government officials in any rendering of the African American foreign policy elite that spans the twentieth century. This standing is the result of a history of racism that once barred African Americans from official political power—a legacy of exclusion that was acute in US foreign policy circles.[60] In light of this history, *Treachery and Diplomacy* foregrounds three broad, porous categories of African Americans who have substantively influenced US Africa policy or public views around it: intellectuals, activists, and government officials. The porousness in these categories finds a ready parallel in the revolving door that shuttles the broader American political elite through the corridors of universities, media outlets, and government agencies.

From their perches as media and academic elites, the African American intellectuals who appear in this text have had little power to formulate US policy toward Africa. A determination to bring public pressure to bear on US policymakers has often compelled these elites to operate as both intellectuals and activists. W.E.B. Du Bois, for example, thrived as a prolific analyst of African history and politics as well as a leading civil rights and international peace activist. Despite their distance from the levers of policy, the attempts of intellectuals to influence public perspectives on US–Africa relations have been thoroughly documented.[61] The editors and journalists of African American newspapers were pivotal in this regard for much of the twentieth century.

Starting in the 1990s, however, this dynamic was undermined as many African American periodicals were shuttered while internet media achieved dominance. In academia, during this same moment, attacks against Afrocentrism and essentialist Pan-African thought called into question the very terms on which many African Americans had long identified with Africa. Both the clarity and the excesses of these critiques came at a cost. A growing preoccupation with Black hybridity untethered from concrete questions of statecraft and political economy threatened the vitality of an older tradition of African American scholarship on Africa's international relations.[62] This tradition was pioneered by the likes of Du Bois, Rayford Logan, Eslanda Cardozo Goode Robeson, and W. Alphaeus Hunton.[63] It had, however, been facing headwinds since the 1950s as African Studies programs beholden to US Cold War imperatives gained stature in American universities.[64] Hence, when Washington expanded military financing and training programs for its African allies at the turn of the twenty-first century, a tradition of African American scholarship that scrutinized the motives and consequences of US foreign policy in Africa was in sharp decline.

As for activists, groups ranging from the NAACP to the African Liberation Support Committee worked ardently to influence African American views on Africa's relations with the West.[65] But as a number of political scientists have noted, the final quarter of the twentieth century marked a decline in the influence of the traditional African American activist or "protest elite."[66] The titles of works chronicling this decay leave little to the imagination: *We Have No Leaders*, *Revolutionaries to Race Leaders*, *The Jesse Jackson Phenomenon*.[67] Much of this research traces the implications of Black gains in electoral politics for Black political progress and Black elite claims to racial leadership. Front and center are tensions between traditional activist elites and a rising tide of Black government officials—tensions that were intensified by the attempts of both groups to cloak their discrete interests in the rhetoric of racial solidarity.

The smallest group of elites, Black government officials, includes members of Congress, State and Defense Department officials, state and city politicians with national prominence, a US vice president, and a US president. Obviously, members of the Black official elite have disparate levels of power in foreign policymaking and various international priorities. Yet each has an institutional base within the US government from which to assert his or her views and some capacity to influence the execution of foreign policy or the allocation of resources in pursuit of policy goals.[68] The ideas and priorities of these officials have at times gained unique significance in US policy toward Africa, in large measure because Africa policy has often been marginal in US foreign affairs.

Also notable is that for much of the twentieth century, Black government officials who received diplomatic appointments often first gained prominence as media elites. Lester A. Walton, for example, US minister to Liberia from 1935 to 1946, first built his reputation as a newspaper editor and journalist.[69] Much the same can be said for W. Beverly Carter Jr., who was publisher of the *Pittsburgh Courier* before being appointed US deputy assistant secretary of state for African affairs in 1969 and serving as US ambassador to Tanzania and Liberia during the 1970s.[70]

Walton was a Democratic Party apparatchik appointed by the Roosevelt administration, and Carter was a Republican stalwart who became a diplomat during the Nixon and Ford administrations. Nearly three decades separated their diplomatic tours in Liberia, but their views on African governance and US–Africa security relations share much in common. Moreover, these men's perspectives parallel many of Du Bois's ideas during the early years of his political life. Indeed, though the African American foreign policy elite has largely comprised liberals, it has been guided by a mélange of Black liberal and Black conservative beliefs that have coalesced to form a global perspective that I deem Black moderate transnationalism. Black moderate transnationalism predates the formal theorization of Pan-Africanism in the early twentieth century and would underpin African American support for US security partners in Africa throughout the Cold War and the War on Terror. This global perspective has a long and complex history that is intertwined with the landscape of domestic African American political ideologies. The salient features of this ideological terrain, as such, warrant a brief review.

A FRAUGHT TRANSNATIONALISM: AFRICAN SOVEREIGNTY AND AFRICAN AMERICAN POLITICAL IDEOLOGIES

As Michael Dawson's research illustrates, Black liberalism is an integrationist political ideology that opposes American racism yet holds firm in the view that America can live up to the ideals of equality enshrined in its founding documents.[71] Black liberals often endorse political inclusion and gradual reforms achieved through protest and political persuasion. Walton, for example, largely limited his criticisms of American racial hierarchy to the ways that middle-class African Americans were demeaned in the American press, underrepresented in government, and confronted with the indignities of Jim Crow. He coveted the approval of philanthropists and the Democratic Party establishment. Accordingly, he argued that African Americans should prioritize propriety and achievement so as to "emancipate" white people from a belief in Black inferiority.[72] This thinking informed his global outlook and espoused hopes that Liberia would forge itself into a model of Black self-government on a continent dominated by European powers. Well into the 1940s, Du Bois had a similar vision for the West African state and was deeply invested in it achieving economic gains to fortify its government's writ.[73] This held true even as Du Bois largely abandoned liberalism and "lost faith in the capitalistic system."[74]

African American liberals who have not "lost faith" à la Du Bois are often critical of capitalism's most rapacious abuses but nonetheless believe that it can meaningfully serve Black interests at home and abroad.[75] Traditionally, Black conservative hosannas for free market economics have been far louder than those of Black liberals, as have their protests against US legislation aimed at redressing historical injustices and engendering racial equality. Yet in practice the boundaries between Black liberalism and Black conservatism are sometimes indistinct.[76] Both ideologies attribute a unique brilliance to America's founding ethos, take a favorable view of capitalism, and traditionally assign Black men a leading role in campaigns of racial uplift. This ideological harmony has been particularly resonant when African American leaders cast their gaze to Africa's shores. Indeed, the liberal Walton and the conservative Carter both implored their African counterparts to embrace a commitment to global capitalist commerce.[77]

Black moderate transnationalism has long evinced a faith in liberal economic policies as a pivotal means for African states to empower themselves and preserve their autonomy. This first applied to Liberia and Ethiopia and later to the African governments that emerged from the mid-twentieth-century wave of decolonization. In 1859 the abolitionist William Whipper offered an eloquent expression of this vision for Africa: "I would collect the resources of her productive industry, and extract the gold from her thousand mountains, and pile them up in every port, until the pedestal of her commerce should attract the attention of the world, to which every nation under heaven should pay tribute."[78]

A focus on stoking transatlantic commerce and entrepreneurialism can be traced to some of the earliest attempts of African Americans to reestablish ties with Africa. It appears across the ideological spectrum throughout the eighteenth and nineteenth centuries, in the emigrationist designs of Black nationalists such as Paul Cuffee and Martin Delany as well as the spirited appeals of moderates such as Whipper and David Augustus Straker.[79] This impulse, however, was more intrinsic to the calculations of Black moderates.

The critical concern for nationalists has always been "various degrees" of separation from white America.[80] Indeed, this guiding concern has led Black nationalism to be commonly associated with radicalism and served to contrast it with moderate ideologies such as Black liberalism and Black conservatism. A similar radicalism would later be attributed to the Black Marxist thought of figures such as George Padmore, who viewed capitalism primarily as an irredeemable system of exploitation.[81]

Both Black nationalists and Black Marxists have called for a fundamental reordering of social relations, often on a global scale[82].

Unlike proponents of moderate Black ideologies, nationalists and Marxists do not renounce violence as a means of defending Black interests or pursuing political change. However, the legitimacy of violent resistance is not an ideological pillar of Black radicalism. Throughout the course of American history, despite the fiery rhetoric of figures ranging from David Walker to Kwame Ture (née Stokely Carmichael), Black radical acts of political violence have been rare. Nevertheless, Black radicals have often rejected the liberal discourse of nonviolence when confronted with American racial terror. As a result, they have been more closely associated with militarism than adherents of Black moderate ideologies. The support that Black moderate elites have offered America's African security allies calls this characterization into question.

David Augustus Straker's late nineteenth-century theories offer an early signpost of the propensity for Black moderate transnationalism to embrace militarization in US policy toward Africa as well as authoritarianism in African governance. Born in Barbados in 1842, Straker graduated from Howard Law School in 1871, was elected to the South Carolina legislature in 1876, and was unseated amid the collapse of Reconstruction the next year. Straker would leave the South a decade later and go on to achieve renown as an attorney and civil rights leader in Michigan.[83] Counting himself among the "sons and daughters of Africa," he attended the 1st Pan-African Conference in London alongside better-known contemporaries such as Henry Sylvester Williams, W.E.B. Du Bois, and Anna Julia Cooper.[84]

In January 1886 Straker published a series of articles in *The New York Freeman* celebrating the Berlin Conference's potential to usher civilization, Christianity, and commerce into Africa. With these articles, Straker presages the outlines of a discourse that prioritizes security and law enforcement in Africa as a prerequisite for development and prosperity. "Africa is our father's land," he wrote: "We must enter Africa with the Anglo-Saxon and build it up and thus make joint title at least to its future greatness and prosperity."[85] Yet Straker noted that because Africa was "barbarous," its indigenous rulers lacked the "vital enforcing power" to coerce their subjects to respect laws that protected individual rights.[86] As such, Western powers needed to teach Africa how to "promote wealth by protecting life and property."[87] In Straker's view, no country was better suited for this task than the United States because of its remarkable progress in overcoming racism by cleaving to its founding ideals.

While Straker was hashing out these theories, the first Black US envoys to Liberia, J. Mylton Turner and his successor John H. Smythe, were working toward their realization. In 1871 Turner was appointed US minister resident and consul general to Liberia by the Ulysses S. Grant administration. Smythe was appointed to the position in 1878 by President Rutherford B. Hayes. Both Turner and Smythe thought that Liberia, with US assistance and benevolence, had the potential to serve as a powerful symbol of Black industriousness and self-determination. Both appealed to Washington to help the ruling Americo-Liberians suppress uprisings from indigenous African groups they were attempting to subjugate, such as the Kru and Grebo peoples. Turner and Smyth did so, much like twentieth-century Black moderates, despite their persistent concerns around the exploitative, antidemocratic practices of Liberia's rulers.[88]

As Khary Polk's pioneering research demonstrates, Major Charles Young would take matters a step further.[89] Young graduated from West Point in 1889 and was widely heralded by fellow African Americans.[90] In 1912 the Taft administration appointed him US military attaché to Liberia. His remit was to gather intelligence and expand US economic and political influence in Liberia, much as he had as US military attaché to Haiti during the prior decade. In this sense, as Polk suggests, Young would distinguish himself as "the leading African American military imperialist in Africa."[91] But Young also genuinely yearned to uplift and bind together people of African descent worldwide. He saw his time in Liberia as an opportunity to advance this transnational agenda and promote the country as a beacon of black self-governance. During two tours in West Africa, Young marveled at Liberia's vast, untapped potential for industrial and agricultural prosperity—prosperity that might benefit enterprising Blacks in Africa and the Americas.[92] Liberia, as such, had to be protected from encroachments on its sovereignty by European powers as well as local African uprisings.

Young was often troubled by the disdain and brutality with which the Americo-Liberian government treated indigenous West Africans. He nonetheless threw himself into the task of advising and training the country's military and commanding Liberian troops as they quashed indigenous rebellions.[93] Young's exploits and those of other African Americans who fought with the Liberian Frontier Force were celebrated by many leading African Americans. The NAACP's *Crisis Magazine* hailed the achievements of men such as Dr. Wilson Ballard, one of Young's subordinates, who received a medal from President Howard of Liberia in 1916 for "bravery in the action against the Krus, a tribe that had never before been subjugated by the Liberians."[94] The magazine likewise informed "young colored men of education, military training, and physical fitness" that to secure appointments in the Frontier Force, they simply needed to write to Major Charles Young.[95]

The rapacity of European colonialism in Africa at the turn of the twentieth century placed many African American leaders in a bind. They believed that the rulers of Ethiopia and Liberia, imperiled bastions of Black sovereignty, deserved the military might to protect their territories from European powers. If this same military might buoyed the expansionist and antidemocratic initiatives of Ethiopian and Liberian rulers who sought to maintain power, this too was viewed by many African Americans as a sign of strength.[96] As Black moderates were demanding greater democratic inclusion in the United States, they often stood behind African rulers who denied vast swaths of their "native" populations similar opportunities. To champion Emperors Menelik and Selassie in Ethiopia was to countenance the subordination of the Oromo, Afar, and Somali. To support Presidents Howard, King, and Barclay in Liberia was to stomach the suppression and displacement of the Kru, Grebo, and Bassa.

While admiration for the Liberian government existed across the African American political spectrum during the nineteenth century, from the outset of the twentieth century the Liberian government drew the lion's share of its African American support from liberal elites rather than radical nationalists or Marxists. These liberals did not advocate emigration to Liberia, but they often defended its government as a loadstar of Black self-rule and supported efforts to expand its military. Marcus Garvey, the twentieth century's preeminent Black nationalist, only briefly embraced the Liberian government in the early 1920s, notwithstanding his concerns about its repressive practices. Garvey sought the C.D.B. King administration's authorization to establish a settlement in Liberia that might help to fulfill his vision of mass Black emigration to Africa.[97] When the King administration rejected the plan, Garvey denounced Liberia's elites for exploiting the country's indigenous population and enriching themselves.[98] While they rejected Garveyism, leading Black Marxists such as Harry Haywood and George Padmore also pilloried Liberia's rulers as tools of Western capitalism throughout the 1920s.[99]

Padmore softened his criticisms of the Liberian government in the mid-1930s after he broke with Communist Party and fully embraced Pan-Africanism. The Trinidadian radical wrote to Du Bois that he considered it a duty to save Liberia, the "black baby," from the "white wolves" of imperialism.[100] At the time, Du Bois was both a leading Pan-Africanist and a Black liberal intellectual, and, like many of his fellow travelers, he was an advocate for the Liberian government. He had, in fact, attended King's inauguration in 1924 as an official US delegate. He also initially supported Liberia's deal with the Firestone Corporation in 1926. That year, Harvey Firestone Sr. collaborated with US officials to pressure the cash-strapped Liberian government into leasing his company a million-acre concession for a rubber plantation. Du Bois vainly hoped that African American managers would be hired to oversee the rubber plantation and help direct its proceeds toward the country's development.[101] Instead, the Firestone Corporation soon dominated Liberia's rubber economy and labor politics, often with the backing of the US State Department. As historian D. Elwood Dunn notes, between 1926 and 1977 Firestone's operations in Liberia earned the company roughly $410 million, and about one-fourth of these proceeds went to the Liberian government.[102]

Du Bois and much of the liberal African American intelligentsia viewed Liberia's rulers as flawed but creditable standard-bearers of Black independence plagued by the avarice of Western powers. As such, they backed the Liberian ruling class even as it deployed the Frontier Force to subjugate the indigenous African majority throughout the early twentieth century. In 1932 Du Bois criticized the Liberian government for the exploitative taxes and labor regime it imposed on the country's indigenous Africans. But in its defense, he noted: "The brutalities of the Frontier Force are brutalities practiced by soldiers everywhere—Americans in the Philippines, the English in Ireland, and the French, everywhere."[103] Apparently, these military excesses had a silver lining: "As for law and order," Du Bois quipped, "one is safer in Liberia than in New York."[104]

In the early 1950s, a far more radical Du Bois and his allies in the Council on African Affairs would detail the abuses of Liberia's government, but during the fall of 1932 the scholar saw little room for nuance in his defense of the West African state. Months earlier, following revelations that Liberia's rulers had profited from conscripting indigenous laborers and shipping them to work on plantations in nearby Fernando Po, the League of Nations had approved a Plan of Assistance for Liberia, and the Hoover administration proposed that the country's government submit to the direct guidance of American advisors. Both proposals posed a threat to Liberian sovereignty.[105]

Even after these proposals collapsed, Du Bois offered few public criticisms of the Liberian government, despite its efforts to maintain a repressive status quo. The scholar was aware of the influence that African governments could derive from cultivating American constituencies. As the editor of the NAACP's *Crisis Magazine*, Du Bois wrote to Liberia's president, Edwin Barclay, and encouraged him to submit an article intended to achieve precisely this aim.[106] Du Bois likewise maintained a friendly personal correspondence with Minister Walton, one of Firestone's strongest advocates. In letters to Walton, he expressed wariness about Firestone's rubber operations but hailed the progress of the Liberian government and reminded the minister of his cordial ties with Liberia's leaders.[107]

Throughout his nine-year tenure, Walton maintained a close friendship with Liberia's governing elite. He would, nonetheless, be consistently frustrated by the graft that marred Liberian politics and the government's inept attempts to cultivate economic development and domestic order. As a result, his views on Liberian autonomy were fluid and contradictory, much like his stances on American racism and Black solidarity. Some scholars contend that Walton was a "race man."[108] Others contend that he "represented no overall black consensus, or even constituency, on African affairs."[109] Walton hoped to see Liberia "preserve its sovereignty" and insisted that America lend a "helping hand." But "if the hand were not of iron in a silken glove," he wrote to the State Department, "any endeavor to accelerate Liberian advancement would end in failure."[110] Apparently, Walton wanted Liberia to assume a "more commanding and respected status among governments," but not commanding enough to ignore Washington's edicts.[111] This was not an uncommon point of view for moderate African American elites.

NAVIGATING "INTERNATIONAL JIM CROW": BLACK MODERATE TRANSNATIONALISM AND THE MILITARIZATION OF US-AFRICA RELATIONS

Scholars have sketched the parameters of moderate transnationalism, under many names and guises, among African American political elites in the first half of the twentieth century. With the exception of Khary Polk, few have placed an explicit focus on its interplay with American security politics.[112] Sundiata, for example, documents the backing that leaders such as Du Bois provided the Americo-Liberian ruling class despite its military excesses and antidemocratic ethos. He argues that this transnational perspective reflected a "simple Pan-Africanism" that was "unable to answer the conundrum posed by the Liberian situation," while "the movement's cosmopolitanism impeded its grasp of African realities."[113]

Cedric Robinson is more withering than Sundiata in his appraisal of "moderate" African American transnationalism from the dawn of the twentieth century to World War II. "The mediating leadership strata of the Black middle class," Robinson argues, was guided largely by "greed and self-deceptions" that bred "identifications with American imperialism at home and Black ruling class oligarchies abroad." According to Robinson, these impulses allowed for "the collusion of Black leaders with the Liberian elite's use of forced labor." Historically, they likewise shaped the initially tepid response of the NAACP executive board to the US invasion of Haiti in 1915 and intensified Black liberal animus toward Marcus Garvey's United Negro Improvement Association. Robinson argues that moderate Black leaders were "alienated" from ordinary, working-class Black people. This divide fueled a "deep resentment" among working-class Black folk that motivated them to take the lead in protesting Italy's invasion of Ethiopia in 1935 while pressuring moderate race "spokesmen" to follow suit.[114]

Jeffrey Stewart offers a more charitable appraisal of elite, African American transnationalism in the opening decades of the twentieth century. He identifies a "new negro foreign policy consciousness" in the ideas of Ralph Bunche and Alain Locke and points to a similar outlook among contemporary Black liberals, such as former US president Barack Obama. According to Stewart, New Negro foreign policy analysts called attention to the pernicious role of white supremacy as a shared justification for imperialism in Africa and racial segregation in the United States. However, he argues that because these thinkers were determined to be taken seriously by the US foreign policy establishment, they often took a restrained and tactical approach to criticizing American racism while downplaying "the naked racial violence" that underpinned imperialism in Africa.[115] I contend that they likewise downplayed the heavy-handed tactics that the leaders of Liberia and Ethiopia employed to maintain power over their "native" subjects.

"New Negro" thought nonetheless represented a break with many nineteenth-century African American foreign policy perspectives because it largely dispensed with a view of Africa as a primitive domain that would benefit from the civilizing influence of Western ideas. Stewart gives New Negro theorists credit for prioritizing the interests and aspirations of Africans and holding fast to a vision of a more equitable international community.[116] Similar views prevailed among the "Bourgeois Radicals" at the center of Carol Anderson's research. Anderson draws warranted attention to the midcentury anti-imperialist and antiracist agitation of figures such as the NAACP's Chairman Walter White and Executive Board Member Channing Tobias.[117] Though "Bourgeois Radicals" and "New Negroes" may have discarded the civilizing impulse that was notable in the theorizing of moderates such as David Augustus Straker, they did not abandon hopes of helping to imbue independent African governments with "vital enforcing power."[118] This military might was necessary for states such as Liberia and Ethiopia to assert their authority in the face of internal threats from restive "natives" and external threats from European imperialists.

While Stewart finds much to laud in the New Negro foreign policy perspective, like Robinson, he acknowledges the deep paternalism of this vein of transnationalism. It was a mindset of Black leaders who were confident that "they know what is best for the masses and masters."[119] Alvin Tillery also notes a running paternalism among African American political elites despite what he views as their largely successful effort to be "sincere brokers" of African American public opinion on Africa.[120] The Black legislators at the center of his analysis take a "strategic" approach to US–Africa relations.[121] For most of these politicians, Africa policy initiatives were intended to come at little or no cost to their Cold War bona fides or the economic concerns of their constituents.

Explicitly and implicitly, these renderings of African American elite transnationalism call attention to the ways that it emerged and often existed in harmony with a statist Pan-Africanism that aimed to profit from the US security agenda on the continent. Leaders such as Walter White and a young Du Bois were indeed firm antiracists and anti-imperialists. Yet they were preoccupied with government power and liberal economic development in independent African states as means to achieve greater parity in relations between Africa and the West. This often outstripped their concern for everyday Africans seeking political participation in states such as Liberia and Ethiopia. Except for the NAACP's brief opposition to the Ethiopian annexation of Eritrea on the heels of World War II, similar priorities would lead Black moderate elites to support African security allies of the United States for much of the twentieth century.[122]

As Walton's and Du Bois' views suggest, however, African American moderates did not all share the same transnational vision. At times there were clear fault lines between Black liberals and Black conservatives, such as the writer George Schuyler, who was unrestrained by a liberal antiracist ethos and fiercely criticized the Liberian government.[123] This was until Schuyler's dogged commitment to the US Cold War agenda and its system of alliances, which exceeded even that of his liberal rivals, made such criticisms inopportune.

There were also cleavages between moderate Black activists and intellectuals, on the one hand, and, moderate Black government officials, on the other. Black diplomats, in particular, were beholden to the aims of the administrations that appointed them and the agendas of their political parties. Ministerial appointments to Liberia were often a reward for this partisan loyalty, and a concession incoming administrations granted African American voters for their support. During the Cold War, Black diplomats and elected officials often framed Africa as a prize to be won in the US competition with the Soviet Union.[124] Moderate activists and intellectuals had more latitude to critique this Cold War calculus and to acknowledge the unique aims of US allies such as Liberia and Ethiopia. While both groups of Black moderates often supported US–Africa security partnerships, activists and intellectuals tended to be open to African states having greater influence within these partnerships.[125] What these Black elites shared was a desire to help seed economic growth in Africa and strengthen African governments in the name of order and stability across the continent. To achieve these aims, they often supported US military aid to African states even as it threatened potential democratic reforms.

At times, as Alvin Tillery illustrates, African American politicians who embraced African leaders allied with Washington used these ties to bolster their clout in debates around US foreign policy.[126] A number of Black legislators, including William H. Gray III and Mervyn Dymally, also sought the ear of African leaders to encourage development policies that might serve the economic interests of Africans and African Americans.[127] Moreover, due to the African American public's intermittent interest in US Africa policy, lawmakers such as Donald Payne and activists such as Jesse Jackson often had a free hand to bestow their blessings on African leaders who were US security allies. Congressman Charles Diggs of Michigan, for example, was among the earliest American legislators to assert the legitimacy of Mobutu Sese Seko's government in December 1965.[128]

There were instances in which the abuses of the US's African allies were so pronounced that some moderate African American leaders were compelled to raise objections. During Liberia's forced labor scandal in the 1930s, Carter G. Woodson, for example, denounced the West African state's leaders.[129] Later, in the late 1980s, Walter E. Fauntroy, the District of Columbia's delegate to Congress, led an effort to scrutinize the Reagan administration's support for Mohamed Siad Barre's repressive regime in Somalia.[130] Particularly as the twentieth century progressed, African American elites' censure and endorsement of the African security partners of the United States often punctuated long stretches of apathy toward the continent. There were historical moments when apathy was politically untenable. This was the case when Italy invaded Ethiopia in 1935, amid the tide of African decolonization in the 1960s, and at the height of the antiapartheid movement in the 1980s. In these moments, African American leaders were forced to respond to pressure from segments of the African American public that were mobilized around African issues.[131]

Despite the inconsistent interest that many prominent African American moderates directed toward the continent, their approval or disapproval of the African security allies of the United States had consequences. African American celebrations of "strong" African leaders among US allies often legitimized increases in US aid to these states and bolstered US security partnerships with them. Black legislators routinely supported security assistance packages for African leaders who were in their good graces.[132] These endorsements also served as a form of US soft power and were underscored in the latter half of the twentieth century by high-profile summits that brought together African and African American leaders.[133] Conversely, the censure of African American leaders often intensified public interrogations of Washington's bonds with its African security allies. At times, this undercut their influence within US–Africa security partnerships. In the 1980s a former director of Human Rights Watch observed that African leaders appeared to take the criticisms of African American lawmakers more seriously than those of their white counterparts. She opined that these criticisms could "not be dismissed as racism."[134]

Perhaps it should come as little surprise that an alloy of apathy, opportunism, and idealism was the basis for many African American politicians' engagements with their country's African security partners. Like most American politicians, they prioritized domestic issues and searched for political capital while attempting to shape and interpret the ideological appeals of their constituents. Widely overlooked, however, is the extent to which the transnational vision that Black moderate leaders held aloft was often a handmaiden for the militarization of US policy in Africa. In this sense, the militant posturing of Black radicals has been far more bloodless than the transnationalism of Black moderates.

Yet, it would do Black moderates a disservice to gloss over the enduring vein of racism in Western foreign relations to which they were responding. A desire to confront this racism may have constrained their criticisms of African security allies of the United States, but their concerns around its persistence were far from baseless. As early as 1915, in the "African Roots of War," Du Bois called attention to the Western capitalist and working classes' shared investment in white supremacy as a motive force for conflict and imperialism.[135] More recently, Errol Henderson has argued persuasively that international relations, a field pioneered by British and American diplomats, was itself underpinned from the outset by white supremacist ideas and "rationalized . . . slavery, imperial conquest, colonization, and genocide."[136] Robert Vitalis has made a similar case, unearthing the origins of the *Journal of Race Development*, known today as *Foreign Affairs*, and chronicling the efforts of figures such as Du Bois, Alain Locke, Rayford Logan, and Merze Tate to contest the early to mid-twentieth century's "white world order."[137]

Among these figures and the scholars who have followed in their footsteps, Tate's insights have perhaps received the least attention. As a pioneering security theorist, Tate offered a unique perspective on the play of realpolitik and racial politics in international relations. Few observers, however, would deem her a "race woman." Du Bois, as is well known, proclaimed: "The problem of the Twentieth century is the Color Line."[138] By contrast, Tate, reflecting her primary concerns, asserted: "The problem of the Twentieth century is not disarmament to assure peace but co-armament to maintain peace."[139] A "pert phrase" this is not.[140] Nevertheless, throughout Tate's analyses of arms control diplomacy, she often drew connections between Western militarism and imperialism, on one hand, and white supremacy, on the other.

In *The Disarmament Illusion*, Tate primarily frames the factors that undermined a century's worth of international arms control diplomacy before World War I in classical realist terms. She limns tensions between status quo and revisionist powers, the frailties of pacific public opinion, and a stark security dilemma among European states giving rise to the war itself. But to offer a comprehensive portrait of the forces that crippled disarmament bargaining, she looks beyond these factors alone. Tate highlights, for example, the role of Western imperialism in fueling competition for naval armaments meant to defend colonial possessions.[141] Du Bois would take her to task for not placing enough emphasis on imperialism, though even he hesitated to question the underlying rigor of her research.[142] Tate also points to the persistent, malignant influence of "the international armament ring" of weapons manufactures, broaching a subject that has yet to receive sufficient analysis in international relations scholarship.[143]

Most important, she drew a subtle connection between the "predatory habits of mind" that marked Western militarism and an intertwined commitment to white supremacy. While the structure of the international system would always open the door for arms competition, security dilemmas, and war, it was Western militarists who pushed their states across the threshold. Of particular significance for Tate among this "influential body" was Captain A. T. Mahan, a prominent scholar of Western sea power, and the American naval delegate to the indecisive First Hague Peace Conference in 1899. Tate suggests that Mahan was appointed to this role because of his skepticism toward arms control which was closely bound to his devotion to white supremacy.[144] Mahan held fast to the view that Blacks were "darkies" and "niggers."[145] As Tate notes, he was adamant that "all that European civilization has to depend upon for its supremacy is its energy, of which international competition and armament are not only the expressions, but essential elements. . . . When these fail and fall the end will be at hand." Mahan was in general agreement with President Theodore Roosevelt, who, according to Tate, shared the view "that sufficient naval and military force should be kept up to make the higher civilizations masters of the world."[146]

In short, security dilemmas alone did not foil arms control diplomacy; it was also undercut by a Western militarism steeped in notions of racial hierarchy. Interests and ideas, particularly ideas around race, are foundational to Tate's approach. We also see this in her second major work, *The United States and Armaments*. Tate notes that in the interwar years, "The determination of the dissatisfied or renovating states to expand endangered the peace of the world even more than did the imperialism of those powers of the nineteenth century which believed that expansion was the 'white man's burden,' the 'mission civilisatrice,' or manifest destiny."[147] Here, Tate's rendering of the nexus of racism and imperialism in the decades before World War I is explicit enough, one would imagine, to satisfy even Du Bois. On first glance, however, it appears that a realist logic crowds out any attention to race in Tate's explanation of the origins of World War II. But Tate's account of the factors that hastened Japan's path to war surveys more than simply the balance of power in the Pacific. In fact, Tate argues that the United States struck the first blow to diplomatic amity with Japan by instituting racist, debasing policies such as 1924's Immigration Act. It was a racism mirrored by the "British Commonwealth policy prohibiting immigration to Australia, New Zealand, and Canada to all but Caucasians."[148]

Tate's analyses of the dynamics intrinsic to war, diplomacy, and collective security prioritize classical realist considerations, but she refuses to ignore the salience of race. Indeed, it was precisely because Tate viewed World War II as a "militarist and imperialist struggle for freedom and power—power for some at the expense of others" that she foresaw the likelihood of a subsequent race war.[149] Of course, this did not happen. Nonetheless, in many other ways Tate, Du Bois, Logan, and a host of

Black moderates' views on the significance of race in international relations withstand scrutiny. The substance of their claims is discernable in a review of US–Ethiopia security relations and Emperor Haile Selassie's attempts to benefit from them in the immediate wake of World War II.

AN EMPEROR'S INFLUENCE: ETHIOPIA, KAGNEW STATION, AND US RACIAL PROPAGANDA

In May 1951, when Ethiopia's Kagnew Battalion arrived in Pusan, South Korea, the Truman White House hailed Emperor Haile Selassie as a guardian of collective security.[150] The Ethiopian battalion joining the US-led UN force was a beacon, Washington declared, in a maelstrom of communist aggression. Truman and Selassie cited the fight against North Korea as proof that the world had learned the costs of apathy during Italy's 1935 invasion of Ethiopia in the predawn carnage of World War II.[151]

A United States Information Service newsreel feted the gallantry of the Kagnew Battalion, showcasing the smart impression it made on crowds of cheering South Koreans as it disembarked from the USS *General J. H. McRae.* The newsreel captured the Ethiopian troops, drawn from Selassie's own imperial guard, shoulder to shoulder with beaming American advisors. These were not the sons of a "semi-barbaric nation"—as US military observers had long claimed—its military art "elementary," its fighting forces compromised by "racial and religious differences."[152] No, now the 1,158 Ethiopian troops "carried with them the wisdom and dignity of an ancient people" as they joined the Americans in the mountains of South Korea.[153] Here, before the world, stood a firm alliance bolstered by shared ideals facing a common threat. The diplomatic record reveals a more complex story.

While Selassie held some belief in the principle of collective security, his offer to send troops to Korea came amid Ethiopian attempts to press the United States into supporting its claim to Eritrea, which had been seized by the recently defeated Italians in 1885. Just as important, Selassie was determined to secure a steady stream of military assistance from Washington. In August 1950, the same week that the emperor announced his decision to send troops to Korea, he sent a memo to the US ambassador in Addis Ababa, prodding the United States to aid the Ethiopian military not only in the immediate conflict in Southeast Asia but also over the long term. The memo made a pointed case in view of Italy's 1949 inclusion in the North Atlantic Treaty Organization (NATO):

> Italy, who yesterday violated her obligations to the League of Nations and the principles of collective security and made a war of aggression against Ethiopia, and who today presents herself as another Italy, has received considerable military and economic assistance from America. . . . But Ethiopia, who has held constantly to the same principles in the past and present and who nevertheless was victim of aggression, has not received any such assistance in her military and economic recovery from aggression.[154]

Selassie noted that not only had formerly fascist Italy received more aid than Ethiopia from the United States, so too had a host of other states that balked at the prospect of sending troops to Korea. Many African Americans who had tenaciously opposed Italy's 1935 invasion of Ethiopia and had long viewed the African state as a touchstone of Black independence also perceived a double standard. Indeed, a deep identification with Ethiopia, as a citadel of African glory, sovereignty, and redemption, could be found among Black populations throughout the Americas, dating back to their earliest exposure to and reinterpretation of the Christian Bible.[155]

An editorial from the Associated Negro Press, "Ethiopia Gives, Doesn't Get," asserted that the "black republic" had not been duly rewarded in US aid for its commitment to the fight in Korea.[156] The United African Nationalist Movement and Greater New York Council of Black Nationalists, groups that coalesced in the wake of Marcus Garvey's United Negro Improvement Association, telegraphed President Truman with a request that the United States donate merchant vessels and battleships to Selassie's government as it deployed the Kagnew Battalion.[157] Interestingly, Garvey himself had condemned Selassie when the emperor fled Ethiopia during Italy's invasion and denounced the deeply stratified order that Selassie had overseen.[158] Nonetheless, African Americans, many of whom were also calling for the full desegregation of the US military during the Korean conflict, were not alone in underscoring the significance of race in US–Ethiopia relations at the time.

Weeks after the Kagnew Battalion arrived in Korea, the Truman administration dispatched Lt. General Charles L. Bolte to Addis Ababa to oversee negotiations with Selassie on the subject of US military aid. To prepare Bolte for his mission, the State Department put together a secret policy statement that noted "the great propaganda value . . . of a contingent of troops from an independent, colored nation in Africa, which would help to offset the Soviet claim that the Korean war is white imperialist aggression against the colored races of the world."[159] This perspective would maintain its salience as negotiations grew contentious over the next two years and Selassie struggled to overcome US reluctance to commit to a military defense assistance agreement with Ethiopia. In a 1953 memo to the Pentagon, the State Department again emphasized, "The presence in Korea of colored troops from an independent African country is of great value to us in the propaganda war as well as in the Korean war. On this basis alone, Ethiopia's request for arms assistance deserves sympathetic consideration."[160]

The Ethiopians were well aware of America's vulnerabilities around racial issues as well as its segregationist policies. Before the Kagnew Battalion set out for South Korea, Ethiopian General Mulugeta Buli informed the US military attaché in Addis Ababa of "his sincerest hope that his men would not encounter any racial discrimination, as they want to fight enemies and not allies."[161] Its soldiers in Korea, however, were only one tributary of influence for Addis Ababa as it bargained with Washington. Even more powerful was the leverage it derived from the Pentagon's determination to maintain access to Radio Marina. This high-frequency radio communications facility was located in Asmara, Eritrea, which in 1952 had been incorporated into Ethiopia as a federated territory. In fact, maintaining possession of Radio Marina was pivotal in the US decision to support Ethiopia's demands for Eritrea's incorporation.[162] The United States had taken over the telecommunications facility, a former Italian installation, from the British in 1942, and it quickly became a valuable relay station and signals intelligence collection node in Washington's Cold War communications network. Of similar, if secondary, importance to Washington was continued access to air and naval bases at Eritrea's Port of Massawa.

The Ethiopians aimed to take advantage of the strategic value the Americans assigned Radio Marina and were determined to avoid "one-sided concessions" in exchange for it. In a 1952 meeting with the US Army vice chief of staff, Minister of Foreign Affairs Aklilu Habte-Wold argued that if Ethiopia did not make a forceful case for its interests, it would appear weak, "and many European bees will want an equal right to sip the Ethiopian honey."[163] Aklilu, much like General Mulugeta, strongly resented midcentury American racism, once remarking while in New York, "if I am ever excluded—even once—from any restaurant here, I swear to you, I will leave this country immediately and never return."[164] According to an Ethiopian foreign policy advisor privy to the diplomatic wrangling around the US–Ethiopia defense agreement, at least one US military official "did not conceal his contempt for a negotiation with a small backward country such as Ethiopia," leaving Aklilu vowing, once again, to never return to the United States once an agreement was reached.[165]

In May 1953, with the fourth rotation of Ethiopia's "colored troops" fighting in Korea and Radio Marina backing its demands, Addis Ababa and Washington signed formal agreements on "Mutual Defense Assistance" and US "Utilization of Defense Installations Within Empire of Ethiopia."[166] The former was largely quid pro quo for the latter, which secured US access to Radio Marina and air and naval facilities at Massawa. But it was a more profitable quid, secured through a more contentious bargaining process, than many Truman officials envisioned. In the wake of these agreements, the United States renamed Radio Marina the Kagnew Station, after the Ethiopian battalion fighting in Korea. Over the next three years, Ethiopia would collect roughly $14 million in US military aid, primarily dedicated to training infantry divisions and supplying artillery, machine guns, and small arms.[167] Well into the 1970s, Ethiopia would receive the largest share of US military assistance to sub-Saharan Africa.[168] Yet this ostensibly tight-knit partnership was fraught from the very beginning.

State Department officials noted that by 1955 the US military assistance program for Ethiopia was in "a very bad way." Ties between US and Ethiopian military officials were "inadequate," US weapons deliveries were "haphazard," and military relations with the Ethiopians had "suffered severely."[169] Selassie's government routinely decried the quality and quantity of US munitions Ethiopia received in comparison to states that had been less supportive of Washington's aims.[170] When the Eisenhower administration resisted Selassie's requests for aid in expanding Ethiopia's navy and air force, Foreign Minister Aklilu fulminated, "Ethiopia must ask itself again, just what place does Ethiopia actually hold in the eyes of the US?"[171]

Selassie's officials impressed on their American counterparts the dangers they perceived from growing discontent within Eritrea and from neighboring Egypt and Somalia.[172] They stressed the risks Ethiopia took by playing host to a US listening station—risks they felt were being insufficiently rewarded. Powerful voices within the Ethiopian Foreign Ministry grew increasingly frustrated with US paternalism and dismissiveness.[173] But, as the *New York Times* reported, "what really rocked Washington was Ethiopia's decision to withdraw her final unit from Korea."[174] In 1955, despite protests from the Pentagon, the Ethiopians informed the floundering US military assistance group in Addis Ababa of their plans to withdraw the fourth rotation of the Kagnew Battalion, by that point patrolling the Korean demilitarized zone.[175]

When this tactic did not produce sufficient results, the Ethiopians pushed even harder. Disgruntled Ethiopian diplomats called for a more nonaligned tack in Addis Ababa's foreign relations, which the emperor tepidly pursued, accepting overtures from China, Czechoslovakia, and, at the end of the decade, the USSR.[176] This approach began to yield proceeds in the wake of the Suez Crisis as Eisenhower grew more concerned with the spread of communism and Arab nationalism in the Middle East, and US access to Ethiopian facilities became more valuable. Despite his general pro-American bent, Selassie made clear his disappointment with US military aid in meetings with US generals, Vice President Richard Nixon, and Ambassador Joseph Simonson, who found Ethiopia to be "more primitive" than he anticipated.[177] As the 1960s dawned, US operations at Kagnew expanded to facilitate communication among naval vessels newly armed with ballistic missiles. It was in this context that the Eisenhower administration became more responsive to Selassie's criticisms, and during the late 1950s and early 1960s US military aid to Ethiopia grew rapidly.[178]

To make amends for "past misunderstandings," Eisenhower authorized the sale and donation of aircraft and naval vessels to Ethiopia.[179] Smelling opportunity, Addis Ababa continued to press its demands for security assistance. The Ethiopians consistently reminded the Americans of the burdens Kagnew Station posed. The base did not go unnoticed. Indeed, in the run-up to the founding of the Organization of African Unity (OAU) in Addis Ababa in 1963, the United Arab Republic and radical pan-Africanist states of the Casablanca Group such as Ghana and Guinea called for the removal of the US listening station from Ethiopian territory.[180]

Selassie, of course, did no such thing. The advantages that Kagnew offered as the emperor spurred the United States to increase its military aid were far too great. US Pentagon and State Department records indicate that Kagnew consistently served as a "hostage to fortune," an effective means of "bargaining leverage," and a powerful source of influence for Ethiopia until 1977.[181] At that point, in the wake of Selassie's overthrow and assassination, Ethiopia's Marxist military government, known as the Derg, abrogated the 1953 US–Ethiopia mutual defense assistance agreement and ordered the Americans to abandon the installation. Kagnew Station's strategic significance had begun to decline in the late 1960s and 1970s amid advancements in US communications technology.[182] Nevertheless, in a failed attempt to keep the telecommunications facility and Ethiopia itself within the Western camp, Washington rapidly expanded US aid to Addis Ababa during the first two years of the Derg regime.

"SAVAGES" AND STATESMEN: THE COLOR LINE AND MIDCENTURY US-AFRICA SECURITY PARTNERSHIPS

From 1953 to 1975 the Ethiopian government negotiated roughly $280 million in US military aid, far more than any other African state.[183] Emperor Selassie used this aid to professionalize Ethiopia's army, a vital instrument in his autocratic order and his country's running conflicts with neighboring Somalia. Throughout Selassie's reign, as Edmond Keller suggests, he maintained "a strong commitment to royal absolutism while at the same time espousing modernization and economic development."[184]

Moderate African American leaders were aware of both facets of this dialectic but called attention to the latter while downplaying the former. Many expressed pride in the staying power of Ethiopia's Christian monarchy and firmly backed US aid to Selassie. Domestically, the emperor oversaw the introduction of Ethiopia's first constitution and the creation of nominally representative institutions, but these reforms did little to threaten his sweeping, traditional powers or those of Ethiopia's Amhara-Tigre aristocracy. Opposition political parties were prohibited. The emperor appointed Ethiopia's prime minister at his discretion. Dissent among students, intellectuals, and subordinate ethnic groups was often met with force.[185] Congressman Adam Clayton Powell Jr. chose to overlook these realities when he hosted Selassie in 1954 as the emperor received a rapturous welcome in Harlem. Powell was confident that the Ethiopian monarchy had embraced "the basic principles of democracy."[186] Later, Charles Diggs was far more fulsome in his praise of Selassie, the emperor's moderate Pan-Africanism, and US relations with Ethiopia. Diggs deemed Selassie "one of the great statesmen of our era" and noted that emperor had rightly earned the sobriquet the "Father of African Unity" due to his integral role in the OAU's founding.[187]

Much of the African American foreign policy elite was guided by a traditional reverence for Ethiopia and an appreciation for the country's reliable backing for Washington's security agenda. But their support for Selassie's autocratic reign and the US military aid that bolstered its viability stemmed from more than that alone. It was also a reaction to the racial animus that white US policymakers directed toward Ethiopia. While African Americans saw a storied and resilient polity in the Horn of Africa, many white policymakers saw a reflection of African barbarism and political ineptitude. Such views were notable among isolationist and arch-segregationist politicians.

For example, North Dakota's Senator William Langer and Congressman Usher Burdick (the former an independent, the latter a Republican) were notorious for their postwar isolationist convictions.[188] On the heels of Selassie's 1954 visit to the United States, Langer made a point of entering Burdick's denunciations of US aid to Ethiopia into the *Congressional Record*. Burdick's thinking was clearly animated by racism as well as isolationism. The congressman claimed that when Italy invaded Ethiopia before World War II, it found thriving slave markets overseen by Selassie himself. Burdick declared that the emperor's "antics indicated that that he was an absolute and ruthless dictator, who had all the barbarous instincts of a complete savage."[189] Reflecting a similar, less brazenly bigoted perspective, Congressman Brady Gentry, from Texas, also questioned "an alliance that obligates us to make a military power of the shoeless, nomadic tribes of Ethiopia."[190]

Even legislators whose proposals for US military aid to Africa reflected greater appreciation for multilateralism were loath to criticize European colonialists. Instead, they often saw the specter of racism emerging among African nationalists. In the early 1960s, Senator Mike Mansfield, a Democrat, argued that the United States should be sensitive to African leader's desire for independence and nonalignment. He proposed that the United States and the Soviet Union agree to stop searching for military bases in Africa and conduct their military aid programs for African states under UN auspices. The senator believed that such policies would serve the interests of Africans and also keep them from directing unreasonable ire at America and Europe. He argued that even though colonialism was in decline, its history and legacy often gave rise to "racism in Africans." He also contended that indigenous African societies had atrophied during colonialism and that the boundaries imposed on these societies when European colonialists carved up the continent would pose serious problems for Africa's new states. A handful of African nationalists would confront these challenges with little malice toward the West, but many others were likely to turn to aggression and a "pan-Africanism on the basis of a militant racism."[191]

Mansfield's views were downright progressive compared to those of some segregationist legislators who were at the heart of the US foreign aid appropriations process. Black journalists made no secret of the "jaundiced eye" with which Dixiecrat members of Congress viewed US security assistance to African states, and they attributed much of this skepticism to racism. Otto E. Passman, a Louisiana Democratic congressman and chair of the House Subcommittee on Foreign Operations Appropriations, was one of Congress's most outspoken opponents of US foreign aid in all its guises. That said, he held unique contempt for the "potentates" and people of Africa, whom the United States was "advancing . . . into a society that they are not ready to accept."[192] Columnist and former diplomat Carl Rowan argued that Passman's bigotry was a stain on US foreign relations, noting a firm belief among African diplomats that Passman's opposition to US military aid for their countries was rooted in racism.[193]

Passman's Democratic colleague from Louisiana, Senator Allen J. Ellender, a member of the Appropriations Committee, was even more opposed to US military aid to Africa and even more convinced that people of African descent were incapable of self-government. He lamented that the Belgians granted independence to the Congo because in his view they had done a "splendid job."[194] During a 1962 visit to Rhodesia, he declared, "It is always the whites who are responsible for any progress made in Africa." The following year he proclaimed that African Americans had turned Washington, DC, into a "cesspool" and observed that conditions in Haiti, Liberia, and Ethiopia were a clear indication of Black people's inability to govern their own affairs.[195]

Ambassadors from twenty African states came together to issue a statement condemning Ellender's bigotry, and Senator Ellender was barred from entering Uganda, Tanganyika, and Congo.[196] The Kennedy administration sought to distance itself from him, but it did so tepidly in the hope of retaining his support for its domestic legislative agenda.[197] However, at the State Department's request, Illinois Democrat Barret O'Hara, chair of the House Subcommittee on Africa, announced that Ellender's views were archaic, detrimental to US–Africa relations, and likely meant to appeal to his constituents in Louisiana who were struggling with a "race question" of their own.[198] This was consistent with O'Hara's standing as a proponent of the Kennedy administration's efforts to build up Ethiopia's navy and army.[199]

When Selassie visited Washington in 1963, the National Negro Press Association took no small pleasure in recounting his tongue-in-cheek response to Ellender's "race baiting" proclamations of African inferiority. Selassie observed that Ellender "obviously is not aware that Ethiopia has administered herself for thousands of years" with much success.[200] Unsurprisingly, Ellender was a dogged opponent of the Kennedy administration's plan to expand US military aid for African states, including Ethiopia, Liberia, and Morocco. He was convinced that arming African governments would only support dictators, produce chaos, and fuel arms races across the continent, predictions that resonated with his notions of African barbarism.[201]

Selassie had journeyed to Washington in October 1963 to negotiate for more security assistance, express disappointment in the recent US decision to offer military aid to Somalia, and update the Kennedy administration on the status of the newly formed OAU.[202] American racism and its consequences for African Americans and US–Africa relations had been on the agenda at the conference in Addis Ababa that led to the organization's creation. Just one month before the OAU was founded in May 1963, the Southern Christian Leadership Conference and the Alabama Christian Movement for Human Rights' desegregation campaign drew the world's attention to Birmingham, Alabama. African leaders bore witness to scenes of peaceful Black demonstrators, many of them children, being pummeled by police officers, attacked by police dogs, and blasted by firehoses.[203]

One of the OAU's earliest resolutions condemned racial discrimination against people of African descent worldwide. The resolution, however, was carefully worded to express both concern for the plight of African Americans and appreciation for US government efforts to confront the racist indignities they faced.[204] Yet even this measured critique was beyond the pale according to Congressman Silvio Conte, a Massachusetts Republican who sat on the House's Appropriations Committee with Otto Passman. "Very few of these countries in Africa," Conte remarked, "have any right whatsoever to criticize the United States in its policy because I saw discrimination in many of the countries I visited in Africa among Africans."[205]

Conte's goal was to charge the Africans with hypocrisy and remind them of their proper place, so to speak, but his observations were not without basis in fact. Nor were many of the bigoted claims of white legislators who scrutinized US foreign aid to Africa during the mid-twentieth century. Conte quite shrewdly referenced Liberia's unjust social hierarchy to make his case. Burdick was correct in asserting that slavery existed in Ethiopia before World War II.[206] Mansfield rightly called attention to the problems that colonial boundaries posed for emerging African states. Ellender's assertion that US military aid to Africa would help to prop up autocrats proved prescient in many cases. In the surrounding decades, radical African American activists, including W. Alphaeus Hunton, who castigated Liberia's rulers, and Kwame Ture, who opposed Selassie's monarchy, would make similar points for vastly different reasons.[207] The same can be said for this text itself.

Many African American political elites embraced a different calculus. They saw their support for African governments as a means of confronting a nexus of racism in US domestic and foreign policy. As such, they often championed US security partnerships with governments such as Liberia and Ethiopia, despite their authoritarian excesses. The *Baltimore*

Afro-American's editorial board captured this sentiment in 1963 when it opposed an amendment curtailing US arms donations to African states that had recently passed the House Foreign Affairs Committee. According to the editorial board, the amendment "smacked of racism" because it limited African governments to US arms intended to preserve internal security while the United States funneled Europe's colonial powers a broad array of offensive weapons, including fighter jets.[208] Even more concerning according to the paper, the amendment's sponsor was Representative William Broomfield, a Michigan Republican who feared that well-armed African governments might initiate collective military action against apartheid South Africa. Broomfield expressed concerns about apartheid's discriminatory policies. Nonetheless, he often opposed meddling in South Africa's internal affairs, celebrated its vibrant trade relations with the United States, and argued that the country's economic vitality benefited its African majority while the economies of other African states languished.[209]

Moderate African Americans leaders were not unmoved by threats to peace and democracy in Africa that were exacerbated by US security partnerships with African states they often supported. Many no doubt would have agreed with a 1953 NAACP resolution that urged US policymakers to make "larger appropriations for economic aid as compared with military aid."[210] At the same time, African American leaders could not help but hear the drumbeat of racial slights and allusions to African inferiority that accompanied the proposals of politicians such as Broomfield, Burdick, and Ellender. Nor could they overlook the segregationist convictions and apologias for white minority rule in Africa expressed by American politicians who often led the charge against US security assistance to independent African governments.

It was in the context of these midcentury political realities that much of the African American foreign policy elite underscored the value of US security partnerships with states such as Ethiopia and Liberia. They aimed to confront racism on a global scale, to strengthen African governments, and to bolster the bargaining power of the African security allies of the United States. As a consequence, African American elites also abetted the militarization of US policy toward the continent and the abuses of African governments themselves. This dynamic certainly benefited Emperor Selassie's monarchy as it painstakingly searched for influence in its security relations with the United States. However, it would be even more beneficial for Liberia, a state whose security ties with Washington were older and whose influence was more sporadic, but which nonetheless possessed strategic assets that Washington coveted.

2

"UNCLE TOM'S" AIR BASE?

Liberia's Strategic Assets, African American Allies, and "Special" Security Partnership with the United States

Liberia was settled in 1820 by formerly enslaved African Americans under the direction of the American Colonization Society, a body white clergy, abolitionists, and slaveholders.[1] The group maintained that Black people could never be woven into America's "fabrics of government," to take a phrase from its third leader, former American president James Madison.[2] Such were the origins of a "special relationship," both hailed and endured by Liberia, that set the tone for the often expedient backing that the United States offered the country throughout the twentieth century.[3] This relationship was disrupted briefly in the 1930s when the Hoover administration broke diplomatic ties with the West African state amid an international outcry over the Liberian government's brutal, forced labor arrangements with the island of Fernando Po.[4]

For W.E.B. Du Bois, Rayford Logan, George Padmore, and even a young Eric Williams, future prime minister of Trinidad and Tobago, the international outcry was shot through with the hypocrisy of imperialists whose sights were set on Liberia's sovereignty.[5] Nevertheless, news of the country's forced labor scheme exposed a record of exploitation that Liberia's African majority experienced at the hands of its émigré African American and West Indian leaders and their allies in the small indigenous elite. Indigenous groups such as the Grebo and Kru bore the brunt of these labor, taxation, and military abuses, which intensified at turn of the century as the Liberian government expanded its authority into the country's hinterland to combat incursions from European powers during the Scramble for Africa.[6]

In the wake of the forced labor scandal, the United States restored relations with Liberia and during World War II built and operated Roberts Field air base near the country's capital, Monrovia. From that point forward, Roberts Field would serve as a source of substantive, if sporadic, influence for Liberia in its security partnership with the United States. This chapter places Roberts Field at the center of twentieth-century US–Liberia security relations and documents the efforts of Liberia's leaders to capitalize on the air base. Monrovia was rarely in a position to make sweeping demands of Washington. I demonstrate the ways that Liberia's leaders nonetheless chiseled away at the hegemon, playing consistently on a US desire to maintain access to Roberts Field and Liberia's other strategic assets. This cautious diplomacy strongly benefited their narrow domestic interests and often benefited from a tailwind of African American support.

THE RISE OF ROBERTS FIELD

In March 1942, with World War II underway, Liberia's Barclay government signed a defense agreement with the Roosevelt administration authorizing the construction of Roberts Field in exchange for a promise of protection from Axis aggression.[7] The base served as an American bulwark against German advances in West Africa and naval operations in the South Atlantic. More important, it was a waystation for US matériel destined for North Africa—some seventeen thousand Allied bombers traversed the airfield at the height of the fighting in that theater.[8] It was also a pivotal means of assuring US access to Liberia's rubber resources.[9]

Lester A. Walton, US minister to Liberia at the time, was one of the first American officials to champion the prospect of establishing a US military outpost at Roberts Field on the eve of World War II. In dispatches to Washington, Walton emphasized Liberia's "strategic geographic importance" and the value of coming to the small state's defense given the potential for German attacks in West Africa. He argued that the US bond with Liberia was "no longer merely a sentimental attachment," but instead a matter of national security.[10] Despite the minister's appeals, the Roosevelt administration was decidedly unsentimental toward Liberia until the United States itself was poised to enter the war.

In early 1939, as hostilities loomed, the US War Department ignored Liberia's pleas for arms and ammunition to better equip its military, the Liberian Frontier Force.[11] Instead, US officials recommended that Liberia seek assurances of protection from France and Great Britain. When France proved receptive and proposed to take the lead in training and equipping the Frontier Force, the United States initially resisted the plan as a French play for influence. It did so under pressure from Harvey Firestone Jr., who was determined to maintain his firm's singular influence in Liberian affairs.[12] By that point, the country's rubber cultivation was almost entirely in the hands of the Firestone Corporation. When President Roosevelt suggested that the War Department grant Liberia a minor concession by offering to sell it a handful of coastal defense guns, US defense officials likewise opposed the idea.[13] They claimed that "if a serious attack were made upon her, Liberia, unaided, could not, of course, resist such an attack," and in any case, "neither the United States nor any other great power has found it possible to train black troops in the use of such guns."[14]

With the onset of World War II and the construction of Roberts Field as a node in Allied operations, US interests in Liberia became unambiguous. In 1942, not only did the United States pledge to come to Liberia's defense, but it also trained three thousand members of the Liberian Frontier Force.[15] Moreover, Washington arranged to build a port in the West African state through a lend-lease agreement that granted the US Navy access to the facility. The same year, Roosevelt drew further attention to the tightening US–Liberia security ties by visiting Roberts Field and reviewing the US troops stationed there.[16] Nearly all of them were

African Americans under the leadership of white officers in America's segregated armed forces.

Minister Walton was not present for Roosevelt's visit. He had been summoned to Washington in early 1942. The State Department denied Walton a role in the pivotal talks that led to the air base's construction, despite his ardent support for the Roberts Field project and his standing as the top US diplomat in Liberia. *The Atlanta Daily World*, a leading Black newspaper, noted: "The question is being raised whether a colored man could not have been entrusted with carrying on the negotiations."[17] An increasingly conservative George Schuyler, known for his criticisms of Liberia's leaders and the Roosevelt administration, took the matter a step further. In the *Pittsburgh Courier* Schuyler speculated that Walton had been "recalled as soon as the Monrovia post became important and high US and British Army and Navy officers might find themselves under his command."[18] After working doggedly to advance US–Liberia security relations, Walton was pushed aside in the run-up to Roosevelt's visit to Roberts Field. He was, instead, tasked with traveling the United States to develop a plan to boost sagging "negro morale" in the war effort.[19]

Walton would be briefly returned to his post, but he nonetheless found his views competing for standing with those of the "Africonciliators" of Roosevelt's informal "Black Cabinet," such as famed educator Mary McLeod Bethune and housing specialist Dr. Robert C. Weaver.[20] It was reported that Bethune even had a hand in choosing Walton's replacement when President Truman took office in 1945.[21] In a sign of class cleavages among African Americans playing out across the Atlantic, many of the African American soldiers who were stationed at Roberts Field openly criticized Walton and his support for the Liberian elite as they exploited the indigenous population.[22]

Walton did not envision Roberts Field as a means to embolden Monrovia in its relations with Washington, though on occasion it would do so. As a US diplomat and Democratic appointee, he was obviously invested in Roosevelt's wartime agenda and, more broadly, American power. For George Padmore, the Black Marxist luminary, malign American power was precisely the problem. Padmore saw Roberts Field as a clear sign that Liberia was "destined to pass more firmly into the orbit of Yankee imperialism."[23] US officials would have disavowed Padmore's rhetoric, but the substance of his claims was clear to some of them. In early 1939, when Minister Walton informed his superiors that Liberia would welcome a US base, the State Department's Division of Near Eastern Affairs replied: "We assume . . . that the Liberian Government has made its anxiety so plain in regard to the menace of aggression by certain European powers that it would be willing to risk the alternative of virtual American domination along the lines you mention."[24]

While less strident than Padmore, Carter G. Woodson's *Negro History Bulletin* suggested that the US presence at Roberts Field gave rise to a question the Liberians would do well to confront: "Has its sovereignty been impaired by this concession?" Noting a history of British and French meddling in Liberia before the war, the *Bulletin* suggested that Liberia might "be exchanging several masters for one."[25] The NAACP did not share Woodson's and Padmore's concerns.

When the war concluded, US defense officials proposed shuttering Roberts Field. The NAACP forcefully opposed the idea. In early 1947 its executive secretary, Walter White, telegrammed the War Department in protest. "We strongly urge you to use every means to have the matter reconsidered," he wrote. "Roberts Field is of strategic importance to Liberian progress and the continued promotion of good relations between Liberia and America."[26] This view was echoed by Dr. Channing Tobias, an NAACP board member and the director of the Phelps Stokes Fund, an education philanthropy and Firestone ally. Tobias maintained that Roberts Field reflected the "importance of the America-Liberia relationship." He emphasized that "Liberia is the only foothold of the African continent that America has. It is strategically, militarily, and socially important."[27]

William L. Dawson, a Democratic congressman from Illinois, encouraged the Truman administration to offer the Liberian government more support due to Roberts Fields's value for postwar US military operations as well as the African state's rubber supply. Dawson noted that his calls to strengthen US–Liberia relations were also borne of his heritage as an African American and Liberia's history as a country founded by Black émigrés from the United States.[28] At the time, Dawson, Perry Howard, a member of the Republican National Committee, and Frank L. Stanley, president of the Negro Newspaper Publishers Association, cochaired the National Committee for the American Celebration of the Liberian Centennial. The committee was composed largely of Black political elites, including Mary McLeod Bethune, Howard University historian Rayford Logan, and Fisk University president Charles S. Johnson. It was at the center of an outpouring of attention that many Black leaders directed to the West African state during the hundred-year anniversary of its independence. When the committee unveiled a plaque commemorating the history of "cooperation and mutual trust" between America and Liberia at the US Capitol, President Truman sent a message of support, avowing that the "United States and Liberia will march together during the next century."[29]

THE POLITICAL IMPORTANCE OF ROBERTS FIELD

The US Army Transport Command pulled its forces from Roberts Field in 1947. Nonetheless, the US Air Force maintained access to the airfield by awarding a contract to oversee its commercial operations to the newly formed Liberia Airways International. Reports of this "fat air base contract" rarely failed to note that Liberia Airways had been established by Homer M. Adams, who had little experience in the airline business and was an aide to the former US secretary of state, Edward R. Stettinius Jr.[30] Stettinius himself had recently established the Liberia Company.[31] These firms and the Liberia Mining Company, which was founded on their heels, were led by former US diplomats and defense officials and their partners in the Liberian government who were determined to profit from the country's rubber and mineral resources.

Liberia's appealing postwar economic prospects were at the heart of a three-article series published by *The Associated Negro Press* in 1948. The series extolled a "new phase" in US–Liberia relations borne of

Washington's recognition of "both the strategic importance of this land . . . and the economic importance of its resources." A "Liberian renaissance" might be abetted by this new era of "American friendship."[32] John W. Davis, a leading Black educator and a director of the Point Four Program, recently established by the United States in Liberia, echoed this sentiment in an article in *Présence Africaine*.[33] For its part, the *Pittsburgh Courier* asserted that Roberts Field and Liberia's rubber resources "put it in a strong position to bargain with American interests."[34]

In 1953, when the US Air Force determined that maintaining the Roberts Field contract could no longer be justified as a strategic measure, the State Department pressured the Pentagon to continue funding the airfield's operations at an annual cost of roughly $260,000.[35] State Department officials, apparently dismissive of America's own racial history, claimed: "In recent years, Liberian leaders have been exposed to racist and nationalist influences, particularly in the United Nations, with the result that Liberian acceptance of United States leadership has shown a tendency to be less automatic and may no longer be taken for granted. Any sign of lessening United States interest in Liberia would aggravate this tendency."[36]

The diplomats also emphasized Roberts Field's domestic "political importance," asserting that "withdrawal of our financial support . . . might be interpreted by important segments of the American public as a decrease of official interest in Africa."[37] Black foreign policy elites, buoyed by a renewed interest in Liberia during the country's centennial, were among the loudest voices in the American public calling for Roberts Field to remain open. Congressman William Dawson, NAACP executive secretary Walter White, Phelps-Stokes Fund director Channing Tobias, the *Associated Negro Press*, the *Pittsburgh Courier*, and *The New Journal and Guide* had all given the airfield and the Liberian government their blessings. These Black moderates acted largely out of a desire to bolster Liberia's standing within the international community and its emerging postwar institutions. They aimed to see the principles of the UN Charter applied to Western relations with Black-governed states.

Many African American leaders and Liberian officials saw Roberts Field as an invaluable outlet for the small state's commodities and a lifeline for its economic development. Its dual role as an outpost for US military power was readily apparent. But Black liberals were far less skeptical of the amalgam of American militarization, American resource speculation, and African development than they were of European imperialism and communism. They believed that strategic ties with the United States would help to shield Liberia, a beleaguered sentinel of Black self-governance, from the machinations of France, Great Britain, and the Soviet Union. This would strengthen the Liberian government, buttress its autonomy, and help to unlock the country's "storehouse of wealth."[38]

Ultimately, the Eisenhower administration decided to continue funding Roberts Field until 1954. At that point, the Liberian government and Pan-American Airways took over the operating costs. In return for Eisenhower's assistance, which included more than $800,000 worth of repairs to Roberts Field, Liberia's Tubman administration granted the Pentagon continued access rights to the facility.[39] Black leaders were not alone in contributing to this outcome, but their influence was significant. Black liberal appeals to the Truman and Eisenhower administrations dovetailed with the interests of former American officials turned financiers and their rent-seeking allies in the Liberian government. These factors, however, should not obscure the centrality of realist calculations in Washington's policy toward Monrovia.

Eisenhower's deputy assistant secretary of defense saw value in Liberia as a "source of natural rubber and high grade iron ore." He believed that in the event of another global conflict, Roberts Field might be necessary if the United States required a "South Atlantic Air Route."[40] Moreover, he noted that the port at Monrovia, which the United States had expanded through a lend-lease agreement, was the only port in West Africa that was not under European control. These considerations justified expending resources to keep Roberts Field functional as well as funding for US military training programs for Liberia's armed forces. Just as important, the Liberian government expressed a vocal commitment to preventing the "ruthless spread of Communism."[41]

Nevertheless, during the late 1940s and early 1950s, African American leaders had routinely reminded the US foreign policy establishment of Roberts Field's political importance. For the Eisenhower administration, Roberts Field and modest support for the Liberian government were ideal political sop. The administration was generally unresponsive to African American's appeals for racial justice and their support for African decolonization. Eisenhower himself met only once, briefly, with a group of Black leaders during his presidency.[42] But officials in the State Department Office of African Affairs recognized that Black elites such as A. Philip Randolph and Adam Clayton Powell Jr. were "influential citizens whom it is desirable not to offend."[43] Their influence with rank-and-file Black voters could not be wholly overlooked. As a Republican president, Eisenhower was interested in chipping away at Black support for the Democratic Party while largely avoiding reforms to America's segregated social order.

As the United States negotiated with Liberia to maintain access rights to Roberts Field in 1954, Secretary of State John Foster Dulles recommended that Eisenhower invite President Tubman to Washington as an official guest. Dulles pointed out that "The African republic has always been of special interest to the American Negro population."[44] He was encouraged to make this recommendation by Jesse Locker, a Black Republican and former Cincinnati city councilman whom Eisenhower appointed ambassador to Liberia in 1953. In a memo to the secretary of state, Locker revealed high hopes: "An invitation of President Eisenhower to President Tubman would no doubt tend to have our people [the blacks] return to the Republican party."[45] This, of course, did not happen during the 1956 US presidential election, but Eisenhower did make notable gains among Black voters. His modest efforts to gain their support were aided by virulent "Dixiecrat" resistance to desegregation in the wake of the Supreme Court's 1954 *Brown v. Board of Education* decision.

Amid the debate over Roberts Field, Eisenhower apparently saw some value in Locker's line of thought. He met with and hosted a banquet for Tubman when the Liberian leader journeyed to the United States in 1954. During the visit, which was sponsored by Harvey Firestone Jr. and followed closely in the Black press, Tubman was lionized by the cadre of American financiers and Black leaders who had pressed Eisenhower to recognize Liberia's potential.[46] Black voters were not allowed to forget that Eisenhower had invited President Tubman as well as President Paul Magloire of Haiti and Emperor Haile Selassie of Ethiopia to Washington. On the eve of the 1956 US presidential election, an Eisenhower-Nixon campaign ad in African American newspapers declared, "They're Everybody's President and Vice President." To back this claim it boasted, "President Eisenhower is the only Chief Executive who entertained within 12 months at the White House three chiefs of state of Negro governed countries."[47]

THE FRIENDS, FOES, AND FINANCES OF PRESIDENT WILLIAM TUBMAN

These American currents of electoral politics, military planning, corporate power, and Black transnationalism converged at a pivotal moment in Liberian history. During the late 1940s and 1950s, the Tubman administration erected an edifice of unprecedented authoritarianism in the West African state.[48] Tubman assumed the presidency in 1944 and was hailed as a reformer by many African American leaders. In the wake of World War II, he oversaw expansions in voting rights that enfranchised Liberian women as well as property holders among the country's indigenous groups. In practice, however, this bolstered an uneasy coalition between Tubman's True Whig Party and the most powerful chiefs among these groups. The reforms did not extend the franchise to Liberia's indigenous majority, which made up roughly 99 percent the country's population.[49] Instead, they served the interests of indigenous rulers and the political class among the Americo-Liberian minority, which had been recruiting select indigenous elites into its ranks since the late nineteenth century.

Some African Americans recognized the limits of the Liberian president's electoral reforms but chose to celebrate their implications.

Rayford Logan observed that while the change in Liberia's electoral laws "does not go the whole way in providing for a democratic form of government, it is an augury for that consummation."[50] Others, such as Charles H. Wesley, president of the State College of Education and Industrial Arts at Wilberforce, Ohio, brought the matter closer to home. "These are steps that can be hailed with enthusiasm," Wesley wrote. "This movement should be encouraged until all barriers to suffrage are wiped out, just as we are proposing to dissolve the poll tax barriers in the United States."[51]

Tubman's reforms were not an "augury" for democratization. As Carl Burrowes's research deftly illustrates, they were a harbinger of the rise of the "paramount presidency" and "chieftaincy model of governance" in Liberia.[52] Tubman would become the country's longest serving president, dying in office after a twenty-seven-year tenure. In the late 1940s, as African American liberals were celebrating his modest reforms, Tubman initiated a withering assault on free expression and Liberia's political dissidents. Relying on its alliance with indigenous elites, Tubman's party transformed the Liberian legislature into a body of loyal partisans that granted the president sweeping "emergency powers" to detain citizens, confiscate property, and grow the Liberian military.[53] Tubman swelled the ranks of the Liberian Frontier Force and used it as a mechanism to consolidate his personal power. US military aid to Liberia was integral to this process.

With US funding, Tubman more than doubled the size of the Frontier Force at the outset of his presidency. In response to the Liberian leaders' appeals for more security assistance, the US Military Mission to Liberia was established in 1951 to assist "in all troop training programs" for the Frontier Force.[54] At the time, Tubman was relying on the twofold pretense of anticommunism and national security to crack down on his political opponents on the eve of a presidential election. Nonetheless, the African American editorial board at Norfolk's *New Journal and Guide* applauded the US training mission as an attempt to assist Liberia in "maintaining internal security." It likewise lamented the prospect of the decline of Robert Fields and its return "to the bush."[55]

Pentagon officials viewed military aid to Liberia as a "low-cost" means of maintaining access to Roberts Field and engendering "good will."[56] A National Security Council memo captured the prevailing view: US military assistance programs were effective "quid pro quo for bases."[57] US security assistance to Liberia may have been modest by Washington's standards, but it was invaluable for the Tubman administration as it cemented a system of authoritarian rule during the 1950s. From 1951 to 1959, the United States provided Liberia more than $12 million dollars in technical assistance through its Mutual Security Program and offered the country military credits for the purchase of roughly $1 million dollars in matériel.[58] During that time, the United States also transferred two naval vessels to the West African state. Including the cost associated with its training mission in Liberia, Washington funneled to the Tubman government roughly $3.9 million in military aid from 1953 to 1963.[59] Should these figures appear paltry, it is worth noting that in 1950 the Liberian government's total revenues amounted to roughly $3.8 million.[60]

During Liberia's 1951 presidential election, some African American liberals who had supported the Liberian government grew disturbed by Tubman's attempts to squelch dissent and cling to power. Because many of these liberals had backed the Tubman regime for more than six years, their attempts to change course were often tentative. The NAACP's Walter White telegrammed President Tubman to raise concerns about reports of political persecution against opposition party presidential candidate Didhwo Twe.[61] Twe was a Kru-Liberian rubber planter who had been educated in the United States and garnered international attention in the 1930s by helping to expose the Liberian government's forced labor practices.[62] In 1951, he fled to New York after being charged with sedition by the Tubman government for requesting that the United States and the United Nations monitor the Liberian presidential poll.[63] Government violence and chicanery prevented Twe's Reformation Party from fielding a candidate. Nearly two dozen of the party's leaders were imprisoned, and Tubman won a second term in an uncontested election.[64]

White's inquiry into Twe's treatment ignited a spat between the NAACP leader and President Tubman that played out in the pages of the

Black press. Tubman scolded White for intruding in Liberia's affairs and parroting Twe's allegations.[65] White, who had recently boasted of the NAACP's efforts to help Liberia avert "economic domination," deemed Tubman's response evasive and "ludicrous."[66] He likened Tubman's thinking to the "attitude of the Dixiecrats in the United States who disenfranchise and exploit Negroes and then denounce outside interference." According to White, Prime Minister Malan of apartheid South Africa took an "identical position."[67]

White's public protest in support of Liberian democracy was short-lived. The US ambassador to Liberia at the time was Edward Dudley, a Black attorney who had worked closely with Thurgood Marshall at the NAACP Legal Defense Fund and whose diplomatic career had benefited from White's support. Dudley sent word to White that it would be best to "slow down" his criticisms.[68] Tubman was happy to enlist the support of African Americans of "substance," but he would not be beholden to them.[69] Dudley believed that Tubman's charges against his political opponents were largely fabricated and that most of them were simply attempting to introduce democratic reforms. But the US ambassador viewed the Liberian president's system of rule as far too entrenched to be challenged by internal or external forces.

Dudley moved quickly to end the tiff between the NAACP and the Liberian government. When Tubman visited the United States in 1954 to seek Eisenhower's assistance in strengthening Liberia's military, Channing Tobias, who was on the NAACP Executive Board, spoke glowingly of the Liberian leader. During the visit, the Liberian government also received praise from Ralph Bunche, director of the UN Trusteeship Division, and Hulan Jack, the Saint Lucian–born borough president of Manhattan.[70] As President Tubman basked in these plaudits, back in Liberia it was suspected that his allies in the True Whig Party had hatched a plot to terrorize their opponents that led to the murder and mutilation of several children.[71] Joseph J. Cheeseman, one of the plot's key figures, was chair of Liberia's newly formed Joint Security Commission, which issued orders to the police force as well as select members of the US-trained Liberian military. Cheeseman had only recently returned to Liberia after studying in the United States and reportedly held FBI Director J. Edgar Hoover in high esteem.[72]

While Black liberals praised the Tubman government throughout the 1940s and early 1950s, radical and conservative Black leaders voiced skepticism. George Schuyler had traveled to Liberia in the 1930s, witnessed the subjugation of the country's indigenous majority, and penned a novel and numerous articles excoriating Liberia's rulers.[73] Schuyler had few criticisms of Firestone, despite evidence of the company collaborating with Liberia's leaders to profit from the abuse and displacement of the country's workers.[74] Up until the eve of Eisenhower's election in 1952, the conservative columnist remained fiercely critical of the Tubman administration. After Eisenhower became president and "save[d] the Republic from socialism," according to Schuyler, the writer interpreted US ties with Liberia through the lens of Cold War realism and moderated his criticisms of the Tubman regime.[75] When a Democrat returned to the White House in 1961, Schuyler did not hesitate to revive his acid prose. He branded Tubman a hypocrite for supporting Algerian independence while overseeing a "one-party dictatorial state."[76]

Prominent Black radicals also intensified their criticisms of the Liberian government during the mid-twentieth century. Days after President Tubman's January 1952 inauguration, the Council on African Affairs (CAA) issued a statement denouncing the Liberian leader as a tyrant who exploited the country's workers to fill the coffers of American corporations.[77] At the helm of the council were Paul Robeson, W.E.B. Du Bois, and William Alphaeus Hunton, three of the day's preeminent Black Marxists and Pan-Africanists. Du Bois, by this point, had largely disavowed the liberalism of his youth.

For nearly fifteen years the CAA had organized campaigns to oppose racism and colonial exploitation in Africa while largely keeping silent about the Liberian government's abuses. In 1944 Robeson voiced his approval when State Department officials met with a group of "liberal-minded" CAA members to exchange views on US lend-lease agreements with Liberia and Ethiopia.[78] At the time, the CAA boasted a largely liberal membership under the leadership of the increasingly radical Robeson and the increasingly conservative Max Yergan. By the end of the decade, Yergan would fully embrace McCarthyism, break with the CAA, and charge Robeson with opening the organization to communist influences.[79]

Unlike Yergan and CAA members Mary McLeod Bethune and Channing Tobias, who fled the "subversive organization," during the 1940s Robeson, Hunton, and Du Bois grew critical of Tubman's push to expand Liberia's strategic and economic ties with the United States.[80] These criticisms became a point of contention between the CAA's moderate and radical factions. After the factions parted ways, the CAA's radicals continued to decry Tubman's tyranny.[81] Moderates like Mary McCleod Bethune and Carl Murphy, publisher of the *Baltimore Afro-American*, moved further into the Tubman camp. Bethune and Murphy attended the Liberian leader's second presidential inauguration as official US delegates and lavished him with praise.[82] In fact, Murphy's newspaper anointed Tubman 1952's "African Statesman of the Year," while his ally in the US Congress, William Dawson, was awarded US "Statesman of the Year."[83]

As early as 1949, Robeson had begun to castigate the American commercial interests that partnered with Tubman for overseeing an "invasion of Africa."[84] In 1950, when Tubman dispatched Liberian troops to quell a labor uprising at the Firestone plantation, Robeson remarked that it demonstrated "the kind of enforcement of exploitation by armed might which the rulers of Africa are employing."[85] Paul Robeson's view of the ways that American capital, racism, and military might intertwined with Liberia's political hierarchies likely benefited from the firsthand insights of his partner, Eslanda Cardozo Goode Robeson. Eslanda Robeson was an accomplished journalist, political theorist, and anti-imperialist organizer whose knowledge of African affairs and connections across the continent were extensive. In 1946, en route to the Belgian Congo, Eslanda Robeson had a layover at Roberts Field. She witnessed its segregated social order, noting that it "was definitely a WHITE American base." The Liberians she saw at the airfield, Robeson observed, were "all definitely servants, obviously removed from white contact."[86]

W. Alphaeus Hunton, the CAA's education director and a Howard University English professor, shared the Robeson's concerns. In the early

1950s Hunton penned exposés outlining Liberia's "urgently needed internal democratic reforms" and the Tubman regime's abuses against Didhwo Twe's Reformation Party.[87] In fact, before the end of the decade Hunton would bring a similar incisiveness to a woefully overlooked manuscript, *Decision in Africa*. The text owes a debt to George Padmore's *The Life and Struggle of Negro Toilers* but surpasses it in scope by detailing Washington's quest for military bases and defense agreements in Liberia, Nigeria, Morocco, Libya, and Ethiopia.[88]

Before Tubman strong-armed his way to reelection in 1951, Du Bois offered largely circumspect public criticisms of the Liberian government. For example, when Tubman embraced the wave of postwar US corporate interest in his country, Du Bois remarked, "Liberia is taking a second step on a dangerous experiment. The first was the Firestone Rubber concession."[89] Despite the mild tenor of these critiques, during his reelection campaign Tubman seized on the ongoing US federal investigation into Du Bois's alleged communist activities. Tubman declared that Du Bois and his associates should "endeavor to work out their own salvation with fear and trembling," rather than provide solace to his political opponents.[90]

The CAA's criticisms were a harbinger of broader disenchantment with Tubman's regime that would take shape among many African Americans as the era of African liberation dawned in the late 1950s. Tubman's moderate Pan-Africanism was increasingly deemed suspect, if it was noticed at all, by younger and more radical African Americans inspired by the tide of African independence. The Liberian leader was out of step with the times, as were his courtly relations with Washington, his skepticism toward strong African multilateral institutions, and his aversion to all but the vaguest critiques of Western racism. Tubman's outlook stood in contrast to the visions of continental unity, progress, and autonomy articulated by the leaders of newly independent states such as Ghana and Guinea. While Nkrumah and Touré condemned neocolonialism in Africa, Tubman bartered Liberia's territory for US military aid.

The Liberian president was admired by African leaders including Senegalese president Léopold Sédar Senghor and Nigeria's Nnamdi

Azikiwe. Tubman had supported Azikiwe's nationalist movement during its successful campaign to overturn British rule.[91] Moreover, the Liberian government and Selassie's monarchy played leading roles in a high-profile but abortive effort to have the International Court of Justice order South Africa to relinquish control over neighboring Southwest Africa (Namibia).[92] Nonetheless, the autocracy over which Tubman presided and his devil's bargain with Washington did little to evoke pride in Africa among African Americans. Many looked elsewhere for models of African self-determination as they increasingly demanded civil rights and political power at home.

In 1959 the seasoned war correspondent, Charles H. Loeb, summed up this discontent, linking Tubman to what he viewed as a growing class of moderate African American leaders. According to Loeb, "The only African leader who might be remotely characterized as an "Uncle Tom" is old man Tubman of Liberia, who for too long has been forced to eat at the white man's table." The journalist likewise saw Congressman William Dawson as a good fit for the lead role in "Uncle Tom's Cabin." Loeb was also unimpressed by Congressman Charles Diggs who was rapidly emerging as a leading voice in US–Africa relations. "The eloquence of Frederick Douglass," Loeb wrote, "has been simmered down to the faltering schoolboyisms of Charles Diggs." In a similar vein, Loeb chided the "cautious militancy" of Adam Clayton Powell Jr. and Dr. Martin Luther King Jr.[93]

But even "cautious militants" often supported and drew inspiration from Africa's newly assertive posture on the world stage. A clear solidarity is discernable, for instance, in Dr. King's account of his trip to Ghana's 1957 independence ceremony and, later, in his work as a member of the American Negro Leadership Conference on Africa.[94] Amid the growing admiration for bold African leadership, Liberia nonetheless maintained a solid base of support among Black liberals. Rarely did they chafe at Tubman's authoritarianism or question the ways that it was underpinned by military ties with the United States. In 1963 Representative Robert N. C. Nix, a Democrat from Pennsylvania, hailed Liberia as "free and independent," with "no Sino-Soviet bloc ties," and firmly opposed to "totalitarianism and exploitation." Nix hastened to mention that the country's "multimillion dollar Roberts Field Airport is a strategic US base, while her well-developed port of Monrovia is a potentially vital submarine facility."[95]

It was not that African American liberals refrained entirely from criticizing the governments of enduring outposts of Black sovereignty. In the 1950s Adam Clayton Powell Jr., for example, produced heavily sanitized accounts of Tubman's "accomplishments."[96] Yet the Harlem congressman also issued clear-eyed denunciations of Haiti's dictatorial Duvalier regime and the US military training mission that had been dispatched to the country.[97] Liberia's origins were an important element of its allure, but there was a unique appreciation for the country's loyalty to America in "peace and war," as Powell put it.[98] Moreover, many Black liberals sincerely agreed with Secretary of Defense McNamara's publicly espoused view that military aid to African states such as Liberia and Ethiopia would contribute to "internal stability from which will flower . . . economic and political developments."[99] They were also enamored with the prospect of Liberia's rubber and iron-ore resources granting, it a "top bargaining position" in world affairs.[100]

When Tubman died in 1971, one of the fiercest American defenders of his legacy was Roy Wilkins, Walter White's successor as head of the NAACP. This comes as little surprise. Not only did the NAACP have a history of support for Tubman, but Wilkins was himself a staunch proponent of integration and global, Black respectability politics. In fact, he cited Nigeria's late 1960s civil war as evidence that African political motives could be just as morally flawed as "the middle-class American ways" that a younger generation of African American radicals were calling into question.[101] Upon Tubman's death, Wilkins painted a portrait of a genteel leader, responsive to the needs of Liberians and Americans, who "helped the United States at a time when it needed help" and reinforced "the balances of political power that bolster hegemony."[102]

Indeed, the Liberian leader had not only nurtured and benefited from a close security partnership with the United States, he had also backed the US position on a host of international controversies, from its intervention in Vietnam to its accommodative stance toward Ian Smith's white-supremacist regime in Rhodesia. In return, as Dunn notes, during

Tubman's tenure, "the US government provided $275 million in grants and loans, approximately two-thirds of total foreign aid received by Liberia from all sources."[103]

Tubman's influence in Washington was largely derived from US policymakers' anticipation of his preferences, gleaned through frequent diplomatic exchanges conducted in the shadow of the myriad strategic assets of the United States in Liberia. In the course of these exchanges, Tubman was often forthright about what he deemed the "quid pro quo" that animated US–Liberia relations. "The United States has done great things for Liberia," he once fumed, "But we have contributed to the United States our blood, our territory, our support at the Councils of State even some time when we do not altogether agree with it."[104] Given the cautious tenor of Tubman's diplomacy, his calculated embrace of African American elites who championed Liberia's cause in Washington is all the more understandable. His successor, William Tolbert Jr., who came to power in 1971, would take a similar tack vis-à-vis the African American elite, and a moderately more confrontational approach to dealing with Washington.

PRESIDENT WILLIAM TOLBERT JR.: GESTURES OF REFORM AND AUTONOMY

Tolbert was more of a reformer than his predecessor. Nevertheless, he had served as Tubman's vice president for nineteen years and, ultimately, reverted to the repressive tactics of the old order when confronted with political dissent. The new Liberian leader freed political prisoners who had run afoul of the previous government, but by the end of his tenure he would respond to demonstrations with an iron fist.[105] Though Tolbert's grandfather had emigrated to Liberia from the United States, he had come of age among the Kpelle people and married a woman from the Vai ethnic group.[106] Touting this background, the Liberian leader made much of his efforts to address the socioeconomic divide between indigenous Africans and Americo-Liberians, a term he reviled as an instrument of foreign meddling.[107] Tolbert also took aim at the corruption and patronage networks that had long diverted Liberia's revenues into the hands of a privileged minority.

Liberia, nonetheless, remained a one-party state whose executive and legislative branches were dominated by Tolbert's True Whig Party. In this context, Tolbert's 1975 election to a full term as president was a foregone conclusion.[108] In the immediate wake of his victory, Tolbert offered Liberians broader space for free expression. However, it was not until his regime was on the verge of collapse that Liberia's rubber-stamp legislature exercised its power to grant legal status to opposition political parties. Tolbert also reinforced his authority and his vision of a "wholesome functioning society" through brutal spectacles, including public floggings for criminals convicted of petty crimes.[109]

While in office, Tolbert made modest progress toward the goal of dismantling Liberia's enduring social hierarchies. Yet, his economic reform agenda was often undercut by his loyalty to his family and allies in the True Whig Party who relied on patronage networks to generate profits for their private enterprises.[110] All the while, Tolbert's standing as one of his country's wealthiest businessmen did little to help his image among everyday Liberia's, many of whom were encouraged by his rhetoric but grew disaffected by the halting pace of progress.[111] The Liberian president's half-hearted reforms and a downturn in Liberia's economy fueled a wave political discontent that would be his undoing. In 1980 he was overthrown and assassinated in a coup orchestrated by members of the Liberian Frontier Force, who called themselves the People's Redemption Council.[112]

Much like his domestic reforms, Tolbert's foreign policies were marked by contradictions. For the first time, Monrovia exchanged ambassadors with Moscow. Moreover, Tolbert openly expressed support for nonalignment throughout the Global South. He was also a proponent of African regional and continental integration and inked a security guarantee with his more radical neighbor, Sékou Touré of Guinea.[113] In the year before his assassination, Tolbert served as OAU chairman and was a leading voice in the organization's condemnations of white-minority rule in Southern Africa. The Liberian government even offered modest financial assistance to African nationalist movements, including the Southwest Africa People's Organization and South Africa's Pan-Africanist Congress.[114]

At the same time, Tolbert remained a moderate, statist Pan-Africanist. He evoked outrage across the continent for meeting secretly with Prime Minister John Vorster of South Africa in 1975, in what the Liberian president called a diplomatic effort to advance a solution to the crisis in Southern Africa.[115] The same year he met with and offered funds to Jonas Savimbi, whose UNITA forces were increasingly viewed by progressive African leaders as South African pawns.[116] While Tolbert held considerable disdain for Liberia's reputation as an "American satellite" in Africa, as a CIA assessment noted, he remained committed to preserving "the essential elements of Liberia's 'special relationship' with the United States."[117]

He was, in short, a man of "temperate views."[118] In matters of racial politics, this had been obvious as early as 1961. That year, in his capacity as a Baptist minister, Tolbert attended the Southern Baptist Convention in St. Louis, Missouri. This was just days after a bus carrying the Freedom Riders had been firebombed outside of Montgomery, Alabama, and the civil rights activists had been brutalized by a white mob. Tolbert avowed that Liberians were "in sympathy with the struggle of our American brothers for common decency," but, as the Black press underscored, he refused to speak directly to the events that had unfolded in Montgomery.[119]

Early in his tenure, Tolbert signaled support for his country's security partnership with the United States by signing an agreement that authorized the construction of a US Coast Guard Omega Navigation Station on a 700-acre plot of Liberian territory.[120] Moreover, during his time in office, the Liberian leader maintained a cordial rapport with Presidents Nixon, Ford, and Carter. In fact, in April 1976, a month after Kissinger proposed smuggling arms through Roberts Field, Tolbert welcomed the US secretary of state to his country, where Kissinger delivered a speech proclaiming a US "dedication to peace, national dignity, and racial justice" in Africa.[121] Some two years later, Tolbert offered Washington more practical assistance by allowing Roberts Field to serve as a staging point for US aircraft shuttling Moroccan troops to Zaire's Shaba province to help President Mobutu fend off an incursion by Katangan rebels.[122]

Still, during Tolbert's presidency, the US–Liberia security partnership grew fractious. In early 1976 Thomas W. M. Smith, the State Department's director of the Office of West African Affairs, noted Tolbert's attempts to chip away at Liberia's image as a US client, but he also observed that relations with the West African government were "generally good." According to Smith, there was one running disagreement. Many Tolbert officials claimed that the United States had not done enough to contribute to Liberia's development, and they clearly viewed "US aid as quid-pro-quo for the location of strategic US facilities in Liberia." This did not mean, in Smith's opinion, that the United States need acquiesce to all of Liberia's requests, but it did require the United States to "remain responsive to Liberian development needs."[123]

Throughout the late 1970s, NSC, CIA, and State Department documents all pointed to the Tolbert administration's inclination toward harder bargaining. Some US officials underscored the danger of Liberia turning to Moscow for assistance if Washington was unresponsive.[124] Others noted the asset specificity of US facilities in Liberia and suggested that these facilities would grow in importance as US access to its listening base in Ethiopia became imperiled by the political turmoil that led to Selassie's overthrow.[125] In response to these trends, during the latter years of Tolbert's tenure, US security assistance and development aid to Liberia saw gradual increases. The country's foreign minister, Cecil Dennis, whom US officials deemed an abrasive negotiator, boasted to his colleagues about his success in extracting these concessions.[126]

After a tumultuous tenure as US ambassador to Tanzania, former *Pittsburgh Courier* publisher W. Beverly Carter Jr. was appointed US ambassador to Liberia in early 1976. He immediately began to play a key role in backing the Liberian's requests for more US security assistance. Just months after he took up his post, Carter appealed to the secretary of defense to reconsider proposed reductions in funding for the US military training mission in Liberia.[127] Carter warned that the Liberians expected increases in US aid to underwrite a five-year self-sufficiency plan for the Frontier Force and that any funding cuts would be a serious blow to relations between the states. The Ford administration agreed. In fact, US military aid to Liberia totaled more than $10 million over the course of the 1970s, nearly a 50 percent increase over the prior decade's allocation and more than enough to keep the senior commissioned officers of the Frontier Force in Tolbert's pocket.[128] It would be enlisted men drawn from indigenous groups who would oversee the Liberian president's demise.

A spirit of camaraderie animated Ambassador Carter's relations with the Liberian elite. Carter and Tolbert held a shared faith in liberal economic development. This contrasted with the ambassador's previous posting in the African-socialist milieu of Tanzania, where he had championed capitalism in spirited but cordial debates with President Julius Nyerere.[129] Carter did not think that Tolbert was as intellectually keen as Nyerere or Nkrumah, whom he had befriended decades earlier when they both attended Pennsylvania's Lincoln University.[130] But the ambassador did believe that the Liberian president was genuinely invested in improving the lives of all his country's citizens. Despite mounting evidence to the contrary, so too did many other Black moderates.

Empathy for Tolbert's government stretched across the Black moderate political spectrum, from the conservative Carter to liberals such as Representative Charles Rangel and the Reverend Jesse Jackson. In 1972 Tolbert invited Reverend Jackson to Liberia as part of a campaign to stoke foreign investment in the country. Jackson readily accepted the invitation as the leader of Operation PUSH, an African American economic empowerment organization. After meeting with Tolbert, Jackson called his talks with the Liberian president the "most important ones that have ever taken place between black brothers on the two sides of the Atlantic." The civil rights leader agreed to encourage African Americans to develop trade relationships with Liberia and to invest in its manufacturing sector. The goal, in Jackson's inimitable phrasing, was to move from "lip service" to "ship service."[131]

While little came of this endeavor, it reflected both the long-standing economic priorities of Black moderate transnationalism as well as a growing consensus around Tolbert's bona fides as an agent of substantive change in Liberian politics. In the 1940s and 1950s Walter White, Rayford Logan, and Mary McLeod Bethune had viewed his predecessor through a similar lens. Even as Tolbert's reform agenda floundered, he nonetheless retained the backing of many African American moderates.

Representatives Charles Rangel, Ralph Metcalf, and William Clay visited Liberia and pledged to be at the forefront of the Congressional Black Caucus's efforts to bring greater recognition to the country's needs.[132] Illinois legislator Lewis A. H. Caldwell and members of Alpha Phi Alpha Fraternity honored Tolbert in 1976 when the organization convened in Monrovia.[133] When A. B. Tolbert, President Tolbert's son and chair of Liberia's House Foreign Affairs Committee, visited Los Angeles in 1978, its first Black mayor, Thomas Bradley, presented him with the key to the city.[134] The same year, during a monthlong tour of Africa, an NAACP task force consulted with President Tolbert as it compiled a series of recommendations to improve "human development" in Africa that were presented to the United Nations and to US policymakers.[135]

Meanwhile, many Liberians began to tire of Tolbert's notions of "humanistic capitalism," which allowed the president to travel the world in a private jet formerly owned by Frank Sinatra while his family expanded its interests in the country's rice, fishing, charcoal, and palm oil industries.[136] In April 1979, as food shortages and unemployment spread throughout the country, Tolbert's minister of agriculture proposed a steep increase in the price of rice, a Liberian staple. This sparked a wave of protests and rioting that led to the deaths of between forty and one hundred people, most at the hands of the Liberian police.[137] In the protests' wake, Tolbert suspended habeas corpus, shuttered the University of Liberia, and oversaw mass arrests, targeting student groups and his political opponents in the Progressive Alliance of Liberia and the Movement for Justice in Africa.[138] Later in the year, Tolbert postponed municipal elections and banned labor strikes.[139]

The Liberian leader blamed the unrest on communists and outside agitators. However, it would have been difficult for the African American foreign policy elite to remain unaware of the nepotism, profiteering, and illiberalism that had overtaken his reform agenda. Despite the fragmented and sometimes opaque allegiances of Liberia's political opposition, it found ways to make itself heard in the United States. For example, in May 1979, less than a month after Tolbert's security forces initiated a crackdown on political dissidents, the Liberian Students Association garnered headlines by holding a sit-in at the New York offices of Winston Tubman, Liberia's ambassador to the UN.[140]

Nevertheless, in October 1979, after Tolbert addressed the UN General Assembly in New York, he was eagerly accompanied on a tour of the Midwest by Representative Charles Diggs and earned the recognition of Mayor Coleman Young of Detroit. Tolbert also attended a reception held in his honor by TransAfrica, a recently formed African American lobby that aimed to support progressive causes in Africa. Its leader, Randall Robinson, appeared lukewarm about the "ceremonial niceties" his group granted Tolbert. Robinson told the press that African Americans felt "a sense of obligation" to welcome African leaders and turned the subject to TransAfrica's comprehensive support for the OAU's positions on African issues.[141]

During Tolbert's visit to the United States, the Liberian leader also met with President Carter, who chose not to dwell on Tolbert's dubious claims that the roots of the April 1979 demonstrations could be traced to the presence of communist agitators in Liberia. Instead, Carter emphasized the importance of the "special relationship" between the United States and Liberia and offered to send a delegation to Liberia to identify ways to enhance relations between the long-standing allies. Carter made clear that the delegation was not intended to facilitate expansions in US aid to Liberia. However, he informed Tolbert that the State Department had just authorized $5 million in direct funding and a $10 million guarantee to support low-income housing construction in Liberia. Carter offered Tolbert little else. He balked when the Liberian president requested that the United States donate funds to help build military housing in Liberia, noting that the country already received more per capita US assistance than any other African state.[142]

With US funding, Tolbert had attempted to modernize the Liberian Frontier Force. But for years, US security aid to Liberia had primarily served the interests of the highest ranks of the Liberian military and the regimes that they protected, namely, Tubman's and Tolbert's. This left an increasingly restive class of enlisted soldiers to live in squalor. President Carter knew that there were mounting tensions in US–Liberia relations, but US officials were also aware of how deeply embattled Tolbert was at home. He was, as such, in no position to drive a hard bargain, even when US strategic assets in Liberia were taken into account. In fact, Tolbert's regime was increasingly viewed as a catalyst for political instability that imperiled US access to its facilities in Liberia.[143]

Internally, US State Department officials noted the "abysmal incompetence of the top officers of the Liberian army." Extending the indictment to the entire Liberian army and police force, they observed that "over two decades of military assistance seem to have had little positive effect." Of course, these officials failed to mention that successive US administrations had helped to prop up the Tubman and Tolbert regimes with military aid. "In the end," they noted, "only the Liberian Government can strengthen the morale and discipline of its security forces."[144]

The senior officers of the Liberian Frontier Force, who had profited most from US military aid and had overseen Tolbert's attempts to squelch the growing unrest, remained largely loyal to the Liberian leader. It was disaffected and poorly paid enlisted soldiers, many of them from the Krahn ethnic group, who saw Liberia's political turmoil as an opening to seize power and exact vengeance on the country's rulers. They did so under the leadership of Master Sergeant Samuel Doe in April 1980, after murdering Tolbert and subsequently executing more than a dozen of his cabinet members.

PRESIDENT SAMUEL DOE: A FRIEND OF THE REAGAN WHITE HOUSE, A DISAPPOINTMENT TO THE AFRICAN AMERICAN FOREIGN POLICY ELITE

When Tolbert's government fell and Doe's junta began torturing, executing, and jailing former Liberian officials, the Carter administration publicly called on the new regime to respect human rights and due process.[145] These were important concerns for some Carter officials.

However, far more attention was paid to preserving US strategic assets in Liberia, protecting the investments of US rubber and mining companies, and warding off communist influence amid the country's political transition. With these priorities in mind, Carter officials quickly decided to offer "muted public criticism" of Doe's abuses.[146] Rather than distancing itself from the new Liberian government or maintaining the status quo of US–Liberia relations, the Carter administration searched for ways to demonstrate that it would be a reliable source of funding and advice for Doe's regime. Carter administration officials recommended resuming and modestly increasing US military aid programs to Liberia that had been suspended in the coup's wake. They also planned to dispatch economic and technical advisors to the country to help shape Doe's fiscal policies.[147]

Despite some early nonaligned posturing by Doe officials, his regime appeared willing to be kept in the fold. With the exception of Ethiopia's Mengistu Haile Mariam, many other African leaders wanted little to do with Doe.[148] The carnival of violence that abetted his rise to power was widely viewed with disdain. Nearly all observers agreed that Doe—a twenty-eight-year-old high school dropout who had risen through the ranks of Liberia's predatory armed forces—was out of his depth as a chief executive. According to the CIA, Doe's regime immediately reached out to the Americans for help.[149] The Carter administration readily obliged.

Months after the coup, Carter authorized a covert operation to assist Doe's government and to train and equip Liberia's intelligence and security services. The stated aims of the operation were "maintaining U.S. interest in Liberia, keeping Liberia moderate and pro West, and encouraging respect for human rights."[150] This initiative was paired with more public-facing measures, which included sending a delegation to Monrovia to counsel moderation and discern means to shore up Liberia's political institutions. At the helm of the US delegation was Representative William H. Gray III, a member of the House Foreign Affairs Committee and the Congressional Black Caucus. Upon his return, Gray penned an article that implored African Americans to play a more aggressive role in US foreign affairs while offering his view of what was at stake in Liberia. The congressman made no mention of the Doe regime's human rights abuses or the aspirations of Liberians who had previously protested the Tolbert government and were now forced to navigate the uncertainties of military rule. Rather, he encouraged African Americans to throw their weight behind an agenda of political stability and economic development for Liberia.[151]

The priorities of Black moderate transnationalism loom large in Gray's analysis. He argued that the profits American corporations reaped in Liberia strengthened their balance sheets, which generated tax revenues and jobs for African Americans in the United States. In a telling example, Gray noted that Bethlehem Steel, a company based in his home state of Pennsylvania, was planning an iron-ore mining venture in Liberia. Moreover, the congressman suggested that Black-owned businesses were mapping out investments in Africa that would be well served by orderly governance. For good measure, Gray speculated that if Liberia's political turbulence was allowed to metastasize, it might destabilize the entire region and require a US military intervention. Under these circumstances, he was confident that African American soldiers would be shunted to the front lines and suffer disproportionate casualties, much as they had in Vietnam.[152] By the close of the decade, the brutality and maladministration of the very regime the Gray was helping to get on its feet would indeed help to fuel a conflagration in the Mano River region.

Some members of the African American foreign policy elite acknowledged the inequalities and discontent that laid the groundwork for Doe's coup. Columnist William Raspberry lamented the executions of his acquaintances among the Liberian ruling class. But he also observed that his friends "had been the oppressors" and according to that logic some of them "deserved it." Still, Raspberry hoped that Doe's regime would not cast aside the legitimate grievances of everyday Liberians in a quest for vengeance against the country's former leaders, whom he compared to Rhodesia's white-minority settlers. This was a comparison that TransAfrica's Randall Robinson likely would have rejected, but in a cable to Doe he too asserted that "the previous government concentrated virtually all political power and wealth in the hands of a minority that refused to concern itself with the broader welfare of the

Liberian people."[153] Robinson nonetheless encouraged Doe to show restraint and seek the moral high ground.

Doe had other ideas. As Burrowes notes, his regime "imprisoned, tortured, and killed more Liberians for political reasons than all its predecessors combined."[154] It also received more US security assistance than all of Liberia's previous governments. Early in Doe's rule, the Reagan administration oversaw nearly $5 million in renovations at Roberts Field.[155] From 1980 to 1985 alone, Liberia took in nearly $72 million in US military aid and $475 million in total US assistance.[156] To advance its staunch Cold War agenda, the Reagan White House vastly expanded Carter's previous efforts to ensure that Doe and US assets in Liberia were protected. Reagan was so committed to supporting key, "anticommunist" African allies that Doe, during the first half of his ten-year rule, had little need to bargain with the United States. Even better for Reagan, Doe was a leader of limited ambition. Regime security obviously mattered to him, but he clung to power largely to enrich himself and his ethnic allies rather than to impose a broader political agenda on Liberia or the region. Into the late 1980s, Doe routinely expressed loyalty to Reagan, and the United States was overwhelming receptive to his requests for assistance.

It was only when Doe's regime started to collapse under the weight of its own brutality and economic mismanagement that Reagan, under congressional pressure, began to turn away from his West African ally. In response, in 1987 Doe called for a review of all foreign assets on Liberian soil, with the goal of demanding more rent from the Americans.[157] By this point, however, access to Roberts Field and the Port of Monrovia was of waning value. Southern Africa was the focus of Reagan's security initiatives on the continent, and airfields in Zaire offered ready access to the region. Worse still for Doe, US communications facilities in Liberia were being driven into obsolescence by advancements in satellite technology.[158]

African American leaders did not stand silent as Doe's regime descended into a vortex violence and cronyism. After its early appeals for restraint went unheeded, TransAfrica began to forcefully criticize Doe's human rights abuses. Members of the CBC were not among the cosponsors of the first pieces of legislation to demand that Reagan suspend military aid to Liberia. But they did express growing concerns around Doe's policies when they communicated directly with his officials.[159] Doubtful that Liberia's 1985 presidential election would be free and fair, the CBC leadership asked to send observers to monitor the poll. When the request was denied, Representative Edolphus Towns threatened to send a team of observers to Liberia anyway, declaring, "If we don't take a stand against what is taking place over there, who else in the US will?"[160] Representative Charles Rangel also championed this effort to "preserve democracy" in the West African state.[161] The election monitors were not dispatched to Liberia, and Doe won his first official term as the country's president, after a campaign marked by extensive suppression of dissent.

The CBC continued to call attention to Doe's persecution of his political opponents, including Ellen Johnson-Sirleaf, a former minister in Tolbert's government who would later be elected president of Liberia in 2006. In fact, Representative George Crockett Jr. made specific reference to Johnson-Sirleaf's imprisonment in 1986 when he became of one of the first CBC members to call for a suspension of US military aid to Liberia.[162] Journalists such as Ethel Payne, who had long chronicled African and African American politics, likewise highlighted the appeals of Liberian political dissidents in exile, such as the Union of Liberian Associations in the Americas.[163] By 1990, as the Liberian military massacred civilians amid a civil war that would lead to Doe's assassination and the fall of his regime, much of the Black foreign policy elite firmly opposed continued US security assistance to Liberia. The CBC's leadership cosponsored legislation to suspend US military aid to the country, and TransAfrica made similar demands of the US State Department.[164]

THE SHIFTING TIDES OF AFRICAN DIPLOMACY, AMERICAN RACIAL POLITICS, AND BLACK MODERATE TRANSNATIONALISM

The wave of opposition to the US security partnership with Doe's regime marked a shift in Black moderate transnationalism. Indeed, in the late

1980s and early 1990s the African American foreign policy elite offered a wide-ranging critique of US–Africa security relations. Liberal Black leaders questioned US strategic ties with Liberia, Somalia, Kenya, Nigeria, Malawi, and Zaire.[165] Since the 1960s their criticisms had largely targeted US military aid to South Africa and Rhodesia. In the decades prior, many had interrogated Washington's bonds with Paris, Brussels, and Lisbon because these loyalties weakened US support for decolonization. As a result of these ties, US taxpayers helped to arm European militaries that suppressed African nationalist movements.[166] In 1949 William J. Walls, a prominent bishop of the AME Zion Church, made this point exactly when he vocally opposed the ratification of the North Atlantic Treaty Organization (NATO) pact.[167] Similarly, during the first half of the century, liberal Black leaders directed their fury at the cozy relations the United States had with European powers who threatened the sovereignty of Liberia and Ethiopia.

This corresponded nicely with the Black elite's opposition to racism at home. They were contesting white dominance in Africa. Autocratic leaders of independent African states that aligned themselves with the United States posed a more complex problem for African American liberals. Across the twentieth century, some offered occasional denunciations of the most abusive African leaders among US allies and adversaries alike, such as Liberia's C.D.B. King, Congo's Moise Tshombe, and Uganda's Idi Amin.[168] Moreover, starting in the late 1970s, leading members of the CBC expressed muted and infrequent reservations around the militarization of US policy toward Africa.[169] They opposed, for example, the Carter administration's efforts to secure US access to Somalia's Berbera air base and questioned the Reagan administration's increases in military aid to states such as Zaire and Sudan.[170] But these issues were tangential to their running and forceful opposition to US relations with apartheid South Africa, a cause rooted in traditional critiques of anti-Black racism in US foreign policy.

In the 1980s the Black foreign policy elite's central interventions in US–Africa security politics revolved around contesting US economic and military ties with South Africa. Amid this tide of activism and legislation, many Black and white conservatives argued that Black liberal denunciations of white-minority rule in Africa were morally inconsistent with their silence around the repressive policies of Black-governed African states.[171] Some Black liberals appeared sensitive to this charge and emphasized that their persistent condemnations of South Africa as well as their more infrequent critiques of states such as Liberia all reflected a commitment to democracy in Africa. Representative George Crockett noted that the Reagan's administration's charitable approach to the Doe administration mirrored its "apologies with respect to South Africa," and the congressman took issue with both.[172]

Conservatives often charged Black liberals with moral inconsistency to deflect the criticism that Reagan's policy of "constructive engagement" with South Africa was yet another example of racism in US foreign affairs.[173] Reagan appeared determined to stop the antiracist commitments of Black liberals from poisoning US foreign policy. This meant dispensing with what his officials deemed "the civil rights tone" that Andrew Young, Carter's UN ambassador, had imposed on the previous administration's relations with South Africa.[174]

Confronting racism in US foreign policy may have blunted African American criticisms of African leaders, but their concerns around its ascendance during the Reagan administration were not unfounded. As is now well known, in a 1971 telephone conversation with President Nixon, then Governor Reagan had choice words for the African delegates who stood against the United States in the UN vote to recognize the People's Republic of China. The governor disparaged the African delegates as "Monkeys . . . still uncomfortable wearing shoes."[175] Nixon cackled and agreed heartily. In a more public allusion to African savagery, Reagan claimed during his 1976 presidential campaign that if Washington abandoned Ian Smith's white-supremacist regime, Rhodesian whites would likely be massacred.[176] Smith himself, it should be noted, died of natural causes in 2007 after residing openly in independent Zimbabwe for more than two decades.

In 1983, after a disappointing visit to US security allies in Africa, President Reagan's deputy assistant secretary of defense for African affairs observed, "One distinction shines through, and can probably not be stated without risking the racial overtone. Where African military elements shine, they are closely run by European officers."[177] While overt expressions of racism are rarely found in the late twentieth-century diplomatic record, at least among declassified sources, the notion that some military capabilities were beyond African comprehension is nonetheless discernible during this period—much as it had been in early and midcentury US assessments of the Ethiopian and Liberian armies. Interestingly, according to a boastful 1985 State Department appraisal of President Reagan's programs in Africa, his foreign service, ostensibly unencumbered by bias, had adeptly exploited "Soviet racism" across the continent and Moscow's ignorance of "African tribal realities."[178]

This matrix of views coheres with what Siba Grovogui rightly deems "the racial ideology that motivated much of the Reagan administration foreign policy toward Africa."[179] Similarly, Darren Brunk has called attention to the pervasiveness of an African "cognitive schema" among US policymakers that was grounded in stereotypes of endemic African savagery and anarchy.[180] Reagan took such ideas for granted despite more nuanced appraisals from career diplomats in Africa and Black congressional leaders laboring to distinguish the stereotypical from the substantive as they assessed African governance. Notwithstanding their racist foundations, these stereotypes often found their greatest confirmation among the Reagan administration's closest security allies in Africa, including Samuel Doe, Somalia's Mohamed Siad Barre, and Zaire's Mobutu Sese Seko. Nevertheless, Reagan officials publicly underscored the fortitude of these African leaders, their alleged commitments to reform, and their loyalty to Washington's anticommunist agenda.[181]

Of these US allies, Mobutu would prove to be the most adept bargainer and reap the greatest rewards from his security partnership with Washington. Unlike Liberian and Ethiopian heads of state, the Zairian president would move beyond bargaining influence derived largely from the anticipation of US diplomatic officials and embrace bargaining tactics that put US goals and security operations at risk. Yet, starting in the late 1980s, Mobutu would finally face a headwind of opposition from African American leaders who were revolted by his kleptocratic and antidemocratic practices. During this moment, African American moderates would take their firmest stance yet against repressive US security allies in Africa. Their critiques, however, would soon give way to hasty plaudits when a "new breed" of African leaders emerged in the mid-1990s.[182]

3

THE HEART OF DARK OPERATIONS

Zaire's Kamina Air Base and Mobutu's Muscle in Washington

In February 1987 Representative Ronald Dellums became the first member of Congress to publicly warn the Reagan administration about the dangers of using Kamina air base to host US operations in Southern Africa. He cautioned that such operations would bolster the Mobutu government as it abused its own citizens while collaborating with Apartheid South Africa and "counterrevolutionaries" in Angola.[1] News had recently broken that a CIA operation was using Kamina air base as a transshipment point for weapons being flown to Jonas Savimbi's National Union for the Total Independence of Angola (UNITA).[2] For more than a year, Representative Dellums, Representative John Conyers, and members of the Congressional Black Caucus had been pressuring the Reagan administration to cut aid to the Mobutu government. Conyers, capturing the spirit of this effort, deemed the close ties between Mobutu and Reagan an affront to human rights and "a direct insult to black Americans."[3]

But the CIA operation at Kamina had powerful supporters on Capitol Hill. Primary among them were former segregationist and ardent anticommunist senators such as Strom Thurmond and Jesse Helms. These conservatives would provide a reliable tailwind for Mobutu's campaign to leverage Kamina air base as a source of influence in Washington as the CIA's operation expanded in Zaire. From 1986 to 1991, the Reagan and Bush administrations funneled weapons to UNITA through Kamina. During this time, Mobutu consistently reminded US officials of the base's critical importance to the operation and the risks Zaire incurred because of his covert assistance to the CIA. Mobutu demanded and received remarkably consistent returns, including increases in US foreign aid and US interventions on Zaire's behalf with international financial institutions. Mobutu's aptitude for extortion was abetted by the covert, makeshift nature of the US operation at the Zairian air base. This not only offered Mobutu greater latitude for experimentation as he sought influence in Washington but also offered unique opportunities for legislators such as Helms and Dellums to push for shifts in policy around the Kamina operation.

US covert operations in Africa such as the one at Kamina were often stopgap measures Washington used to "fill the holes" in its regional policies, and their broader strategic aims were often "cryptic."[4] This stemmed from a running dearth of US intelligence regarding most security crises in Africa, indifference toward long-term foreign policy planning vis-à-vis the continent, and rival agendas among American diplomatic, defense, and intelligence agencies. As a result, to borrow a phrase from Chester Crocker, Ronald Reagan's assistant secretary of state for African affairs, the US government was not always "obliged to make up its mind about which foreign policy was its real foreign policy."[5] This ambiguous and fragmented approach to US policymaking provided Mobutu outsized influence and an incentive to make the most of this influence before the operation that rendered him momentarily indispensable came to an end.

This chapter traces Mobutu's efforts to exploit US reliance on Kamina air base. Kamina was a centerpiece of the Reagan administration's push to oppose Soviet influence in Southern Africa. The CIA operation was a reprisal of the program that Kissinger had been forced to abandon in the mid-1970s, despite his illicit plans for Roberts Field. Against this backdrop, Mobutu's diplomatic campaign to capitalize on Washington's regional security agenda was more confrontational, improvisational, and effective than those of earlier US security partners, such as Ethiopia and Liberia. Moreover, the Kamina case brings into focus racial cleavages around the CIA operation in Zaire, primarily between Black members of Congress and their white counterparts, many of whom were skeptical of majority government in Southern Africa and civil rights reforms in the United States. African American members of Congress played a pivotal role in undercutting the influence Mobutu derived from the Kamina operation. This reflected a gradual about-face for the liberal African American foreign policy elite, much of which had long held out hope that Mobutu's government would develop into a source of stability and economic dynamism in Africa.

"A STAGING AREA . . . IN TIMES OF CRISES": A HISTORY OF US STRATEGIC INTEREST IN KAMINA

On the afternoon of October 21, 1985, President Mobutu paid a visit to the US Pentagon. In a meeting with Casper Weinberger, Reagan's secretary of defense, the Zairian president revealed plans to expand his army by seven brigades and requested that the United States train and equip these new troops. He insisted that since Reagan had taken office, Zaire had been inadequately rewarded for its long-standing alliance with the United States. "Is Zaire being told it is no longer strategically important?," prodded Mobutu.[6]

Weinberger assured Mobutu that the United States considered Zaire a valuable ally, emphasizing, however, that Congress had hamstrung the Reagan administration's military aid initiatives. Mobutu was not pleased. He reminded Weinberger that since 1961 the United States had viewed Zaire's Kamina and Kitona military bases as strategically vital redoubts in Central Africa. His country remained, Mobutu argued, more important to American interests in the region than states such as Sudan that were receiving more military assistance than Zaire. Weinberger committed to do as much as he could to help Mobutu, and the Pentagon "scrambled" to arrange a joint training exercise with US and Congolese troops as well as repairs to Kamina.[7]

Mobutu had only slightly exaggerated the importance of Kamina and Kitona to America's early Cold War calculus. In fact, denying the Soviet Union access to these bases played an important, and largely overlooked, role in the US decision to undermine and plot the assassination of Patrice Lumumba, Congo's first prime minister. US policy toward Congo upon its independence was guided by concerns that instability and Lumumba's "Soviet-oriented neutralism" would make the new state fertile ground for Moscow's machinations, thus facilitating the rise of communist regimes among Congo's many neighbors.[8] In addition, there was a desire to advance US business interests by maintaining access to Congo's mineral resources. In the context of these broader motives, Pentagon documents reveal a specific fear that Kamina and Kitona would be tangible and dangerous strategic spoils for the Soviet Union if Lumumba were to expand his ties with Moscow. In August 1960, less than two months after Congo's independence, the US Joint Chiefs of Staff warned that Kamina could provide a ready "focal point for Communist subversion."[9]

Under the terms of a Treaty of Friendship between Belgium and the Congo drafted prior to Congo's independence, Belgium maintained access to Kamina and Kitona and could keep troops stationed at both facilities.[10] Congolese soldiers, still under the command of Belgian officers committed to the colonial status quo, mutinied less than a week after the state achieved independence on June 30, 1960. Amid the unrest that followed, Belgium sent paratroopers to the Congo and deployed soldiers from Kamina and Kitona with the stated intention of protecting Belgian nationals. In addition to fighting mutinying Congolese troops and evacuating Belgian citizens, these paratroopers supported the secession of Congo's mineral-rich Katanga province under the leadership of Moise Tshombe. On July 11, 1960, with the full support of the province's Belgian mining giant, Union Minière du Haut Katanga, Tshombe declared Katanga independent.[11]

Lumumba denounced the Belgian intervention as an act of aggression that violated the Treaty of Friendship and alarmed the United States Joint Chiefs by repudiating the unratified accord. Less than a month later, after the adoption of a United Nations (UN) resolution calling for the withdrawal of Belgian troops from the Congo, the US Joint Chiefs expressed an urgent commitment to keeping Kamina and Kitona in friendly hands. They predicted that Kamina, due to its "strategic location in the heart of Sub Saharan Africa," would be a key "staging area for military operations in times of crises" for the United States, the North Atlantic Treaty Organization (NATO), or UN forces. More critically, the Joint Chiefs suggested that if the base came under Soviet control, it could provide a source of military assistance for communist coups in neighboring African states and threaten "free world" air and sea communications. Soviet control of the Kitona air base, located along Congo's Atlantic Coast, could threaten Western access to the ocean shipping lanes of Southern Africa and facilitate rapid communist troop deployments into West Africa. As such, the Joint Chiefs declared that "all possible steps be taken to deny these facilities to the Soviet Bloc."[12]

Because the Belgians faced pressure to abandon Kamina and Kitona, the Joint Chiefs recommended that the United States take action to ensure that the UN, rather than the Soviets, take immediate control of these facilities. Moreover, they recommended the initiation of military assistance programs to keep these bases operational. Their final and most telling recommendation—given the key role that the CIA ultimately played in destabilizing the Lumumba regime—was "covert action, including the introduction of agents, in all of the above to ensure a pro-Western orientation." This was considered an essential component of a long-term strategy to keep the bases in "friendly hands."[13] The Joint Chiefs' preoccupation with Kamina and Kitona was so unique that upon receiving their recommendations, Under Secretary of State C. Douglas Dillon remarked that to his knowledge, this constituted the first time the Department of Defense had suggested that America had "any specific strategic interests in Africa south of the Sahara."[14] This point of view had been prominent within the State Department when the Congo crisis began, and American diplomats had taken scant measures to ensure that Kamina and Kitona remained in friendly hands. However, after the Joint Chiefs made their position regarding the strategic value of the bases clear, the State Department placed greater emphasis on "assuring the continued security and maintenance" of these facilities.[15]

The month after the Joint Chiefs of Staff issued its assessment regarding Kamina and Kitona, the CIA provided large-scale covert financial assistance to Mobutu, then a colonel in the Congolese Army, and encouraged him to stage a coup that deposed Lumumba's government on September 14, 1960.[16] In the immediate wake of the coup, Mobutu ordered the expulsion of all Soviet bloc officials from the Congo. On January 17, 1961, Lumumba was assassinated through a coordinated plot by forces loyal to Mobutu and Tshombe, both of whom were supported in this effort by the United States and Belgium.[17]

The United Nations took control of Kamina in autumn of 1961 and used it as a key base to deploy troops and aircraft to end the Katangan secession in January 1963.[18] After UN troops withdrew from the Congo in June 1964, Kamina almost immediately came back into play. In the fall of that year, the United States airlifted Belgian troops from the air base to assist Congo's recently installed Premier Tshombe and Mobutu, now major-general, in crushing a rebellion by the Conseil National de Libèration. These Lumumba loyalists, known as the Simbas, were holding roughly 1,600 Americans and Europeans hostage in their eastern stronghold, Stanleyville. In the wake of this operation, code-named Dragon Rouge, Mobutu made Washington aware of his penchant for brutality by allowing his troops and hired mercenaries to massacre between ten and twenty thousand Congolese in Stanleyville.[19]

US assistance to Tshombe and Mobutu in quashing the Simba rebellion was opposed by a broad cross-section of African American Civil Rights leaders. Dr. Martin Luther King Jr. of the Southern Christian Leadership Conference, James Farmer of the Congress of Racial Equality, Dorothy Height of the National Council of Negro Women, A. Phillip Randolph of the Negro-American Labor Council, Roy Wilkins of the NAACP, and Whitney M. Young of the National Urban League all made their concerns known in a December 1964 letter to President Lyndon Johnson. They urged the White House to withdraw support for Tshombe, who they asserted was "held in disrepute throughout most of independent Africa."[20] Malcolm X, whose disagreements with these Civil Rights leaders were legion, strongly agreed, excoriating Johnson administration policy in Africa: "They send the Peace Corps to Nigeria and hired killers to the Congo."[21]

Tshombe had long been viewed with skepticism by African Americans across the political spectrum who held him, along with Washington and Brussels, responsible for the assassination of Patrice Lumumba. While many moderate African American leaders took issue with Lumumba's assassination, they had hesitated to offer the slain Congolese prime minister full-throated support, deeming him uncooperative with UN efforts to end the Congo Crisis and opposing his invitation to the Soviets to help end the Katangese secession. More radical African Americans viewed Lumumba's attempt to retain power as part of a global struggle against racism and imperialism.[22] The Black Marxist labor activist Ismael Flory asserted that Lumumba's assassination was "a crime against humanity perpetrated by the government of the U.S. Just as the blood of over 5,000 lynched black bodies from the South is on the hands of that government." Tshombe was thus an "Uncle Tom," a corrupt and opportunistic henchman of racist world powers.[23] Richard Wright drew a direct parallel with America's domestic politics: "We have agents-provocateur in the Black Belt, as well as the Congolese in their strife-torn land . . . playing the role that is being played by Tshombe in Katanga. He is a puppet, and I have met puppets in New York's Harlem and on the Southside of Chicago."[24]

In short, African Americans directed the lion's share of their ire at Tshombe rather than Mobutu. Though the two had collaborated to bring about the downfall of Lumumba's regime, Tshombe was held more responsible for the balkanization of the Congo and the chaotic aftermath of independence. Nevertheless, Tshombe had reliable allies in the US Congress. He was embraced by a group of staunch anticommunist senators, some of whom, such as Connecticut's Thomas J. Dodd and Illinois's Everett Dirksen, were largely supportive of civil rights. Tshombe's firmest bloc of assistance, however, could be found among segregationist southern senators such as Georgia's Richard Russell, Mississippi's James Eastland, and South Carolina's Strom Thurmond.[25]

It is no exaggeration to say that Tshombe had the support of some of America's most powerful white supremacists. Senator Russell wrote in private correspondence: "Any southern white man worth a pinch of salt would give his all to maintain white supremacy."[26] For Senator

Thurmond, Tshombe was not just a bulwark against Soviet encroachment in the Congo, he was a "staunch defender of Western principles of civilization."[27] Just months before Dr. King and Malcolm X condemned US support for Tshombe, the two had met for the only time on Capitol Hill as Strom Thurmond was poised to participate in a filibuster against the Civil Rights Act of 1964.[28] Thurmond often favored Tshombe over Mobutu, but during the Reagan years the southern senator would warm to the Zairian president. In the 1980s, Thurmond would work alongside former segregationist Senator Jesse Helms as well as Senators Jake Garn, Orrin Hatch, and Malcolm Wallop—who as one journalist put it, "read speeches that sound as though they were . . . written in Pretoria"—to provide a bulwark of support for the CIA operation at Mobutu's air base.[29] This cadre of conservatives thus offered the Zairian president crucial assistance in maintaining his influence in Washington.

By the late 1980s, many liberal African Americans leaders began to stand on the other side of this equation, openly questioning US ties with Zaire and Mobutu's human rights record. However, in the early 1960s when Mobutu began his rise to power atop the Congolese army, liberal African Americans were far more receptive to his ascent than their later denunciations would suggest. He was widely viewed as a strongman, but when contrasted to Tshombe, Mobutu was cast as a vitally needed source of stability for the conflict-weary Congolese people and a leader who was not as indebted to the Belgian business interests that fueled the Congo crisis.

This penchant for seeing the best in Mobutu became obvious as early 1963 when the Zairian colonel was invited to the United States to tour the country's military installations. Black periodicals depicted Mobutu as a mild-mannered former journalist who was well positioned to reorganize Congo's unruly army by appointing a handful of Western-trained Congolese soldiers to key positions in the force.[30] They observed that he was a staunch Catholic and anticommunist, and perhaps the only Congolese official who could restore order to the Central African state.[31] This sentiment persisted among Black liberals after Mobutu seized power in a coup in late 1965.

That year, Congressman Charles Diggs led a study mission to Africa and met with Mobutu on the day the Johnson administration decided to recognize his government. Diggs and the congressional mission reported that they were impressed by Mobutu's commitment to empowering the Congolese people and strengthening the state's economy.[32] Back home, the *Chicago Defender* hailed Mobutu as a deft political operator who had remained in the shadows of Congolese government for too long, even if he had not come to power in "the best democratic tradition."[33] In short, in his burgeoning effort to consolidate Congo's security ties with Washington, Mobutu quickly gained the support of much of the moderate African American foreign policy elite.

ANGOLAN INDEPENDENCE AND US-ZAIRE RELATIONS

By the close of 1965, Mobutu had begun to steady the foundations of his autocratic rule as Congo's head of state. Over the next three decades, with US, French, and Belgian assistance, he would aggressively consolidate his power as Congo's military dictator. To understand why Kamina would become a powerful source of leverage for Mobutu vis-à-vis Washington during the 1980s, it is first necessary to assess American efforts to counter "communist influence" in Southern Africa dating back to the eve of Angolan independence. Shifts in the tenor of Zaire's ties with the United States during this period loom large. In the context of these periodically fraught relations, Mobutu would refine his efforts to capitalize on American intelligence shortfalls, strategic vulnerabilities, and fears regarding the international balance of power.

Mobutu's desire to expand his influence in Southern Africa and potentially annex Angola's oil rich Cabinda province fueled his attempts to draw America into Angola's civil war in 1975.[34] The Popular Movement for the Liberation of Angola, which was poised to take power upon Angolan independence, stood squarely in the way of these ambitions. Antipathy between Mobutu and the MPLA had taken root in the early

1960s as Angola's fragmented anticolonial forces initiated the first acts of large-scale violence in their war of independence against Portugal. Mobutu backed the MPLA's rivals, Holden Roberto's National Liberation Front of Angola (FNLA). Roberto, who would become Mobutu's brother-in-law, had begun to establish himself as a leading Angolan spokesman for decolonization in the mid-1950s. In 1959 he traveled to Washington to meet with Senator John F. Kennedy and praised Kennedy's rhetoric in support of the self-determination of African states.[35] Roberto's "pro-Western leanings" were clear, and he espoused a vague mixture of populism and free-market economics at a moment when both Washington and Kinshasa were increasingly suspicious of the MPLA's pragmatic Marxism.[36] As a result, much to the consternation of Portugal, its NATO ally, the United States began providing Roberto small amounts of financial support in 1961.

Later, China also provided the FNLA support, largely in the form of military training. However, throughout Angola's anticolonial conflict, the FNLA was almost completely beholden to Mobutu for its survival. Zaire was the base for virtually all its political and military infrastructure. In fact, the extent to which the FNLA relied on external assistance was Jonas Savimbi's stated justification for breaking with the group in 1966 and forming UNITA. Not long after UNITA's founding, despite his strident nationalist rhetoric, Savimbi would begin to actively collaborate with the Portuguese colonial authorities as they fought the FNLA and MPLA.[37] The MPLA received much of its financial support throughout the 1960s and early 1970s from Yugoslavia, while also benefiting from sporadic infusions of military assistance from the Soviet Union and Cuba and military staging bases in Zambia and Congo Brazzaville.[38]

In April 1974 a military junta took power in Portugal and aimed to end the country's colonial wars. To this end, Portugal and Angola's three competing nationalist groups—the MPLA, FNLA, and UNITA—signed the Alvor Agreement in January 1975. It called for a transitional government led by the three nationalist movements to govern Angola until national elections and full independence in November 1975. Within weeks of the Alvor Agreement, the Ford administration allocated $300,000 to the FNLA, and less than two months after the transitional government took power, the FNLA initiated a series of attacks against MPLA positions in and around the Angolan capital, Luanda.[39] The MPLA responded with a counteroffensive in late May 1975, and, despite a series of ceasefires, the fighting escalated into a nationwide civil conflict.

It was at this moment that Savimbi captured the attention of powerful allies in the US State Department and CIA, laying a foundation for a relationship that would span the next sixteen years—with Mobutu's consistent facilitation. Though UNITA's military presence proved meager, Savimbi began to cooperate with the FNLA in early 1975 and seek the assistance of the US and South African governments. At the same time, he vigorously and often brutally consolidated power in the central Angolan highlands, while proclaiming an opposition to communist influence and a commitment to democratic governance. Despite rumors that Savimbi had once been a Maoist, Secretary of State Henry Kissinger and Director of Central Intelligence William Colby saw potential in Savimbi's charisma, political acumen, and staunch anticommunist posturing. Just as important, the Ford administration began to grow concerned by intelligence reports indicating a major increase in Soviet and Cuban support for the MPLA.[40]

Much of the intelligence guiding US policy in Angola in early 1975 came from the CIA station in Kinshasa and its contacts within the Mobutu regime.[41] For Mobutu, the choice between the pliant, deeply indebted FNLA and the unpredictable Marxist MPLA was clear. Despite Mobutu's efforts to support the FNLA, including sending Zairian troops into Angola to fight alongside Roberto's forces in the spring of 1975, by the summer of that year it was obvious that the MPLA was seizing the military advantage. In response, Mobutu began increasingly insisting that the Ford administration provide aid, routed through Zaire, to Roberto and Savimbi. This demand came at a particularly tumultuous moment in US–Zaire relations. Mobutu's influence in Washington and receptiveness to American counsel had both begun to wane in the early 1970s. During this period, US military aid to Zaire sharply declined. Mobutu still openly proclaimed that America was "Zaire's friend in its first hour," but by 1973 he began to express sharp dissatisfaction with the terms of this friendship.[42]

In a bid for autonomy, Mobutu broke ties with Israel and expanded relations with China and North Korea. Under the rubric of "Authenticité," he changed Congo's name to Zaire and initiated sweeping reforms meant to "put an end to exploitation" by external forces.[43] This effort to cultivate what Mobutu deemed a more authentically African identity for the Congo held considerable appeal for some Pan-Africanists and Black nationalist groups in the United States.[44] Others refused to relinquish deep skepticism of Mobutu due to his role in Lumumba's assassination and long-standing ties with the CIA. Nonetheless, by hosting the 1974 "Rumble in the Jungle," during which boxer Muhammad Ali defeated George Foreman, Mobutu aimed to draw attention to Zaire as an epicenter of Black autonomy and cultural vitality.[45]

Despite Authenticité's grand cultural ambitions, ongoing property expropriation and patronage politics in Zaire intensified a downturn in the country's economy. At the same time, the Ford administration offered little assistance and insisted that Mobutu impose austerity measures to improve Zaire's economic straits. In response, Mobutu publicly condemned America's "passive" Africa policy, declaring in early 1975: "Your country has done nothing to help free Africa from colonialism and apartheid."[46] Five months later, Mobutu accused the CIA of colluding with Zairian military officials to orchestrate a coup in Kinshasa and expelled the American ambassador. While there was no evidence to support this act of political theater, Mobutu made clear the consequences of Washington's inattentiveness to Zaire's economic turmoil and the looming threat of an MPLA government in Angola.

As relations between Kinshasa and the Ford administration began to weaken, Mobutu's support from African American legislators such as Charles Diggs and Andrew Young Jr. proved beneficial. In 1975, at the African American Institute Conference in Zaire, Mobutu played generous host to the largest group of Black congressional representatives that had visited an African state.[47] During the conference, in a cable to Washington, Diggs firmly supported Mobutu's criticisms of the newly appointed US assistant secretary of state for Africa, Nathaniel Davis, who had been implicated as a key figure in the coup that had recently unseated

Chile's Salvador Allende. Diggs noted prevailing speculation "that Africa continues to be of minimal priority for the U.S. and that AF bureau will become the dumping ground for retirees and other diffucult [*sic*] candidates to assign."[48]

In June 1975 Kissinger encouraged Ford to approve a $50 million increase in assistance to Zaire. The secretary was determined to avoid a breach in relations with Mobutu, particularly as reports of growing Soviet and Cuban support for the MPLA mounted. The same month, the administration began to finalize its plans to extend covert military aid to Roberto and Savimbi with Zaire's assistance. Between July and August 1975, the United States provided nearly $25 million of covert military aid to the FNLA and UNITA under the auspices of a CIA operation known as "IAFEATURE."[49] Ultimately, CIA efforts to support Roberto's forces would be inadequate, and in December 1975 the MPLA, with the assistance of Cuban troops and Soviet arms, would rout Zairian and FNLA troops in northern Angola. Likewise, the Ford administration's clandestine assistance to Savimbi could not forestall the MPLA's rise to power after Angola's independence in 1975. Even as South Africa invaded southern Angola in the autumn of that year while also providing military aid to UNITA, the MPLA, with the support of its allies, managed to withstand Savimbi's guerrilla attacks and establish a functioning government in Luanda.

American military support for the MPLA's opponents ran through Kinshasa, not Kamina, and three months after IAFEATURE began, its cover was blown. Ford administration sources described the operation to the *New York Times* in September 1975, emphasizing that "the main purpose of the covert American effort in Angola was to underline the Administration's support for President Mobutu."[50] Senator Edward Kennedy, a Democrat who was leading a groundswell of opposition to the program, drew similar conclusions, charging that the administration "appears to have followed Zaire's attempt to insure influence over a future Angolan government."[51] Indeed, during the planning of IAFEATURE, Kissinger stressed behind closed doors that it was a "joint endeavor" meant to mend American relations with Zaire.[52] But once the operation was exposed, he defended it along broader geostrategic lines, claiming that the United States could not stand idle as the Soviet Union extended its sphere of influence in Southern Africa.

The Congressional Black Caucus condemned IAFEATURE and its covert status. The CBC argued that the program's aid for UNITA and the FNLA helped to escalate the civil conflict in Angola while aligning the US with racist South Africa's campaign to destabilize the MPLA government.[53] Moreover, on the heels of the fall of Saigon in April 1975, much of the US public feared the prospect of another protracted conflict resembling America's failed effort in Vietnam. Much like their partisans in the Congressional Black Caucus, many Democrats, such as Senator Dick Clark, were leery of increased "US identification with South Africa," one of UNITA's key supporters.[54] As such, less than six months after the launch of IAFEATURE, Congress passed Section 404 of the International Security Assistance and Arms Export Control Act of 1976. Known as the Clark Amendment, this statute prohibited American assistance to any military or paramilitary force in Angola without congressional authorization.[55] Though the CBC condemned IAFEATURE, in its wake Representative Diggs nonetheless called for the Ford administration to offer emergency aid to Mobutu's regime because of the "economic losses" it had incurred as it supported the operation.[56]

While Mobutu failed to keep the MPLA from coming to power, he had used a well-timed mixture of political theater, exaggerated reports of a Soviet threat, and vital operational assistance to the CIA to assert his leverage as a key American ally and demand concessions from Washington. He would use this strategy to much greater effect a decade later when Kamina air base became an integral element of Reagan's efforts to aid Savimbi. At the outset of the Carter administration, however, the rapprochement in US–Zaire relations came under threat.

Carter had come to power on promises of increased American attention to human rights. Worse still for Mobutu, Carter claimed during his campaign that the Russians and Cubans supporting the MPLA in Angola "need not constitute a threat to United States interests."[57] However, in March 1977 and again in May 1978, former Katangan gendarmes exiled to Angola made incursions into Zaire's Shaba province. In 1977 the Zairian army turned back the gendarmes with the assistance of Moroccan troops, French aircraft and advisors, and a US donation of roughly $15 million in nonlethal military supplies. The next year, French and Belgian troops flown to Zaire on transport planes provided by the Carter administration routed the Katangans. Carter overcame a reluctance to intervene in support of Mobutu on both occasions.[58] Administration officials believed the Katangans posed a serious threat to Mobutu's regime and, should Mobutu fall, the Soviets were poised to exploit the power vacuum that would emerge. Kamina once again demonstrated its strategic value as a key support base for both of these infusions of Western assistance that rescued Mobutu's regime.[59]

As the chair of the House International Relations Committee, Charles Diggs was mindful of the geo-strategic implications of the Shaba invasions, but he was also increasingly concerned about Mobutu's kleptocratic administration of the Congolese State. In mid-1977 Diggs's committee proposed a 50 percent cut in new US military sales credits to Zaire. Diggs framed the move as a warning shot to a loyal but recalcitrant ally rather than a signal that the United States was poised to abandon its Central African security partner. He noted that Washington was still committed to offering Mobutu military and economic assistance, remarking that "one could hardly say that we are turning our backs on Zaire."[60] To do so would have been to overlook Kamina's strategic significance. The air base served as a key logistical hub for the Carter administration's infusions of assistance to Mobutu during the Shaba crises and, as such, a lynchpin for US efforts to keep the Soviets at bay in Central Africa.

KAMINA AND THE REAGAN AND BUSH ADMINISTRATIONS' SOUTHERN AFRICA STRATEGIES

By autumn 1985, when Mobutu met with Weinberger and requested that the United States train and equip seven brigades of Zairian troops,

American officials were well aware of Kamina's value as a staging point for interventions in Africa. Two months after the Weinberger-Mobutu meeting, the CIA would begin negotiations with Mobutu to secure access to Kamina as a base to fly arms to Savimbi's UNITA forces in Angola.[61] President Reagan saw UNITA's insurgency as a vehicle for rolling back the influence of the MPLA's primary backers in Southern Africa, the Soviet Union and Cuba. Moreover, he was determined to avenge the "stinging defeat" suffered by the Ford administration in Angola with the collapse of IAFEATURE.[62]

Savimbi's prodemocracy pronouncements found a ready audience among ascendant, hardline anticommunists in Congress and the Reagan administration. This group's support for Savimbi and Mobutu derived largely from its fervent opposition to Soviet influence in Africa. But this anticommunism was deeply intertwined with anti-Black racism. Reagan's own racist ideas about Africans have been widely noted.[63] Likewise many conservative Senators such as Strom Thurmond, Jesse Helms, Jerimiah Denton, and Orrin Hatch who backed the CIA operation at Kamina readily cloaked their racist views in the language of populism, small government, antiterrorism, and a global confrontation between Western and Eastern values.[64] Among this group were some of the fiercest opponents of domestic civil rights reforms as well as emerging legislation to sanction the apartheid government in South Africa.[65] This clique of conservatives largely ignored Savimbi's autocratic leadership of UNITA and his penchant for silencing dissent through torture and public executions.[66]

As these conservatives tightened their bonds with Savimbi, they increasingly encountered opposition from members of the Congressional Black Caucus and Africa advocacy groups such as TransAfrica.[67] For leaders of these groups, the racism of Thurmond, Helms, and their compatriots was obvious in their foreign policy preferences. This racism was clearly revealed in their willingness to support white minority regimes in Southern African as well as African leaders who collaborated with these regimes, such as Mobutu and Savimbi.[68] In this context, members of the Black Caucus proposed a spate of amendments in the early 1980s aimed at limiting US aid to and trade with South Africa, and by the middle of the decade they had begun to push for similar reductions in US assistance to Mobutu.[69]

In August 1985 conservatives scored a victory with repeal of the Clark Amendment and proposed a range of initiatives in the White House and Congress to begin immediate aid to Savimbi. At the time, the State Department's Africa Bureau urged restraint because it was in negotiations with Pretoria and Luanda to advance Chester Crocker's linkage strategy, which called for South Africa to end its occupation of Namibia in exchange for the withdrawal of Cuban troops from Angola.[70] These voices of caution stood little chance against the ascendant Republican right wing and Savimbi's well-connected lobbyists Paul Manafort and Christopher Lehman, whose firm aggressively made the case for supporting UNITA.[71] In November 1985, once the Clark Amendment's repeal took effect, Reagan used a presidential finding to authorize covert, lethal aid to UNITA. By March of the following year, this operation was fully underway, and Kamina began to serve as the conduit for antitank and antiaircraft arms that the CIA supplied to Savimbi's forces.[72]

Four months after initiating the Kamina operation, the CIA completed a secret assessment of relations between Zaire and Angola. It found that long-standing tensions between the two states had recently intensified due to fears that each was supporting insurgent groups based in the other. As Zaire and the United States used Kamina to arm UNITA, Mobutu's regime grew concerned that Angola would rearm Katangan exiles in Northern Angola. In its redacted form, the CIA assessment of deteriorating Zaire-Angola relations makes no mention of the agency's operation at Kamina. The report does note, however, that by mid-1986, not only were Zaire and Angola at odds, but "tensions in relations" between Zaire and the United States were also mounting. Moreover, the CIA viewed Mobutu's "recent contrariness" and his tepid attempts to improve Zaire's relations with the Soviet Union as part of an effort to gain increased aid from Washington.[73]

In short, as Mobutu was searching for "greater leverage" in Zaire's relations with the United States, Kamina was taking on increased significance in the CIA program to assist UNITA. As such, from a bargaining standpoint, it was in Mobutu's interest to cultivate American dependence on the facility, and the CIA concluded that he would "continue to provide use of airfields, personnel, and intelligence support to facilitate the transfer of matériel to UNITA."[74] This view was echoed in a 1986 dispatch from the US ambassador in Kinshasa to the State Department. The ambassador warned that US–Zaire relations were nearing a "crisis point" and that a "concerted effort" should be made to address Mobutu's concerns, especially given his recent "agreement to permit US covert aid to UNITA to pass through Zaire."[75]

From its earliest days, Reagan's administration had publicly lauded Mobutu as a stabilizing force in Africa while failing to protest the Zairian president's kleptocratic impulses, blatantly authoritarian policies, and long record of human rights violations. Despite these rhetorical gestures, Mobutu remained consistently disappointed by the rewards, in economic and military aid, for his fidelity to the Reagan agenda. Prior to the onset of the Kamina operation, his influence in Washington had begun to wane significantly.

The economic leverage that Mobutu once generated due to US interest in Zaire's mineral resources, particularly cobalt, had been declining since the 1970s. By the mid-1980s, the United States could easily weather a disruption in Zairian cobalt supplies and develop alternative, North American sources for the mineral. The Reagan administration increasingly indicated to Zaire, as the US Embassy in Kinshasa put it, that "the days of a free ride" due to its cobalt reserves were over.[76] Similarly, by the mid-1980s, American private investment in Zaire hovered at the relatively small sum of roughly $200 million, while estimates of American exports to Zaire were a little more than $80 million.[77] In short, the disruption of this commerce would hardly have sent shockwaves through the US economy.

Zaire consistently voted in accordance with American interests at the UN and, in May 1982, became one of the first sub-Saharan African states to reestablish relations with Israel. Kinshasa renewed ties with Tel Aviv primarily in the hope that Washington would respond with significant increases in aid. However, Mobutu's discontent grew when US assistance increased only marginally, from $31 million in 1982 to roughly

$38 million in 1984.[78] In 1983, at Washington's urging, Mobutu sent troops to support Chad against a Libyan-backed insurgency. Though Reagan publicly praised Mobutu for his "courageous action," US military aid to Zaire in the wake of the anti-Libyan intervention remained limited.[79]

Mobutu still maintained the allegiance of influential voices on Capitol Hill and within the Reagan administration. But the notion that if he lost his grip on power, Zaire would descend into ethnic and regional sectarianism—opening the door for Soviet influence—no longer evoked the widespread concern that it had in the 1960s and 1970s. As an indication of how much the "Mobutu or chaos" thesis had worn thin, at the beginning of the Reagan administration a CIA intelligence assessment outlined the contours of a potential "post-Mobutu regime." It suggested that while a post-Mobutu regime might face civil unrest, in all likelihood it would be friendly toward the United States and almost immediately look to Washington for "strong support."[80]

Mobutu's dearth of influence also allowed the Reagan administration to work in tandem with Zaire's other major donors to pressure him to enact economic reforms. The International Monetary Fund (IMF) suspended loan programs with Zaire in 1980 and 1981 due to Mobutu's refusal to cut the Zairian budget deficit. In 1982, after initially expecting Washington to intervene to help convince the IMF to establish a new agreement, Mobutu became convinced that the United States was blocking his efforts to renegotiate new loans from the organization.[81] In 1983, to secure more IMF funding, Mobutu found himself forced to implement reforms, including cuts in government spending and a devaluation of Zaire's currency.[82] Two years later, Mobutu's standing with the IMF had improved, but the austerity measures had intensified domestic discontent with his regime and done little to stabilize Zaire's economy. Yet, in the run-up to the Kamina operation, the Reagan administration offered minimal assistance to help Mobutu navigate Zaire's economic morass by way of aid increases or expanded efforts to encourage the IMF to offer Zaire better terms for upcoming loans.

Mobutu bristled at the "paternalistic" nature of the relationship he had forged with the United States. Much as he had in the early 1970s, he attempted to cultivate a more nonaligned image by, for example, publicly expressing interest in Soviet proposals to improve relations with Zaire. In 1982, when American military aid was temporarily withheld from Zaire due to the Brooke Amendment, a congressional provision that suspended funding to countries that failed to make debt payments to the United States, Mobutu responded by publicly renouncing all US aid. However, once the suspension ended, he ultimately accepted $31 million from Washington. In 1984, not long after Mobutu expelled the United States Peace Corps from Zaire under the pretense that its officers were fomenting dissent, the American Embassy in Kinshasa attributed much of Mobutu's recalcitrance to "a residual discomfort with the subordinate role he saw himself playing."[83] Soon, however, Kamina would become a central component of Reagan administration policy in Southern Africa, and Mobutu would use the air base as vital source of leverage to challenge his most powerful ally.

A "MASTERPIECE" FOR MOBUTU

A primary reason for the Reagan administration's decision to provide UNITA covert, rather than overt, assistance in November 1985 was that military aid to Savimbi's forces would have to come through a neighboring African state.[84] Zaire and Zambia were the White House's preferred options, and both states would need to publicly deny this violation of Angola's sovereignty. Zambia had assisted UNITA during the 1970s, yet by 1985 it saw the rebel force as a South African puppet. As a result, Lusaka would not assist in the Reagan administration's plan. Hence, Mobutu's willingness to assist the Americans in arming UNITA while publicly denying his role in the operation offered him powerful currency in a region where the United States had few alternatives. Not only was Mobutu's cooperation indispensable to the Reagan administration's plans, but Kamina also offered unique advantages not found elsewhere in the region. Built to NATO specifications in 1952, the base had two staggered, 9,000-foot runways. As such, any aircraft in the US inventory could land and depart quickly.[85]

While the operation would grow rapidly, the CIA began the flow of military equipment to Savimbi in March 1986 using a single C-130 transport aircraft, chartered from St. Lucia Airways and emblazoned with the airline's logo, to ferry supplies from Kamina to UNITA's Jamba headquarters in southeastern Angola.[86] So pleased was the agency with the efficiency of the operation that its deputy director, Robert Gates, later called the airlift "a masterpiece of logistical planning."[87]

The CIA operated at Kamina for six years without a formal leasing agreement. In such an accord, leasing terms and costs would have been clear. This might have capped Mobutu's expectations for the amount and nature of economic concessions the United States would offer in exchange for his cooperation. However, under the more ambiguous terms of the CIA's arrangement with Mobutu, little clarity existed about the limits of the quid pro quo that the United States would provide. As a result, Mobutu managed to extract broader rewards. His gains ran the gamut from unprecedented American interventions on his behalf with multilateral creditor institutions to sharp increases in security assistance programs to Zaire. Mobutu fully exploited Reagan's personal commitment to arm UNITA, which the president expressed to him through direct correspondence and during Mobutu's visits to the White House.

The Angolan conflict stood as a pivotal test of the Reagan doctrine and its premise of rolling back communism by supporting prodemocracy "freedom fighters." Within the administration, more moderate officials saw the aid as a means of strengthening Savimbi so that his forces could increase the costs of the conflict for the Angolan government, leading to a military stalemate that would force the MPLA to the bargaining table. More hardline adherents of the Reagan doctrine wanted to arm UNITA so that it could forcibly expel the Cubans and overthrow the Angolan government. By 1985, both factions believed that UNITA was in a perilous position.

In the months before the Clark Amendment's repeal took effect, the MPLA government in Luanda, supported by Cuban troops and Soviet arms, initiated a military offensive against UNITA forces in southern

Angola. When UNITA's defeat appeared imminent, South Africa intervened with the largest deployment of troops it had sent to Angola since 1975 and repelled the MPLA forces.[88] In 1986, when UNITA began receiving American antitank and antiaircraft weapons, Reagan officials sounded hasty notes of vindication due to the "remarkable effectiveness" of the renewed spate of guerrilla strikes launched by Savimbi's rebels.[89]

Despite Zaire's pivotal role in facilitating the introduction of these weapons, for much of 1986 relations between Washington and Kinshasa remained strained. In a December 1986 meeting with Reagan, Mobutu made clear that he wanted assistance in getting "relief from a four-year IMF program that had caused serious rioting" in the other African countries that were also under its strictures. Whether America increased its aid by "$12 or $2 million," Mobutu remarked, if the Reagan administration did not also help with the World Bank and IMF, Zaire would still "pay out much more than we take in."[90] Treasury Secretary James Baker, who was present, cautioned Mobutu not to take unilateral steps that would preclude a new IMF agreement, alluding to Mobutu's recent threat to roll back a slate of conditionality measures. Still, Baker insisted that the United States was committed to assisting Zaire with its creditors. Mobutu countered that he had listened to the Americans' assurances for four years but had not seen a decrease in his debt service payments.[91]

This time—now that Mobutu's air base was critical to Reagan's Southern Africa policy—the US response would be different. In a press conference after the meeting, Reagan announced, "We have encouraged Zaire to hold firm to the responsible economic reforms it is attempting, while promising to do our best to ease the way."[92] During Mobutu's visit to Washington, as Reagan offered the Zairian president accolades, John Conyers of the Congressional Black Caucus publicly vowed to pressure the White House to cut ties with Zaire because of its government's human rights abuses. Nonetheless, the administration would work aggressively to secure Zaire "room to maneuver" with the IMF and World Bank.[93]

By May 1987, Zaire had negotiated a new standby agreement with the IMF to provide an estimated $370 million loan over the course of the next three years. The Reagan administration publicly denied pressuring the IMF to offer Zaire the new agreement. Yet, its behind-the-scenes lobbying was quickly exposed. C. David Finch, the IMF director of exchange and trade relations and one of the fund's lead negotiators with borrowing states, resigned in protest after Zaire's new deal was struck.[94] Finch suggested that the IMF's most powerful member, the United States, was using the fund as a political instrument to reward its allies. The IMF board nonetheless defended the terms of the Zaire agreement, arguing that, due to sharp decreases in the prices of Zaire's key mineral exports on international markets, the state's economy was "fundamentally weak and vulnerable."[95]

The same month as the IMF deal, the Paris Club, under pressure from Washington, rescheduled Zaire's debt repayments for the next fifteen years, including a six-year grace period. In response, an official in Zaire's Ministry of Finance said that the agreement was "without precedent" and that "no country in Africa has been treated as generously before."[96] While these deals were being negotiated, press accounts began to emerge identifying Kamina as the base through which American arms were being funneled to UNITA and linking this operation to the Reagan administration's heightened interest in Zaire's negotiations with the IMF and Paris Club. In the decades since these financial agreements, there has been a solid consensus among scholars that the generous terms of these deals for Zaire were America's quid pro quo for access to Kamina.[97]

Throughout 1987, the CIA provided UNITA with $15 million worth of arms, primarily antitank and antiaircraft weapons. The United States signaled its commitment to this program by increasing its budget to $30 million in 1988 and $50 million in 1989.[98] As more evidence surfaced that Kamina was a conduit for the CIA's arms program for Savimbi, the MPLA government repeatedly threatened military action against Zaire. Meanwhile, African states such as Zimbabwe, Tanzania, and Botswana roundly condemned Mobutu as a pawn of both the United States and South Africa, UNITA's primary supporter. To avoid further regional isolation, Mobutu consistently denied that the CIA was operating at Kamina.[99] But he rarely failed to mention the operation when negotiating increases in military aid from the Reagan administration. For example, in 1988 the US ambassador to Zaire informed Washington that Mobutu "noted once again his support for US Angolan policy and the costs that support entails for Zaire. He specified that Zaire lies in public to protect the relationship but receives nothing in return."[100]

Mobutu also informed the American ambassador that a joint military exercise between Zairian and US troops was approaching, and that one way for Washington to immediately augment its security assistance efforts would be to leave behind all the military equipment that the Pentagon was airlifting to Zaire to support the exercise. However, this would not be the only form of military aid that Mobutu would demand from the United States to maintain his commitment to keep the Kamina operation covert. By the end of 1988, US military sales to Zaire would increase by more than 30 percent despite mounting congressional pressure to withhold security assistance due to the Mobutu regime's worsening human rights record. Conservative estimates suggest that in total, Mobutu acquired $65 million in security assistance, largely in grants and military training programs, for providing US access to Kamina while publicly denying the operation.[101] Much of this aid came from the Reagan administration, but in response to Mobutu's confrontational diplomacy, the George H. W. Bush administration would also pay a price to maintain access to Kamina.

PRESIDENT BUSH'S "OLD FRIEND" LOSES HIS LEVERAGE

A December 1988 peace agreement, brokered by the United States and the Soviet Union, among Cuba, Angola, and South Africa outlined a timetable for Namibian independence and set the stage for withdrawing both Cuban and South African troops from Angola.[102] Despite the loss of South African support, UNITA continued its insurgent campaign against the MPLA government. Though it had helped to mediate the regional peace agreement, the Bush administration nonetheless refused to extend official diplomatic recognition to Angola. It remained outspoken about its determination to keep arming Savimbi until the Angolan government opened negotiations that would lead to national reconciliation and some form of MPLA–UNITA power sharing.[103] Bush's ties to Mobutu, dating from his days as CIA director, buttressed this position, as did the Kamina operation's far-right supporters in Congress. Moreover, Savimbi's lobbyists, who ran a sophisticated public relations campaign for UNITA throughout much of Reagan's second term, also maintained an extensive network of influence within the Bush administration. In fact, under lobbyist and right-wing congressional pressure, the administration later pivoted from support for the vague notion of national reconciliation in Angola to demanding free and fair elections with UNITA participation.[104]

The Bush administration maintained its support for UNITA despite increasing evidence of its humanitarian abuses, such as the abduction and conscription of civilians and the use of land mines to disrupt the agricultural economy of Angolan villages that did not support Savimbi's insurgency.[105] In fact, in 1989 Washington increased military aid to the insurgent force by more than $20 million.[106] Because this expansion of aid came through the CIA operation at Kamina, Mobutu was once again poised to benefit. However, by this point Zaire's relations with Angola had begun to improve, and Mobutu sought to burnish his credentials as a statesman by mediating peace talks between the MPLA and UNITA.

As these talks progressed, Mobutu began publicly to oppose American weapons aid to Savimbi, and in June 1989, the MPLA and UNITA declared a ceasefire at the Zairian president's resort at Gbadolite.[107] In the wake of this short-lived agreement—June to November 1989—Mobutu halted the flow of American arms to UNITA by shutting down the CIA operation at Kamina.[108] It was in his interest to appear to be an honest broker and to avoid condemnation from neighboring African states by openly undermining the agreement he had helped to mediate. However, Mobutu's relationship with Savimbi quickly deteriorated, and UNITA's supporters in Washington were desperate to restart the Kamina operation.

In October 1989 Senator Jesse Helms expressed mounting outrage that "the supply lines have been cut."[109] That same month, when Mobutu visited the White House, Bush appealed to the Zairian president to "turn back on the flow of supplies to UNITA."[110] After offering a bevy of plaudits for Mobutu's efforts as peacemaker, Bush asked what steps he could take to mend the relationship between Mobutu and Savimbi. The American president pledged to remind Savimbi of just how much goodwill he owed the Zairian leader. Bush also encouraged Mobutu to keep in mind UNITA's loyal following in the United States, noting, "I don't want to see you lose support among the American public for your magnificent achievement when UNITA's support dries up because the pipeline is closed." Mobutu responded to Bush's pleas with platitudes about putting aside the past and focusing on the future. When Assistant Secretary of State Henry Cohen inquired as to whether this specifically meant reopening the supply pipeline, Mobutu remained noncommittal. "Almost," he replied. He then raised a proposal to take all the debt Zaire owed the United States and convert it into Zairian currency "to increase North–South dialogue and solidarity."[111]

While the Bush administration was not desperate enough to entertain this proposal, it nearly doubled foreign military sales to Zaire by the end of 1989.[112] The month after his White House visit, Mobutu allowed the Kamina operation to proceed. Days after the program was reinitiated, one of the cargo planes airlifting supplies from Kamina to the UNITA headquarters in Jamba, Angola, crashed. According to a State Department official, "Mobutu went nuts," calling the CIA station chief in Kinshasa the night of the crash and demanding that "you guys quit screwing up."[113] The CIA was forced to acknowledge publicly that it chartered the aircraft, and the crash brought renewed scrutiny to Zaire as a conduit for arms to Savimbi, further discrediting Mobutu as an impartial mediator between UNITA and the MPLA.

Still, the Bush administration increased its dependency on Mobutu by expanding the arms program at Kamina as it intensified its support for UNITA. In 1986 the CIA had used a single C-130 aircraft to transport military supplies from Kamina to Jamba during a four-week window from March to April, for two weeks in May, and on one occasion in October.[114] From 1987 to mid-1989, the CIA airlifts from Kamina increased to roughly twice a week. By June 1990, once Kamina had reopened and the Bush administration redoubled its support for UNITA, the CIA was using three C-130 aircraft to make nightly deliveries to Jamba.[115]

In November 1990 the House of Representatives passed restrictions on the covert aid the Bush administration could provide UNITA. This initiative took shape under the leadership of the CBC and Ron Dellums, then a member of the Armed Services Committee's Subcommittee on Military Installations and Facilities. It was backed by his liberal Democratic colleagues and a handful moderate Republicans. The House capped US aid slated for delivery to UNITA in 1991 at the previous years' expenditure levels.[116] Even this, however, was a compromise proposed by Democratic Congressman Stephen Solarz because Dellums had called for a full suspension of covert assistance to the Angolan rebels.[117] For Dellums, any aid to UNITA was "morally indefensible," and as early as 1988 he had likewise begun to introduce legislation to halt US assistance to Mobutu.[118]

Even more noteworthy, it was the CBC's leadership that forced a rare open debate on the House Floor about the covert operation at Kamina that was arming Savimbi's forces.[119] It was this scrutiny that would ultimately hasten the demise of the Kamina operation and along with it US aid to Mobutu. The Bush administration vehemently defended its assistance to Mobutu as a strategic necessity. At the time, a high-ranking administration official put it bluntly: "The point is, we need him."[120] Nonetheless, in late 1990 the US Congress cut all US military aid to Zaire. Moreover, it routed development assistance to the country through nongovernmental organizations rather than Mobutu's government.

The Bush administration could no longer fill Mobutu's coffers but refused to abandon its ally. By 1991, popular pressure in Zaire and eroding support from the West finally forced Mobutu to feign reforms that gave rise to the prospect of a democratic transition. The Kamina operation, however, did not end until the summer of that year. As such, the Bush administration continued to demand that Mobutu "be included in any coalition government" that might be formed, despite calls from the Zairian opposition and much of the international community that he immediately relinquish power.[121] In June 1991, following a short-lived, American-backed peace accord between the Angolan combatants and amid mounting evidence of humanitarian violations by Savimbi's forces, the Bush administration reluctantly ended the CIA operation at Kamina. Having lost his last significant point of leverage in Washington, by the following year Mobutu began to be pressured by the Bush administration to transfer "all day-to-day powers." Still, Bush never directly called on his "old friend" to leave office. Administration sources claimed that this was primarily due to Mobutu's long history with the United States and his invaluable support for the CIA arms program for UNITA.[122]

At the dawn of the 1980s, Mobutu's standing in Washington had been dubious. But from 1986 to 1991, his skillful attempts to leverage Kamina reliably garnered the allegiance of the Reagan and Bush administrations. The Zairian president's effort gained further traction due to support for the Kamina operation among a coterie of conservative legislators. These lawmakers' racial politics were reflected in their support for white minority regimes in Southern Africa and their legacy of opposition to civil rights reforms. Mobutu's influence would ultimately be undermined by the prospect of a negotiated settlement in Angola and by scrutiny from the Congressional Black Caucus amid a growing movement to end white rule in Southern Africa. Yet, while it was in play, Mobutu's bargaining chip at Kamina yielded sharp increases in military aid, invaluable US assistance with global financial institutions, and a campaign by the Bush administration to ensure the Zairian president a gradual transition from power.

4

MAKING BLACK FRIENDS

The Rise of the New Breed and the Coalescence of the US Counterterror Agenda in Africa

In the mid-1990s the United States abandoned Zaire, its Cold War ally, and forged security partnerships with Uganda and Ethiopia under the aegis of an emerging counterterrorism agenda. Focusing on this pivotal moment, this chapter traces the efforts of the Clinton administration to craft a discourse around a "new breed" of exceptional African leaders. It argues that this discourse helped to consolidate US security ties with Uganda and Ethiopia while obscuring the militarization of US foreign policy in East Africa.

The new breed comprised a rotating cast of emerging African leaders whose commitments to human rights and broad political participation were routinely overstated by Clinton officials. The moniker was most often applied to President Yoweri Kaguta Museveni of Uganda, Prime Minister Meles Zenawi of Ethiopia, President Isaias Afwerki of Eritrea, and Vice President Paul Kagame of Rwanda, that country's de facto leader. The murky new breed discourse received powerful backing from African American political leaders guided by a moderate transnational ethos. Central to this tide of support was a cadre of Black Clinton appointees, including Assistant Secretary of State for African Affairs Susan Rice and Special Envoy for Democracy and Human Rights in Africa Jesse Jackson, as well as key members of the Congressional Black Caucus. The new breed caricature of African leadership rested, in part, on the credibility of these elites who readily called on their racial identities and a history of the African American freedom struggle to back their claims.

Clinton's caricature met momentary success as a public justification for strengthening US relations with Uganda and Ethiopia. Far less effective were Washington's efforts to co-opt the new breed's regional security agenda and to assert control in its intensifying relations with Uganda and Ethiopia. Instead, these new breed governments began to accrue outsize influence in Washington and to leverage their security relations with the United States in pursuit of their own agendas, setting the stage for a similar dynamic in the War on Terror.

A NEW DAY IN AFRICA? A POST-COLD WAR PUZZLE FOR THE AFRICAN AMERICAN ELITE

On February 1, 1989, Ugandan president Yoweri Museveni hailed the opening of Black History Month with a speech at the Martin Luther King Jr. Memorial Library in Washington, DC. Museveni spoke for more than an hour to an audience convened by the library itself and the Links Incorporated, the avowedly elitist Black women's organization. He decried the "bleeding of Africa" during the transatlantic slave trade and the "neocolonialist structure" that burdened Uganda after independence. Museveni told the crowd that the Amin and Obote regimes preceding his presidency wrought extraordinary suffering while gutting his country's economy and healthcare system. "The quiet casualties of neglect and mismanagement are more damaging than the casualties of open conflict," the Ugandan president remarked, revealing a penchant for combat honed at the helm of an insurgent army that had swept him to power three years earlier.[1]

Under his leadership, Museveni declared, a new day was dawning in Uganda, unmarred by butchery at home and parasitic allies abroad. What could African Americans do to help? For the Ugandan president, Garveyite notions of a mass return to Africa were out of the question.

Rather, he encouraged African Americans to offer Uganda their "engineering and electronics skills," to "channel investments" to his country, and to "form a big lobby for Africa."[2] Two years later, Francis Katana, Uganda's chargé d'affaires in Washington, would remind the world of this vision of African and African American relations as he rushed to Museveni's defense.

In a letter to the *Washington Post*, Katana rejected the idea that Museveni held little solidarity with African Americans, a theme that had emerged in a recent article by the *Post's* Africa correspondent, Neil Henry.[3] Closer ties between Africans and African Americans, Katana argued, were clearly important to Museveni. He cited not only Museveni's 1989 Black History Month Speech, but also the Ugandan president's meetings with Mayor Andrew Young of Atlanta and members of the CBC during the same visit to Washington.[4]

Katana's recollections do not capture the full story. During his 1989 US visit, Museveni walked a characteristically fine line on questions of racial solidarity. In an interview with *USA Today*, he observed, "The Black people you see are our people. They contribute to the good of the United States and I think you have an obligation to assist us."[5] But Neil Henry reported in the *Post* that when Museveni was asked by a group of African Americans what they could do for Uganda, his reply was curt: "Nothing. Why do you think you can do anything for us?"[6] The day of his departure, in a speech before the World Affairs Council, the Ugandan leader took pains to underscore the role African rulers played in facilitating the transatlantic slave trade, condescendingly noting, "This is the point I made in the 1960s to some of my Afro-American brothers who were trying to say, 'Black is beautiful.' I responded to them, 'Not all black is beautiful.'"[7]

For many African Americans, grounds for skepticism toward Museveni could also be found in his burgeoning bonds with the Republican establishment. Uganda's registered lobbyist in Washington was Dennis Revell, Ronald Reagan's son-in-law, whose wife, Maureen Reagan, established a rapport with Museveni during a 1988 visit to Uganda.[8] Indeed, during his US trip in 1989, Museveni paid former President Reagan a courtesy call at his Los Angeles offices and had a cordial meeting with newly elected President George H. W. Bush at the National Prayer Breakfast.[9]

Museveni first met with Reagan when he was president in 1987, during the Ugandan leader's earliest visit to the United States. Reagan declared that Museveni had "ended the terrible human rights abuses of an earlier era" and put aside his concerns over the Ugandan government's expanding economic ties with the Gaddafi regime in Libya.[10] The American president applauded Uganda's emerging stability and reinitiated US aid to the East African government. Despite this budding collegiality with the American right, during his 1987 US visit Museveni had spent far more time among African American activists and political leaders, both elite and grassroots, than when he returned to the United States in 1989.

In 1987 the Ugandan president had "unprecedented contact with leaders of the African American diaspora," the *Baltimore Afro-American* reported.[11] He met with then presidential candidate Jesse Jackson, Mayor Marion Barry, Mayor Andrew Young, State Senator David Patterson of New York, and members of the CBC.[12] Museveni was also feted in Harlem while addressing members of the Patrice Lumumba Coalition, a Pan-Africanist group pushing for national liberation in Southern Africa. In fact, he was delighted when Audley "Queen Mother" Moore, the legendary Black nationalist, marked the occasion by presenting him a copy of *The Philosophies and Opinions of Marcus Garvey.*[13]

Upon his return to the United States in 1989, there were no grassroots gatherings on Museveni's agenda. The Black political elite, however, were allowed to rub shoulders with the Ugandan president. For example, Congressman George Crockett Jr of the House Foreign Affairs Committee helped to welcome Museveni to Washington at a reception at the Dirksen Senate Office Building.[14] This was a notable turn of events. Had it been up to Crockett, Museveni may have never come to power. In 1984, when Uganda's Obote government came under fire for human rights abuses as it strained to suppress Museveni's insurgent National Resistance Movement, Crockett condemned the "paltry" military assistance that the United States was providing President Obote's army.[15] The Michigan congressman suggested that an expansion in US military training programs for Uganda's forces would help them better contend with insurgencies without committing human rights violations. Crockett's support for security aid to Obote was a rare point of agreement between the ardent liberal and the Reagan administration.[16]

A pioneering attorney and jurist, Crockett had been elected to represent Michigan's 13th district in 1980. He replaced Representative Charles Diggs, the US Congress's leading voice in African affairs for nearly three decades. Crockett routinely opposed increases in military aid to US allies such as Liberia, Zaire, and Sudan.[17] He was also a fierce critic of the Reagan administration's support for Israel, South Africa, and the Contras in Nicaragua.[18] Why would such a reliable opponent of Reagan's security policies argue that more military aid be sent to Obote's regime despite mounting evidence of its abuses? The Michigan congressman offered little explanation for his stance, aside from decrying the hypocrisy of pouring US aid into repressive regimes in Central America while denying African states similar assistance that might help to stoke their economies and professionalize their militaries.[19] Crockett likewise revealed little about his opinion of Museveni after the two met in 1989.

On balance, Crockett's overtures to Obote and Museveni, avatars of different shades of authoritarian rule, were a rare departure for one of Congress's most outspoken liberals and proponents of human rights. Soon, leading members of the African American foreign policy elite would more readily trod a similar path in their relations with a new breed of African leaders. In fact, Crockett's stance resonated with a penchant for militarization in Black moderate transnational thought that was poised to intensify during the Clinton administration.[20]

In the late 1980s and early 1990s, Black liberal politicians, intellectuals, and activists briefly intensified their scrutiny of US security policy and alliances in Africa. But by the mid-1990s, many among the Black foreign policy elite slowly, often warily, accepted a logic that deemed military intervention a necessary balm for humanitarian crises in Africa and the Caribbean. Many among this elite were supportive when US famine relief morphed into urban combat in Somalia. They pressured President Clinton to dispatch Marines to Liberia and Haiti to stem civilian suffering. They backed sweeping expansions in US military training for African forces. They embraced a new breed of African leaders who saw armed interventions as a solution to the continent's civil conflicts. These interventions often took the guise of "peace operations," backed by Washington and organized by men who had come to power by the force of arms. Clinton officials at times counted Ghana's President Jerry Rawlings and Congo's President Laurent Kabila in the ranks of the new breed, but its central figures were Museveni, Meles, and Kagame. Over time, these men came to benefit from the support of a growing cadre of African American diplomats, activists, and politicians possessed of a new common sense about the virtues of "humanitarian war."[21]

This common sense was not a fringe position or a crude embrace of military solutions for the Global South's political challenges. It took hold amid a broader move to the right among American liberals, a growing synergy between Bush Republicans and Clinton Democrats, and an attendant push for military action to bring order and protect US allies in the Balkans and the Persian Gulf. Lofty aims justified the growing appetite for intervention among Black leaders who championed restoring democracy and protecting civilians abroad. But this impulse toward the use of force broke with a skepticism toward the projection of US military power that remained salient among many Black voters whom these officials represented.[22] Antiwar fervor in Black America exploded during the Vietnam conflict and was reinforced by opposition to often covert US meddling in Africa and the Caribbean throughout the Cold War.

Nevertheless, the interregnum between the Cold War and the War on Terror posed new questions for African American leaders concerned with Africa's future. How could they help to stoke development in African economies ravaged by leaders who were quickly losing the support of Washington or Moscow? Now that historical parallels between white rule in Africa and anti-Black racism in the United States no longer held fast, what new calculus could Black leaders use to determine which African leaders and parties warranted support? How could they shine a light on the promise of Africa's "second independence" and at the same time highlight the plight of civilians caught in the continent's simmering conflicts?

As they found answers to these questions, Black liberal leaders would face little scrutiny from Black Americans who were demobilizing in the wake of the antiapartheid movement. There was a waning investment in the complex, internal politics of Africa's many states. At the same time, more radical, grassroots Pan-Africanist organizations with long histories of anti-imperialist activism were increasingly sidelined by a new class of Africa advocates that rose to prominence during the latter stages of the sanctions and divestment campaign against South Africa. Among these advocates and consultants, the campaign's success was often framed as a victory for American values, multiculturalism, and bipartisanship.[23]

It was in this context that the siren song of militarized humanitarianism caught the ear of the Black liberal elite. In keeping with the precepts of Black moderate transnationalism, their willingness to support a larger role for the US military in Washington's Africa policy was often framed as a response to a deep vein of racism. This was "racism of obliviousness" that consigned Africa to a subordinate status in US foreign affairs.[24] It reflected a callousness that resonated for many Black politicians with Washington's negligence toward underresourced Black municipalities throughout the United States. Many Black leaders rued Africa's perennial "backwater" status as well as Washington's declining foreign aid to the continent and its inattention to the horrible toll of Africa's conflicts.[25] In this light, President Clinton's shift to airstrikes and special operations raids in Somalia or his support for new breed leaders smitten with combat represented, at the very least, long overdue US attention to Africa. Armed humanitarianism was better than outright neglect fueled by bigotry.

Throughout the 1990s, the proceeds of the African American elite's growing support for militarization in US policy toward Africa largely redounded to the continent's new breed, whose key figures, Ethiopia's Meles Zenawi and Uganda's Yoweri Museveni, would later become close US security allies in the War on Terror. For the Clinton administration, the new breed was the embodiment of "African solutions for African problems," from conflicts in Liberia and Zaire to the emerging threat of Islamist extremism in Sudan and Somalia.[26] It was they whom the

Clinton administration called on when, as the US ambassador to Uganda in 1994 declared, the State Department wanted, "to pay Africans to do some of these dirty jobs."[27]

The Clinton administration's early security ties with Africa's new breed can be largely attributed to the continent's waning strategic significance after the Cold War. Just as important was the administration's aversion to direct military interventions in Africa's conflicts after the US casualties in Somalia in 1993. But the consolidation of these security ties was hastened and often facilitated by members of the African American political elite amid a growing US preoccupation with terrorism in Africa. From a practical standpoint, this meant support and praise from Black liberal leaders for African presidents like Museveni, who, as Donald Payne observed, "seemed to have the right attitude."[28] From an ideological standpoint, this impulse to strengthen US–Africa security ties represented the resurgence of a Black liberal appetite for targeted bellicosity and heavy-handed leadership in Africa as regrettable preconditions for stability and economic progress. It reflected a mounting consensus among the African American foreign policy elite about the peace and prosperity that might emerge when the "right" African leaders with the "right" US security assistance managed to quell the continent's conflicts. While elements of this perspective had deep roots in Black moderate transnational thought, the seeds for its resurgence in the 1990s were sown by the US intervention in Somalia.

CRISES IN SOMALIA AND HAITI: STOKING THE BLACK APPETITE FOR FORCE

Black leaders were overwhelmingly supportive in December 1992 when President George H. W. Bush deployed US troops to Somalia with the stated goal of creating a secure environment for humanitarian relief. Bush's decision to launch Operation Restore Hope was hailed by civil rights stalwarts Roger Wilkins and Reverend Jesse Jackson, New York mayor David Dinkins, Afrocentric luminary Molefi Kete Asante, the

NAACP, and the CBC.[29] "Normally, I am opposed to military solutions," Congressman Charles Rangel of New York commented, "but because the military response is of a humanitarian nature, I welcome it."[30] Frank L. Morris Sr., a prominent dean at Morgan State University, was ebullient: "We can finally feel good about the use of US military power."[31]

This chorus of approval contrasted sharply with the CBC and civil rights establishment's near unanimous opposition to the First Gulf War—but reports from Somalia were grave.[32] Roughly a quarter of a million Somalis had perished amid a famine and fighting that began when Mohamed Siad Barre, the late Cold War ally of the United States, was deposed in 1991. At the height of the famine in August 1992, according to the International Committee of the Red Cross, 4.5 million Somalis were going hungry while warring militias routinely hijacked and plundered UN relief shipments.[33]

In the months running up to Operation Restore Hope, editorials in the Black press railed against a racist double standard in US foreign policy. While the "white world" was prepared to intervene in the Balkans, it stood flat-footed as Somalis starved. As NATO's intervention was getting underway in Bosnia, the *Miami Times* suggested that the reason a similar operation had not been conducted in "Somalia is that Black life is seen as having less worth, pure and simple."[34] In the *Cleveland Call and Post*, Congressman Louis Stokes argued that President Bush refused to commit US troops to the UN mission in Somalia because he was "no more concerned about the fate of people of color overseas than he is about the civil rights of African Americans, Hispanic Americans, and Asian Americans."[35]

This line of criticism had been central to Black leaders' criticisms of President George H. W. Bush when the Liberian civil conflict began in the closing days of 1989. Jesse Jackson had deemed the absence of US diplomatic initiatives aimed at ending the crisis clear evidence of racism, a "sort of Tarzan foreign policy."[36] Congressman Donald Payne had pushed the Bush White House to deploy Marines to Liberia in order to set up safe zones for civilians. Payne was offended when the United States rushed to "save an undemocratic monarchy" in Kuwait while doing nothing for a "country our freed slaves had founded." But when Bush deployed Marines to Somalia, the New Jersey congressman was pleased, despite his opposition to the "use of force to solve international disputes." Operation Restore Hope proved, according to Payne, "that the new world order was also for helping Black people."[37]

For critics on the Black left, the chances of the operation helping Black people were slim. Many of these critics were troubled by the haste with which stalwart opponents of American intervention rushed to back the operation. Taking aim at Jesse Jackson, Samori Marksman observed, "Our very prominent brother who wants to keep hope alive was one of the first to endorse Bush's Operation Restore Hope with the invasion of Somalia."[38] Marksman, the pioneering, Black Marxist journalist, condemned the intervention as an imperialist power play masquerading as altruism. Marksman held that Bush was committed to maintaining a US strategic presence in the Horn of Africa and the Middle East while protecting the flow of oil through the Gulf of Aden. He derided Black liberal leaders who supported the operation for a facile understanding of the nuances of African politics and a dearth of "Pan-African patriotism."[39] According to Marksman, their support played into racist portrayals of Somali savagery, bolstering notions of a "White Man's Burden" and the civilizing impulse that were central to the intervention.[40]

Skeptical Black radicals also noted a history of US alliances with colonial powers in Africa and US support for a host of despotic African leaders, including Somalia's own, recently deposed Siad Barre. They decried the Bush administration's foot-dragging and its attempts to stall a truly multilateral UN relief effort when the Somali famine was cresting in mid-1992. Grassroots forums critiquing the "new militarism" in US affairs and among the Black liberal elite offered a venue for these concerns.[41] Pan-Africanist and anti-imperialist critiques came from Elombe Brath of New York's Patrice Lumumba Coalition, Serge Makandi of the Movement of Congo Trade Unionists, Somali academics Said Samatar and Asha Samad Matias, and the luminary Kenyan writer, Ngũgĩ wa Thiong'o.[42]

Black radical criticisms of the operation often highlighted themes of racism and imperialism, but they largely aligned with opposition to the intervention among other voices on the progressive left. Announcing its opposition to Operation Restore Hope, *The Nation* editorialized that the military action "would likely project American power in the region into the next century."[43] Former attorney general and progressive activist Ramsey Clark observed: "We sat back while they starved by the tens of thousands and now we think we can feed people with guns."[44] Rakiya Omaar, the Somali director of the human rights organization Africa Watch, was fired when she opposed the organization's support for Operation Restore Hope. Omaar claimed that the operation was liable to "create more problems than it could ever solve."[45] Omaar's deputy, Alex de Waal, likewise resigned in protest and condemned the "disaster pornography" that served as a pretense for intervention.[46]

However, a distinctly different vein of criticism reinforced Black liberal suspicions about the stereotypes that led Washington to cast a blind eye toward African crises. "The Somali is treacherous. The Somali is a killer," wrote the US ambassador to Kenya, Smith Hempstone, in a leaked cable that urged Washington to avoid this African "tar baby" and its "natural-born guerillas."[47]

African American leaders were far from alone in their support for Operation Restore Hope. It had the endorsement of the Security Council, President-elect Bill Clinton, and the leaders of African governments in Kenya and Nigeria.[48] Nevertheless, there was some ambivalence among the Black liberal elite. "It is a position we take reluctantly," said Randall Robinson, head of TransAfrica, the most powerful African American lobby for Africa and the Caribbean, "but considering the fact that the lives of millions of Somalis are at stake, we must advocate this drastic action."[49] Robinson was adamant that US troops deployed to Somalia should form part of a multinational force and emphasized his opposition to trusteeship arrangements that would compromise the country's sovereignty. Congressman John Conyers tempered his support with similar concerns: "The intent is not to create a New World Order colonialism."[50] Likewise, *Washington Post* columnist Dorothy Gilliam viewed the operation with hope and distrust, noting a history of Western exploitation and military misadventures in Africa. "What will happen the first time a warlord kills a US marine?," she asked presciently.[51]

This question was difficult for Black leaders to ignore given the Bush administration's posturing. Lieutenant General Colin Powell, chair of the Joint Chiefs of Staff, made no secret of his bent for preemptive military action in Somalia and his commitment to a doctrine of overwhelming force. Though he rose through the ranks of the Reagan and Bush administrations, Powell was well regarded by many Black liberals who saw his ascent within the US defense establishment as a marker of progress. "We're not just going to ride shotgun," the general declared on the eve of the intervention, "waiting for people to shoot at us then shoot back."[52] An anonymous Pentagon official struck a similar, ominously colorful note about the deploying troops: "If you're going to send a bear, send a grizzly."[53] As this rhetoric swirled, the *Michigan Chronicle* offered Operation Restore Hope its blessing with a pointed warning: "African Americans are wary of sending American troops to shoot at Africans. We admit that the precedent this . . . will establish is frightening."[54]

Such fears intensified in the fall of 1993. In June of that year Mohamed Farah Aidid's Somali National Alliance killed twenty-four Pakistani UN peacekeepers. In response, US forces, nominally under the auspices of the United Nations Operation in Somalia II, initiated a manhunt for Aidid, the country's most powerful clan leader. After three months of US raids and airstrikes that killed dozens of Somali civilians, the campaign culminated in the infamous Battle of Mogadishu, during which eighteen US soldiers and some three hundred Somalis perished.[55] The corpse of a US ranger who was killed in the battle was dragged through the streets of Mogadishu in a scene that received heavy media coverage. The incident sparked a public and congressional backlash against US participation in the UN mission, and many of the CBC's members began to support growing calls for an immediate US withdrawal from Somalia.

Black leaders who believed that the United States should remain in Somalia argued that the Clinton administration would be abandoning its espoused humanitarianism and turning its back on civilians trapped in a civil conflict.[56] Some wondered, according to congressional delegate Eleanor Holmes Norton, if the public would have reacted as strongly to news of a dead Black soldier, rather than a white one, being paraded through the streets of Somalia's capital.[57] Amid the growing furor, Congressman Dellums met with President Clinton and encouraged him to keep US Army logistics troops in Somalia while soliciting the aid of neighboring governments and the OAU to negotiate a ceasefire.

Just days before the Battle of Mogadishu, Dellums had sent a letter to the White House in which he expressed similar priorities and criticized the "unnecessarily militaristic" turn the US mission had taken in Somalia during its manhunt for Aidid. As both a firm supporter of Operation Restore Hope and a consistent critic of US military policy, Dellums wrote that US combat troops in Somalia had become "more a part of the problem than the solution."[58] This was a point of view that could also be found in some quarters of the Black press. In the progressive *San Francisco Metro Reporter*, columnist Emory Curtis argued that Clinton's "new Democrats" held much in common with their Republican predecessors and that Clinton had emulated a Bush tactic by "personalizing the conflict with Somalia through Aidid much as Bush did with Panama through Noriega."[59]

In his meeting with Clinton after the Battle of Mogadishu, Dellums recommended that the president avoid establishing a hasty timeline for a US withdrawal from Somalia.[60] Clinton promptly ignored this advice by announcing that US troops would be pulled from the country within six months. Though African American reactions to the announcement were mixed, many who were disappointed by Clinton's decision were reminded of America's historical indifference to suffering in poor, Black countries. This perspective was reinforced by the commentary of white politicians who deemed Somalia "primitive" terrain and blasted Clinton for allowing a US solider to be "dragged through the dust of some African village."[61]

Many Black liberals believed that because Clinton bowed to pressure to leave Somalia, he would also eschew forceful action to stem the humanitarian crisis that was simultaneously unfolding in Haiti. They took care to draw distinctions between the two crises and argued that a US military intervention in Haiti should remain an option for the Clinton administration.[62] In late 1991 Haiti's democratically elected president, Jean Bertrand Aristide, was overthrown in a military coup and forced to flee the country. Over the course of the next two years, the military junta that seized power from Aristide was responsible for the deaths of nearly five thousand Haitians, and its human rights abuses included widespread torture and kidnapping.[63] Amid this crisis, Clinton reneged on a campaign promise to end the Bush administration policy of forcibly repatriating refugees who attempted to emigrate from Haiti to the United States. In protest, TransAfrica's Randall Robinson began a twenty-six-day hunger strike to pressure the Clinton administration to change its stance.[64]

By the fall of 1993, much of the Black foreign policy elite supported calls for a US-led, multinational force to be sent to Haiti with the goal of restoring Aristide to power. Their patience had worn thin after a series of diplomatic initiatives failed to coax Haiti's military junta, led by General Raoul Cédras, to relinquish power. They argued that Clinton had a moral imperative to act, especially given the history of US support for dictatorial regimes that had destabilized the island nation. They also predicted that, unlike in Somalia, if Aristide were returned to office, the United States would have a progressive, democratically elected government with which to partner.

Jesse Jackson declared that America's inattention to Black countries like Haiti represented the "soft underbelly" of US foreign policy, and that the island's antidemocratic leaders should not "make us back down."[65] The CBC agreed. Its leaders, including Donald Payne, John Lewis, and Major Owens, backed proposals for a US intervention. However, there were voices of dissent. Roughly a dozen CBC members opposed the idea, and a handful of expatriate Haitian activists in the United States expressed concerns that US soldiers sent to Haiti as peacekeepers might turn on the country's civilians if they came under fire.[66]

Still, many Black liberal leaders saw armed humanitarianism as the best means to bring an end to the suffering of the Haitian people. Some went as far as to suggest that in addition to an intervention force, the United States should conduct "surgical airstrikes" in Haiti to send a message to the country's recalcitrant leaders.[67] At the same time, conservatives smugly noted the appreciation for US military power that they saw taking hold among traditionally antiwar Black liberals. In the *Washington Post*, hawkish columnist Richard Cohen cheered the CBC's more bellicose approach to US foreign policy. In an interview with Cohen,

Donald Payne appeared to relish the CBC's prominent role in shaping a more aggressive foreign policy toward Somalia and Haiti, observing, "It means we're up to the plate and being considered players."[68]

Clinton routinely looked to Black liberal leaders to enhance the public credibility of his policies toward Africa and the Caribbean, but he was far less comfortable with them having a direct hand in shaping those policies. After the Somalia debacle, as the president vacillated on the question of deploying troops to Haiti, he privately rued the influence of key members of the Black foreign policy elite. In a meeting with State Department officials, Clinton scoffed, "We can't let ourselves be driven into military action on anything just because Randall Robinson decides to kill himself."[69] Despite his pique, Clinton had expressed a general inclination toward intervening in Haiti. While Black politicians were not alone in pressuring the president to follow through on this impulse, they emerged as the most vocal and determined proponents of the Haitian intervention after the US casualties in Somalia.

Along these lines, Black liberals parted company with more radical Black leaders such as Ron Daniels, a revered progressive and Pan-Africanist organizer and a former ally of Reverend Jesse Jackson. Daniels was firmly against the intervention and lamented that many Black leaders had been seduced by the allure of armed humanitarianism in both Somalia and Haiti. He argued that Clinton ultimately wanted to see pliable, pro-Western governments installed in both states. According to Daniels, the Clinton administration was deeply skeptical of Aristide's rhetoric of class struggle and his plans for economic redistribution in Haiti. Daniels asserted that the United States had not seriously contemplated taking action to restore the deposed Haitian president until his constitutionally mandated term in office was near its conclusion, and that it would readily embrace the country's exploitative, promarket elite once Aristide's tenure came to a close.[70] From this perspective, the intervention was clearly not in the interest of progressive, grass-roots Haitian reformers. Black liberals on the other side of the debate would ultimately win the day.

In September 1994, with the backing of a UN resolution, Clinton ordered nearly twenty-five thousand US troops to Haiti to force the

Cédras regime to surrender power. Before the US force arrived in Haiti, a diplomatic mission led by former US president Jimmy Carter, General Colin Powell, and Senator Sam Nunn managed to strike a deal with Cédras that set in motion a peaceful transfer of power to Aristide.[71] The Haitian president made a triumphant return to the island the following month, accompanied by the US secretary of state, Reverend Jesse Jackson, and members of the CBC.[72]

This outcome was heralded as a victory for Clinton and Black liberal leaders who were invested in Haiti's future, but it came at a cost. The Black foreign policy elite had grown more comfortable with military interventions as a solution to humanitarian crises. This new disposition would not manifest itself in a concerted effort to push Clinton to intervene in Rwanda as a genocide convulsed the country in 1994, largely because Black leaders' attention was focused on Haiti. But this appetite for intervention would help to allay African American skepticism toward an emerging group of African leaders, including Museveni and Meles, who were not afraid to take up arms to solve regional problems. Indeed, Black liberal officials had lobbied the Clinton administration to seek these leaders' help in mediating the crisis in Somalia.[73] In the wake of the Battle of Mogadishu, as is well known, the Clinton administration became extraordinarily reluctant to intervene with US troops in Africa's conflicts. It was in this context that Museveni and Meles began to position themselves as invaluable US allies, while angling for increases in aid and attenuations in criticisms of their saber-rattling and illiberal domestic policies.

THE UNITED STATES INVESTS IN AN "AFRICAN RENAISSANCE"

Museveni and Meles took pains to distinguish themselves in comportment, military competence, and economic planning from African leaders such as Daniel arap Moi and Mobutu Sese Seko, who had aligned with the United States during the Cold War. The "new generation" of African leaders, according to National Security Advisor Anthony Lake, had transcended "the heady era of independence and subsequent period of blaming everything on the colonial legacies."[74] More important, they offered a broader range of security capabilities that could assist in US plans—at a price they readily demanded. No longer were Washington's alliances in the region simply a matter of maintaining US access to African ports, airfields, and military bases. These, of course, remained valuable bargaining chips for African leaders. Now, however, these leaders could also derive influence by offering to deploy their troops into conflicts and humanitarian crises when the United States was hesitant to act. Museveni, for example, sent Uganda's soldier's as far afield as Liberia in 1994, at the request of the United States and with its funding, to support ECOMOG's peace operation.[75] New breed leaders also offered human intelligence and on-the-ground surveillance in African regions where the United States had drawn down its diplomatic and intelligence personnel in the Cold War's wake.[76]

By the mid-1990s US security interests in Africa had waned sharply. US priorities, such as they were, derived from fears around the "deterioration" of states across the continent.[77] In a February 1995 meeting with President Clinton and Prime Minister Jean-Luc Dehaene of Belgium, Vice President Al Gore summarized these concerns while plotting a dubious African geography. "Uncontrolled population growth, environmental destruction, sales of dangerous weapons, etc. These forces are combining to destabilize countries to the point that it is . . . a mess," Gore observed. "And it is happening all over," he continued, "from Sierra Leone to West Africa."[78]

Notably, Gore did not cite terrorism as a principal threat. Clinton officials had publicly raised concerns around terrorism in Africa, with an emphasis on threats from Libya and Sudan.[79] But by the early 1990s, Libya was seen as a declining source of peril. Sudan had indeed been designated a state sponsor of terrorism in 1993, but it was just as likely to be condemned for human rights abuses against its own citizens. Washington's push to "bring more pressure" against Khartoum's National Islamic Front government began to gain steam in 1994.[80] And it was two years later that the "Sudan menace" began to firmly push counterterrorism to the top of the US security agenda in Africa.[81]

Gore's privately expressed concerns were very much in step with a public discourse around endemic African anarchy and tribalism that emerged with renewed vigor in the Cold War's wake. This view was reinforced for many US officials by the ill-fated UN mission in Somalia, the Rwandan genocide, and so-called Black on Black violence in South Africa on the eve of apartheid's demise.[82] A prominent distillation of this "afro-pessimism" could be found in Robert Kaplan's *Atlantic* article "The Coming Anarchy" (1994). Kaplan conjured a landscape of feckless African leaders, states collapsing under environmental pressures, and "juju warriors influenced by the worst refuse of Western pop culture and ancient tribal hatreds."[83]

Clinton remarked that he had been "gripped" by Kaplan's observations.[84] Indeed, more than a year after its publication, Kaplan's analysis remained so prominent that the State Department's Bureau of Intelligence and Research (INR) dispatched an assessment of it to every African diplomatic post. The agency found Kaplan's claims myopic, hyperbolic, and unduly pessimistic. It highlighted incipient economic and political progress in Africa. Nonetheless, according to the INR: "The medium-term prognosis for the continent is more tribal warfare in the Rwandas, Burundis and Sierra Leones, and more famines in the Horn of Africa. But Rwandan-style killings do not threaten the vital interests of the US and Europe."[85]

This resonated with the views expressed by State Department African Affairs Bureau Chief George Moose not long after his appointment in 1993. A career diplomat and the first African American to hold the post, Moose acknowledged that Kaplan's article had been widely read within the administration. He agreed that there were "genuine problems" in Africa, yet at the same time he cited "contradictory trends" unfolding across the continent—some troubling, others encouraging—making special note of Uganda's recent progress.[86] Over the course of the next half-decade, however, the Clinton administration would increasingly abandon the "contradictory trends" thesis. Instead, to serve its geostrategic interests, the administration would champion narratives of a dawning "African renaissance" and promote a conveniently embellished vision of economic resurgence and democratic ascendance among its

African allies.[87] To bolster this vision, it would publicly transpose the racist hyperbole of afro-pessimists with a caricature of its own: the new breed of African leaders.[88]

While this move has been widely attributed to the naiveté or exuberance of a cadre of State Department officials who rose to prominence around 1997, the new breed caricature began to gain ground within the Clinton administration as early as 1994.[89] The idea of a new breed with whom the United States was determined to refashion US–Africa relations was largely illusory. Its consequences were all too real and enduring. State Department officials framed this fresh portrayal of African leadership as a rejection of racist discourses and a means of transcending long-held stereotypes. In fact, this caricature helped to render palatable the expanding US security alignments with the Meles and Museveni governments. It likewise diverted attention away from the coalescing hard-power objectives of these ties, counterterrorism primary among them. This smokescreen served to intensify US security relations with Uganda and Ethiopia in the mid-1990s, relations that would wane by the turn of the century and be revitalized with the onset of the War on Terror in 2001. During this foundational moment for twenty-first-century US–Africa security affairs, American portrayals of African governance pivoted between extremes—African renaissance and African anarchy—driven by Washington's realpolitik and informed by American notions of racial difference.

A NEW BREED WITH AN AGENDA OF ITS OWN

The Clinton White House made a determined effort to jettison the paternalistic rhetoric of Cold War patron-client relations. Instead, the administration began to aggressively promote an agenda of partnerships in its security relations with African states while anointing a "new generation" or "new breed" of African leaders.[90] Meles, Museveni, and Kagame were most emblematic of this new breed, according to administration officials and pliant Western journalists. US officials labeled these men pragmatic, engaged, active, dynamic, and articulate.[91] These African leaders were, in a word, exceptional. This view buttressed the new breed's regional and international influence, yet these leaders needed no plaudits from Washington.

The new breed caricature was, in fact, the Clinton administration's opportunistic characterization of a regional bloc that had been coalescing of its own accord and with its own nascent agenda since the early 1990s.[92] New breed leaders easily discerned Clinton's opportunism. Some questioned the homogenizing tone of the Clinton administration's new discourse around African leadership. On the eve of the president's 1998 trip to Africa, David Shinn, US ambassador to Ethiopia, cabled the State Department to warn that Prime Minister Meles was uncomfortable with being shunted into the administration's archetypical "new generation of African leaders."[93] Meles was pleased with Ethiopia's expanding relations with the United States but was concerned that the new breed discourse papered over important distinctions in the governing philosophies of a diverse group of African leaders.

Meles acknowledged that he collaborated with Museveni, Afwerki, and Kagame on regional issues and that they were all less likely to be deferential to the West than their predecessors. But the prime minister emphasized that these leaders had varied domestic priorities and different approaches to governance and political participation. According to Shinn, Ethiopian officials were also concerned that the new breed discourse underscored the personalities of African leaders as opposed to the aspirations of their constituents. Shinn recommended that Clinton officials "play down" the rhetoric of a new generation of African leaders when the president visited Ethiopia, notwithstanding their running efforts to popularize the discourse and its clear resonance in the American press.[94] The ambassador largely limited his observations to Ethiopia, but he suspected that other new breed African leaders shared Meles's reservations.

In other words, even a leading member of the new breed was hesitant to be labeled as such, despite the rewards that this standing would yield in US economic and military aid. By pressing forward with this caricature of African leadership until it became patently untenable, Clinton officials gave credence to growing cults of personality in new breed governments. By the mid-1990s, leaders who benefited from this dynamic, particularly Meles and Museveni, were turning a recently espoused penchant for liberalization into fledgling economic growth.[95] They publicly eschewed dependence on Western aid while calling for greater discipline, austerity, and responsiveness from African leaders. Initially, these claims escaped scrutiny due to the horrendous human rights records and flawed economic policies of the new breed's predecessors. In Uganda, Museveni had come to power after fighting the notoriously brutal Idi Amin regime and the brief Obote and Okello governments that arose in its wake. Meles and Afwerki had collaborated to overthrow the Derg military junta in Ethiopia, whose worst atrocities had led to the deaths of more than two hundred thousand during the country's "Red Terror" between 1977 and 1979.[96]

Museveni and Meles were, without doubt, far less corrupt and repressive than their predecessors. There was nonetheless a clear penchant within the Clinton administration to overstate the progress represented by their governments. For new breed leaders, the administration's stated commitment to "democratization and human rights" in Africa was clearly tangential to a focus on state building, regime security, and visions of a new regional order.[97] In fact, democratization and human rights were hindrances to the often illiberal policies that the new breed pursued to achieve these goals.

The "wave of change" Clinton officials identified rolling across the continent in the 1990s was not wholly a chimera.[98] The decade opened with the release of Nelson Mandela and the fall of apartheid. Multiparty elections were becoming routine across the continent, with fifty-four of them, most free and fair, being held in twenty-nine countries from 1990 to 1994.[99] However, this trend was not in evidence among the new breed governments with which the Clinton administration partnered in East Africa. The commitments of Meles and Museveni, for example, to broadening political participation while respecting human rights and civil liberties were dubious at best. US officials were aware of this from these leaders' earliest moments in power. In a harbinger of sporadic crackdowns to come, only days after

Meles's TPLF took control of Addis Ababa in May 1991, its forces opened fire on demonstrators outside the American Embassy who were protesting US support for an Eritrean referendum on independence.[100] For his part, Museveni remained firmly committed to "no party" movement politics.[101] Both men scoffed at "democratic tutorials" from Washington.[102]

Still, the Clinton administration publicly touted these leaders' economic reforms and gradual embrace of democratic values. At the time, some critics saw this as a strategy of disengagement, a means of justifying declining US aid and attention to Africa, whose problems would now be taken in hand by a group of capable leaders.[103] Early public references to the idea of a new breed by Clinton officials can be found amid administration exhortations against throwing US aid dollars into Africa's "bottomless pit."[104] Yet, over time the new breed caricature would come to shoulder both fiscal and strategic aims, even as it revealed itself to be demonstrably, even embarrassingly, suspect.[105] Much of the power of this caricature was derived from the contrast it drew between the new African leaders and the African heads of state with whom the United States aligned during the Cold War. No contrast was as stark as that drawn with Zaire's Mobutu Sese Seko.[106]

MOBUTU AS AN OLD FRIEND AND A NEW FOIL

Since Mobutu's rise to power in 1965, US officials across administrations had privately deemed him "corrupt," "flamboyant," "vain," and "lazy."[107] In 1993 the Clinton administration changed tack by openly criticizing the Zairian president. Not long after, the White House began to hold aloft its new breed of African leaders, signaling a determination to dispense with outmoded security alignments with abusive African governments. The speciousness of this commitment would be revealed over the course of the next four years as the Clinton administration publicly condemned Mobutu while celebrating Meles and Museveni—and closely collaborating with all three leaders.

US officials did not call on Mobutu to leave office until his regime was on the verge of collapse, but it was clear from the earliest days of Clinton's presidency that his administration wanted to distance itself from the Zairian president. Still, it held fast to the vague premise that Mobutu had "a role to play" in Zaire's democratic transition, which began unfolding fitfully after a wave of popular agitation in 1990.[108] In this context, the Clinton administration offered little support to Zaire's elected transitional government or its prime minister, Etienne Tshisekedi. Though it recalled the US ambassador to Zaire to protest Mobutu's track record, the State Department also chided Tshisekedi for inflexibility as Mobutu schemed to maintain power.[109] TransAfrica's Randall Robinson put it plainly in February 1993: It is "not clear that we are prepared to invest any real political capital in removing Mobutu."[110]

The limits of Clinton's commitment to a democratic transition in Zaire became further apparent in the wake of Rwanda's April 1994 genocide. Mobutu's government was pivotal in authorizing clearances for French, US, and other Western personnel to access Eastern Zaire as more than one million mainly Hutu refugees fled into the region. These Western diplomats and security officials assisted the UNHCR and other relief organizations operating in Zaire's Kivu provinces.[111] At the same time, Zairian troops became a running source of instability and criminality during the unfolding refugee crisis.[112] Worse still, Mobutu began to allow former Interahamwe and Rwandan Armed Forces fighters who had carried out the genocide, and who were now among the Hutu refugees, to rearm and train as they launched cross-border raids into Rwanda from camps in Zaire.[113] The regrouping Hutu militants, the perilous humanitarian status of peaceful Rwandan refugees in Zaire, and the general inadequacy of relief operations all fueled a growing regional emergency.

The Clinton administration had been broadly condemned for obstructing UN action to halt the Rwandan genocide. No small measure of this criticism, during the genocide and its wake, argued that US obstruction was underpinned by stereotypes of intractable and inevitable African conflict that had been reinforced by Washington's failed mission in Somalia.[114] Determined to avoid another round of condemnation, the

Clinton administration began "enlisting help from Mobutu" to address the unfolding humanitarian crisis in Central Africa.[115] In response, Mobutu's officials assisted the United States in identifying drop zones for relief supplies in Eastern Zaire and granted US access to Goma's airfield during Operation Support Hope, a humanitarian relief campaign conducted by the US military from July to September 1994.[116]

As we have seen, Mobutu was skilled at using strategically valuable sites as a source of leverage in his relations with the United States. US military personnel ruefully observed that he clearly saw the refugee camps and crisis in Zaire as "an opportunity to bargain with his former Western backers."[117] For two years after Operation Support Hope, the United States solicited the Mobutu regime's aid in controlling arms flows into Eastern Zaire and developing a plan for the repatriation of refugees to Rwanda.[118] Washington likewise supported efforts to "resurrect" Zaire's military as a means to bring order to the refugee camps.[119] In short, as the US African Affairs Bureau chief observed at the time, "Zairian cooperation is key."[120]

Critics charged that the US readiness to work with Mobutu during the refugee crisis, rather than taking more extensive action on its own, had begun to restore the Zairian president's international influence while bolstering his grip on power at home.[121] The White House was sensitive to these charges. In a thinly veiled effort to undercut them, it attempted to publicly collaborate with Zaire's prime minister, Kengo wa Dondo, rather than Mobutu himself.[122] Clinton officials cast Kengo as a reformer and technocrat bent on confronting the corruption of Mobutu's government.[123] But Kengo had been a Mobutu protégé and ally, serving as Zairian prime minister and foreign minister throughout the 1980s while graft and despotism ran unabated. He had been designated prime minister in 1994 to undermine the Zairian opposition and the democratic transition itself. When he was embraced by Washington, Kengo had undertaken only modest economic reforms and confronted only the most brazen cases of government corruption.[124]

In 1994, amid mounting support for Kengo in Washington, Clinton returned an ambassador to Kinshasa. Anticipating disapproval of this move to tighten relations with Zaire, the State Department's Africa

Bureau sought "to maintain a low profile through the confirmation process."[125] Though Washington rejoiced at his halting reforms, Kengo was largely beholden to Mobutu. Much like Mobutu, he would also manipulate the refugee crisis by issuing unrealistic timelines for the repatriation of Rwanda refugees in order to foment domestic support.[126] Meanwhile, Washington never really sidelined Mobutu. In April 1996, for example, the CIA's deputy director met with the Zairian president to develop a plan to gradually transition refugees out of Zaire's camps and back into Rwanda.[127]

This fork-tongued US policy—privately collaborating with Mobutu while publicly excoriating him—persisted right up to the point that Rwandan troops and Alliance des Forces Démocratiques pour la Libération du Congo-Zaïre (AFDL) insurgents, both backed by Uganda, began to make serious gains in their campaign to overrun Mobutu's regime. In late 1996, as Rwanda's intervention hastened Mobutu's downfall, Clinton's national security adviser, Anthony Lake, met with President Jacques Chirac of France. While Chirac wanted to see Mobutu fully restored to power, Lake saw Mobutu as instrumental, at the very least, to resolving the unfolding crisis through a negotiated settlement. Both men agreed that Uganda was providing invaluable support to the Rwandan forces in the Congo and that Museveni could compel Kagame to abandon the fighting for negotiations.[128]

Chirac deemed Museveni "an intelligent but perverse man with an extraordinary capability to say yes to everyone but then never to deliver," who could only be swayed by an appeal from Libya's Muammar Gaddafi, a leading supplier of aid to Uganda. Lake disagreed, arguing that Museveni "needs us to some degree with respect to Sudan, and we do have more influence with Meles. He has some influence with Museveni. Our influence is small, but we should use it."[129]

Despite the Clinton administration's public rhetoric, Lake was clearly willing to appease both the new breed of African leaders as well as the old breed, among whom Mobutu was a convenient, public foil. When Rwanda pressed forward, lending invaluable muscle to the AFDL, and Uganda continued to support the invasion, the United States publicly criticized the intervention while quietly offering Rwanda and Uganda operational assistance.[130] It called for a ceasefire and encouraged neighboring countries to stay out of Zaire, but it continued training programs with Rwandan troops and expanded military aid to Uganda.[131] The Clinton administration also backed Museveni and Kagame's successful effort to ensure that AFDL leader Laurent Kabila came to power after the rebel force unseated Mobutu in 1997, a victory that would have been unlikely without Rwandan and Ugandan assistance.[132]

Kagame, Museveni, and Kabila—new breed leaders—effectively liberated the Clinton administration from its fraught relations with Zaire, relations in which Mobutu still held some influence, notwithstanding his regime's decay. This strengthened Washington's bonds with Museveni in particular and heightened US efforts to embellish the caricature of Africa's new breed, despite its creeping authoritarianism. The caricature would provide useful diplomatic cover as the United States assisted Uganda in confronting Sudan, as Lake hinted, and ramped up its own counterterrorism agenda for the continent.

From a bargaining standpoint, it is also worth noting that the United States was under few illusions about its limited capacity to influence Museveni and Meles. Mobutu's fall offered a convenient means for Washington to cut ties with his regime. But at the same time, Museveni and Kagame essentially cornered Clinton into supporting the terms and timing of their agenda in Zaire while Meles actively participated in planning the intervention. One US diplomat put it bluntly: "We underestimated them."[133]

Also notable is the declining value of Mobutu's strategically valuable territory during the refugee crisis relative to the military capabilities that new breed leaders brought to the table. In overthrowing their exponentially larger neighbor, Kagame and Museveni burnished reputations for military prowess and put on full display the capacity of their battle-hardened forces to effectively operate across borders. These same capabilities could be marshalled to effectively support US aims moving forward—for a price.

During the Cold War, the United States largely looked to its African security allies for basing agreements that helped Washington to balance against Moscow. The asset specificity the United States associated with bases and strategically important sites in Africa would remain a valuable source of influence for African governments during the War on Terror. But this moment in the mid-1990s begins to reveal the broader repertoire of strategic assets that African states would be able to leverage in Washington over the next two decades. Primary among these assets was the capacity to conduct sustained regional military operations supported by effective intelligence collection capabilities. In other words, regional muscle mattered more now, and states such as Uganda were better poised to make the most of this dynamic than long-standing US allies such as Kenya, whose militaries remained largely untested beyond their borders.

THE FRONT LINES OF THE US WAR ON TERROR IN AFRICA

The attention Clinton officials lavished on new breed leaders was rarely extended to grassroots or civil society groups in their countries. Such groups were largely ignored, for example, in the administration's 1995 Greater Horn of Africa Initiative, which had the espoused aim of supporting "food security" and "conflict resolution" in the region.[134] Moreover, US pronouncements of a new breed and dawning renaissance did not lead Clinton officials to completely abandon the empirically dubious rhetoric of "failed states" and "basket cases."[135] Some Clinton officials were emphatic that the mid-1990s offered a brief "window of opportunity" for Africa to escape its dysfunction, that the renaissance was a "last chance," and that international patience was "wearing thin."[136] Indeed, traditional stereotypes of African anarchy and dysfunction would regain prominence by the end of the 1990s when Ethiopia and Eritrea engaged in a border conflict, and Ugandan and Rwandan forces fought each other while playing leading roles in Congo's second civil war.

The White House's espoused commitment to antipaternalistic engagement on the continent was generally well received among Washington's growing Africa-advocacy civil society groups.[137]Amid this firmament of support, the soaring rhetoric of an African renaissance and a new breed of leadership obscured an overriding US concern with hard strategic interests, counterterrorism primary among them. By 1996 the Clinton administration envisioned key roles for Uganda, Ethiopia, and Eritrea in its effort to weaken the Islamic government in Sudan. It accused Sudan of opening its doors to Islamist militants, hosting their training camps, and providing them a safe haven only second to that of its close ally, Iran.[138] The administration condemned Omar al-Bashir and Hassan al-Turabi, the architect of the National Islamic Front, for turning Sudan into a staging ground for groups such as Hezbollah, Palestinian Islamic Jihad, and Osama bin Laden's al-Qaeda.[139]

In June 1996, nineteen US airmen were killed in the Khobar Towers bombing in Saudi Arabia, an attack which the United States attributed to Iranian sponsorship. The next month, US fears around terrorism spiked again with the explosion and crash of a TWA flight out of New York's JFK airport as well as a bombing at the Atlanta Olympics, neither of which would ultimately prove to be the work of international terrorists. Under election-year criticisms, the Clinton administration began to craft a more aggressive military strategy in Africa. It convened Western leaders, plotted preemptive strikes and covert operations, and, as the *New York Times* reported, began to "Chart [a] War Against Terrorism."[140]

Museveni was a ready collaborator in Washington's campaign to oppose the Bashir government. The standing enmity between Uganda and Sudan was reflected in Khartoum's support for the Lord's Resistance Army as it pillaged Northern Uganda and Kampala's backing for the Sudanese People's Liberation Army as it fought to break away from the National Islamic Front government. In 1995, after Sudan launched air raids against Uganda amid deteriorating relations between the neighboring states, US military advisors worked closely with Ugandan troops to fortify the state's northern border.[141]

In the early 1990s, despite US pressure, Meles was hesitant to turn against Sudan because of the support he had received from the National Islamic Front government when he was a rebel leader. As one Ethiopian diplomat reportedly put in June 1995, "How can Ethiopia, with a 45 percent Muslim population, engage in holy anti-Islamic war against the

Sudan, as Clinton's special envoys urge us to do? Why is America so off-beam these days?"[142] Within weeks of this query, Sudan supported an assassination attempt against Egyptian president Hosni Mubarak during an OAU summit in Addis Ababa and later refused to extradite the suspected assassins to Ethiopia. In response, Meles took a hardline stance against Khartoum, condemning it as a source of regional instability.[143] Moreover, along with Uganda and Eritrea, Ethiopia began to firmly embrace plans to undermine the Sudanese government. Thus, while State Department officials attributed the closer US ties with these states to the progressive reforms of a new breed of African leaders, Clinton's CIA and NSC saw them as "frontline" allies in a regional pincer movement targeting Sudan.[144] In April 1996, for example, Director John Deutch of the CIA marked the deepening of his agency's ties with the Ethiopian government during a three-day visit to Addis Ababa.[145]

Among US officials, Meles was seen as more reserved and technocratic than the notoriously folksy and garrulous Museveni. Moreover, Museveni's deeper commitment to economic liberalization put US diplomats at greater ease. However, even as US ties with Uganda and Ethiopia tightened amid rising concerns around terrorism in Washington, relations with both governments remained "difficult to manage."[146] The limits of US influence with both Meles and Museveni would become increasingly apparent throughout the 1990s.

After seizing power in 1986, Museveni had become adroit at nurturing relations with successive US administrations while parrying Washington's criticisms of his government's illiberalism, its close ties with Libya, and its use of torture in quashing insurgencies.[147] As for Meles, despite persistent mutual suspicion, the George H. W. Bush administration had helped to ease his transition to power when it mediated negotiations that gave rise to a new Ethiopian government in 1991.[148] However, the Ethiopian prime minister quickly made US officials aware that he would not be beholden to Washington.

This dynamic is clearly rendered in an October 1996 intelligence assessment that the State Department drafted to prepare Secretary of State Warren Christopher for a visit to Addis Ababa. Meles, according to the assessment, was a "congenial interlocutor" who had impressed many senior US officials but was "not easily swayed . . . and prone to perceive even mild criticism as an unacceptable intrusion in Ethiopian affairs." Moreover, there had been a role reversal on the question of Sudan, with Meles now urging the United States to "maintain unremitting pressure" on the National Islamic Front government and recruiting Washington to his more aggressive efforts to see it overthrown. Meles was also, the assessment held, intent on garnering firmer US backing as he confronted warlords in neighboring Somalia who were supporting insurgents in Ethiopia's Ogaden region. For the Ethiopians, according to the State Department, the threat posed by violence spilling out of Somalia, whose central government collapsed in 1991, was a "more immediate and serious menace than that posed by Sudan."[149]

At the end of 1996 the Clinton administration authorized $20 million in military aid to Ethiopia, Uganda, and Eritrea. Most of it went to Ethiopia, which also received $106 million in US foreign assistance that year, making it the largest recipient of US aid in Sub-Saharan Africa. The State Department publicly asserted that the military aid was for defensive purposes. However, congressional officials confirmed anonymously that the United States expected these states to funnel some of the equipment included in the aid package to the SPLA as it prepared to mount a major offensive against the Sudanese government. When news of the military aid leaked, it was reported as "the first post–Cold War era example of Washington's giving military support to African countries that have vowed to overthrow another African government."[150]

Meles and Museveni were also beneficiaries and ardent supporters of Clinton's African Crisis Response Force (ACRF), a program launched in 1996 with the stated aim of creating and training a standing African peacekeeping force. When it was proposed, amid US concerns that ethnic violence in Burundi might escalate to genocide, ACRF encountered widespread skepticism among African leaders.[151] For many, including Nelson Mandela, the proposal wreaked of American paternalism.[152] For others, it signaled a US impulse to disengage from Africa in the face of looming crises while creating an armed force that might use peacekeeping as a hollow justification for regional interventions. One anonymous US State Department official declared that ACRF was proposed precisely so that Washington would not face an "our troops or no troops dilemma."[153] The program met such a cold reception that the Clinton administration was forced to rebrand it as the African Crisis Response Initiative (ACRI). Nonetheless, Meles was one of the first African leaders to endorse ACRI, and Museveni's troops were among the earliest to receive training under the initiative.[154]

Clinton announced that African forces that received training through ACRI were provided only nonlethal military equipment. However, in a sparsely attended 1997 Pentagon press briefing, the Special Forces commander who coordinated ACRI's on-the-ground activities clarified that the donations of nonlethal equipment included ammunition. The ammunition was for training as well as "force protection." ACRI's coordinator noted that in earlier humanitarian interventions, every African unit that was participating in the initiative "had been in some kind of firefight, even if it was just acts of banditry, in some cases the nonbelligerents became belligerents."[155] This track record hinted at a dangerous ambiguity around the parameters of "peacekeeping." Later that year, this ambiguity became obvious when, instead of being dispatched on a peace mission, Uganda's ACRI-trained military unit was deployed to fight bandits and insurgents in the country's Kabarole district.[156] Notably, in the run-up to the deployment, local journalists had made no secret of the Ugandan military's growing litany of abuses and human rights violations in Kabarole.[157]

From these inauspicious beginnings, ACRI would go on to become a key operational framework for regional US military training programs in Africa. It would serve as a basis for programs such as the Bush administration's African Contingency Operations Training Assistance initiative, which explicitly included the provision of lethal matériel to African militaries with the aim of supporting more muscular peace operations.[158] These programs would also provide a ready, guiding framework for many of the regional counterterrorism initiatives that the George W. Bush administration launched in Africa during the War on Terror. When the administration began the first of these counterterrorism programs, the Pan-Sahel Initiative, states such as Mali were prime candidates for inclusion, in part because of their earlier participation in ACRI.

EAST AFRICA'S TALENTED TENTH

During Clinton's March 1998 tour of Africa, the president visited Senegal, observed an ACRI training exercise for the country's soldiers, and delivered a short speech touting the initiative.[159] Barring this brief display, Clinton officials labored to direct media attention away from US military goals and programs in Africa as the president traversed the continent. Throughout the trip, the administration bombarded the press with statements underscoring its desire to forge new economic partnerships in Africa while downplaying the budding US security partnerships with regional governments. Not only was Clinton's trip framed as a means to showcase Africa's economic potential, but it was also billed as an attempt to "demystify" the continent, embrace its rising status in world affairs, and partner with a new generation of African leaders.[160] As Clinton put it during the visit, "I do believe there is an African renaissance, and I believe their future is a part of our future."[161] Those who were most intrinsic to Washington's vision of Africa's future were leaders such as Museveni, whom Secretary of State Madeline Albright dubbed "a beacon of hope," even as he entered the twelfth year of his presidency determined to maintain a system of No Party rule in Uganda.[162]

During Clinton's visit to six African countries, administration officials intertwined grand aspirations for US–Africa relations with a carefully parsed racial discourse. A stage-managed medley of rhetoric and posturing signaled that Clinton's African excursion was not simply a matter of the future of US ties with the continent. The trip was also, this narrative held, a sincere attempt to reckon with America's history of racial injustices. Clinton called attention to the vile history of transatlantic slavery and expressed regret for the opportunistic Cold War policies of the United States and its indifference to Africa's humanitarian crises. He comforted survivors of the Rwandan Genocide and visited forts in Ghana and Senegal through which millions of Africans passed as they were sold into slavery in the Americas. This journey of racial healing was meant to affirm Clinton's ostensibly fresh and enlightened view of Africa. The growing US preoccupation with terrorism on the continent was consigned to the shadows.

Clinton stopped short of offering an apology for American participation in the slave trade, the subject of a public debate that surrounded, and for some stained, his voyage of racial reconciliation. In Uganda he nonetheless acknowledged that "European-Americans" had been "wrong" to enjoy the "fruits" of the brutal enterprise. "Although I must say," Clinton added, "if you look at the remarkable delegation we have here from Congress, from our Cabinet and Administration . . . you can see there are many distinguished African Americans . . . who are making America a better place."[163] Clinton had, in fact, recruited dozens of his Black liberal allies to accompany him to Africa.

The African American foreign policy elite swelled the ranks of the president's entourage. From within the administration, Clinton was joined by Secretary of Transportation Rodney Slater, Secretary of Labor Alexis Herman, Assistant Secretary of State for African Affairs Susan Rice, half a dozen Black members of his staff, and the Reverend Jesse Jackson, who had recently been appointed special envoy for democracy and human rights in Africa. Nearly a dozen members of the CBC also accompanied the president, including William Jefferson, Donald Payne, Maxine Waters, Charles Rangel, and Sheila Jackson Lee. The mayors of Denver and Detroit served as representatives of Black leadership in municipal government. The corporate wing of Clinton's delegation featured Robert Johnson, president of Black Entertainment Television; Carl Ware, a vice president at Coca Cola, and a host of prominent Black banking, insurance, and healthcare executives. Civil society leaders and activists rounded out the group, representing the NAACP, the National Urban Coalition, Africare, and the African Development Foundation.[164] Clinton was even joined by famed radio personality Tom Joyner, whose syndicated show was broadcast across dozens of stations and claimed millions of loyal African American listeners.[165]

Clinton and his entourage made their appreciation for Africa's new breed leaders unmistakable when they visited Uganda for a summit hosted by Museveni and attended by Meles, Kabila, and the presidents of Rwanda, Kenya, and Tanzania. On the eve of the summit, Susan Rice remarked that Uganda had "pursued important political and economic reforms, which are obviously by no means perfect, but [are] important strides."[166] Rice would note in a memoir published two decades later that by aligning itself with new breed icons like Museveni, the Clinton administration was "casting our lot with undemocratic leaders." "Security interests," Rice recalled, sometimes "took precedence over democracy promotion." While she expressed no regrets for establishing partnerships to confront the terrorist threat in Sudan, Rice wrote that the administration would have been better served by "avoiding praise for individual leaders and speaking out more forcefully about their failings and abuses."[167]

Failings and abuses were not up for discussion during Clinton's 1998 meeting with the new breed in Uganda. Clinton and his Black allies talked up the achievements of the assembled African leaders. The local press reported concerns among the Ugandan opposition that Clinton had arrived to "swoon over Museveni" despite his ban on multiparty politics.[168] Reverend Jackson, however, came to the Ugandan government's defense, declaring, "This is not a military state. This is a democracy in development."[169]

While speaking at the groundbreaking ceremony of a Coca Cola Bottling Plant in Kampala, Jackson appeared to prioritize economic progress over representative institutions. "Democracy is of course important," he proclaimed, "but investment like Coca Cola is long-term sustainable growth." Jackson lamented that Dr. Martin Luther King Jr. was not present to see the plant's construction because King had struggled not only for Black voting rights but also the "right to economic benefits."[170] Representative Rangel, who also presided over the groundbreaking ceremony, remarked that while in Uganda he would be parsing the terms of a trade treaty meant to serve African and American interests. Rangel assured the local press that once the treaty was established, BET's CEO Robert Johnson would widely publicize its benefits.

Rangel was referring to the African Growth and Opportunity bill, the lynchpin of Clinton's legislative agenda for the continent. Passed by the House on the eve of the president's trip, the bill was celebrated as a groundbreaking effort to break down trade barriers by offering the exporters of eligible African countries preferential, duty-free access to American markets. It was not universally supported by the African

American political elite. TransAfrica's Randall Robinson argued that African countries that were granted access to the bill's benefits would be pressured into supporting Washington's foreign policies and opening their economies to US corporate domination. "It should be called the African re-colonization bill," Robinson observed wryly, "It is the same exploitative message in a different private-sector package."[171] Congressman Jesse Jackson Jr. opposed the bill on the premise that it would primarily serve the interests of multinational corporations while threatening African autonomy and the jobs of American workers, particularly those in his Illinois district.[172]

By contrast, Jesse Jackson Sr. was far more sanguine about the legislation. He was now a Clinton appointee and, along with the president's traveling entourage, played a pivotal role in defending the administration's plans. Jackson argued that African Americans should take the lead in implementing Clinton's economic agenda for Africa. "We who were taken into slavery," Jackson avowed, "go back with a meaningful capacity to help both America and the African family."[173] Charles Rangel, one AGOA's staunchest proponents, riffed on a similar theme. "As African Americans none of us knew the country or the year that our ancestors were kidnapped from the continent," he wrote in the *Amsterdam News*, "but landing on African soil for the first time armed with legislation and the president's commitment to help, we finally understood the feeling enjoyed by other ethnic Americans."[174] Rosa Whitaker, Clinton's assistant trade representative for Africa, framed the bill as a vehicle to liberate Africa from "global economic apartheid."[175] Once Clinton left office, Whitaker would go on to work as a paid consultant and registered foreign agent for the Ugandan government and establish close ties with Museveni.[176]

The fanfare around Black solidarity, fresh African leadership, and an unfolding African renaissance obscured the expanding US counterterrorism agenda in Africa and the flaws of its new breed allies. African American leaders expressed a host of noble reasons for participating in Clinton's excursion. Many framed the trip as a means of celebrating and reinvigorating ties with an ancestral homeland. Others were particularly moved when Clinton's tour visited South Africa, then under the leadership of President Nelson Mandela. For example, Congresswoman Maxine Waters and NAACP chair Kweisi Mfume recalled a long history of African American opposition to apartheid and their often thankless efforts to convince US policymakers to take African issues seriously.[177] Nearly all of Clinton's Black travel companions suggested that their historical and cultural bonds with Africa helped to fuel their investment in the president's campaign to spur prosperity across the continent.

These appeared to be sincerely held convictions. They were derived from the traditional priorities of Black moderate transnationalism—strong and stable African governments and mutually beneficial economic arrangements for Africans and African Americans. To advance these priorities, in a historically resonant gesture, much of the African American foreign policy elite endorsed new breed African leaders who were more committed to military might than to democratic governance. Fittingly, these leaders sought both regime security and regional influence by facilitating the US security agenda in Africa.

On rare occasions when journalists pressed Clinton officials about the new breed's checkered track record, the response was cagey. US diplomats argued that Museveni, Kagame, and Meles had supported insurrections in neighboring countries only to foster long-term regional stability. Some claimed that the Clinton administration's tolerance for the new breed's halting democratic reforms stemmed from an appreciation for the unique historical challenges faced by countries such as Uganda and Ethiopia. One diplomat was far more straightforward about the new breed's growing influence given the strategic priorities of the United States: "It has to be recognized that we are not dictating the shape of things out here."[178]

The Clinton administration found itself increasingly unable to dictate the terms of its expanding security partnerships with its new breed allies. But the administration was, in fact, able to dictate the terms of a narrative that shielded these partnerships from scrutiny while celebrating Museveni, Meles, and Kagame. During Clinton's tour of Africa, the administration positioned African American leaders as the tip of the spear of this exercise in obfuscation. While White House officials noted that the president's trip was meant to awaken Americans of all races to Africa's potential, they highlighted the unique role that African Americans were poised to play in engaging their African "counterparts."[179]

Clinton emphasized the ethnic and emotional ties that his African American allies shared with Africa. Meanwhile, these allies explicitly called on the legacies of notable African Americans who venerated the continent, including Marcus Garvey and W.E.B. Du Bois.[180] Indeed, in Museveni, Meles, and Kagame, Clinton's compatriots identified something akin to East Africa's Talented Tenth, an apt corollary to their own class of elite, well-educated Black Americans. This was a late 1990s revival of Du Bois's transnational coterie of "leading negroes."[181] Much like Du Bois's Talented Tenth, this new breed of African leaders was distinguished by its education, worldliness, and familiarity with "Anglo-Saxon culture."[182]

The new breed benefited from a hierarchical model of racial leadership fostered by the African American liberal vanguard. This elite-driven political strategy allowed both groups to project their influence on the world stage. It was part and parcel of a surging Black moderate transnationalism that bolstered the statist Pan-Africanism of new breed leaders such as Museveni and Meles. Both ideological tendencies, as noted, have historical roots that are intertwined with authoritarianism and militarism in African governance.

Moderate transnationalism flourished among the African American foreign policy elite in the 1990s. Its resurgence was abetted by a waning of grassroots energy around anti-imperialism throughout the African diaspora after the collapse of the last white-minority-ruled regimes in Africa. Largely free from the pressure of their constituents, African American leaders returned their focus to transatlantic entrepreneurialism and the opening of African markets to US investments.[183] This effort was framed as a means to create jobs and opportunities for Africans and African Americans while helping to alleviate endemic poverty in Africa.[184] The entrepreneurial aspirations of Black moderates received a tailwind of support from Clinton's Department of Commerce and US groups such as the Corporate Council on Africa.

Commerce summits and conferences that brought together African and African American leaders became a prominent feature of the 1990s landscape.[185] These conferences were often orchestrated by African Americans with enduring ties to corporate America, such as Leon H. Sullivan, and sponsored by companies like Chevron and Philip Morris.[186] They drew the support of a broad range of African American political elites, ranging from Coretta Scott King to Minister Louis Farrakhan.[187] These affairs were hosted by African leaders such as Ivory Coast's Felix Houphouet-Boigny and Gabon's Omar Bongo Ondimba, who had shown little commitment to democratic governance.[188] In a sense, Clinton and his Black entourage's 1998 tour of Africa was an addendum to this conference circuit that disguised the abuses of the new breed security partners of the United States.

The new breed discourse was not only valuable for the Clinton administration as it burnished a pledge to engage Africans as full partners. It also helped the administration to capitalize on the enthusiasm of many African American officials who hoped for more sustained and principled US engagement with Africa and who often saw racism as a motive for US inattention to the continent.[189]

Despite the Clinton administration's plaudits for a new generation of African leaders, some scholars and civil society groups remained skeptical. In fact, while Clinton was in Africa, Ethiopian expatriates held demonstrations in Atlanta, Washington, DC, Ottawa, and London to protest US support for Meles's government.[190] While avoiding the racist tropes of early 1990s afro-pessimism, a handful of scholars likewise highlighted the contradictions of a new breed that had come to power through insurgencies and readily sponsored rebels and interventions in neighboring states. During Clinton's trip, Mahmood Mamdani, then a professor at the University of Cape Town, largely dismissed the American president's gestures of reconciliation. Mamdani criticized Clinton's fixation on economic liberalization rather than political reform in Africa as well as his plan to place Uganda at the center of ACRI's regional peacekeeping programs. Mamdani also took the United States to task for backing Museveni as he worked to criminalize the Ugandan opposition.[191]

Nelson Kasfir, a Uganda expert and professor of government at Dartmouth College, noted at least one reason for Clinton's growing admiration for Museveni: "The West looks for very simple indicators. . . . What do white people look for? Stability, that's all. . . . Uganda has all the trappings of stability."[192] This critique could have been extended to much of the African American foreign policy elite during the 1990s as they strained to promote Black transatlantic entrepreneurialism and liberal economic growth in Africa.

For new breed skeptics like Georges Nzongola-Ntalaja, J. Oloka-Onyango, and Okbazghi Yohannes, it was clear that the United States was willing to downplay the abuses of the Congolese, Ugandan, and Ethiopian governments. The immediate goal, according to these scholars, was to contain Sudan, while the long-term goal was to craft alliances that would expand US access to African resources and markets.[193] To achieve these ends, the United States stoked the militarism that was central to the new breed's regional collaborations—a militarism that would ultimately help to fuel Congo's second civil war and the Ethiopia-Eritrea border conflict.[194]

A RENAISSANCE DISCARDED

By the end of Clinton's term, both Uganda and Ethiopia had been suspended from ACRI due to their roles in regional conflicts.[195] Mounting evidence confirmed that Ugandan troops were committing human rights abuses at home and in the Congo, where they were also pillaging timber and mineral resources.[196] In May 1998, just over a month after Clinton returned from Africa, Ethiopia and Eritrea went to war. Beneath the border conflict were disputes over currency, Ethiopian access to Eritrean ports, and the intransigence of the increasingly personalized regimes of Meles and Afwerki—both of whom had been members of Clinton's new breed.[197]

Three months later, al-Qaeda operatives bombed the US Embassies in Kenya and Tanzania. After the East Africa embassy bombings, counterterrorism began to take center stage in the rhetoric of Clinton officials, quickly displacing visions of an African renaissance. Some of the officials most closely associated with the African renaissance narrative, such as Susan Rice and Madeline Albright, were among the most hawkish members of the Clinton administration in the wake of the embassy bombings. They strongly supported Clinton's botched, retaliatory air strikes on Sudan, as did leading members of the CBC, including Senator Carol Moseley Braun and Representatives Eva Clayton and Albert Wynn.[198]

For some time, Albright had been calling for a firmer antiterror stance against Khartoum, even as a handful of State Department officials argued for expanding dialogue with the regime rather than ratcheting up military pressure. After the embassy bombings, counterterrorism began to predominate US plans for Africa, driving a veritable collapse of Clinton's caricature of exceptional African governance as the lynchpin for a new era in US–Africa relations.[199] With Clinton's new breed fueling wars in the Congo and the Horn of Africa while Uganda and Ethiopia cautiously normalized relations with Sudan, this convenient fiction quickly became unsustainable.[200]

Newspaper headlines trace the arc of this transition: "Back to Hell in the Horn of Africa," "Death of the African Dream," "It's Time to Be Candid About Africa's Leaders."[201] Inside the Clinton White House, officials equivocated, insisting that they had always understood the underlying "fragility" of Africa's institutions and drawing vague analogies with the European renaissance during which "wars and plagues were the norm."[202] As they backed away from the new breed discourse, Clinton officials claimed that the press had blown their commitment to the idea out of proportion.[203] By 1999, mentions of Uganda's domestic stability and economic success had virtually disappeared from official US statements, though ongoing military intelligence cooperation continued apace.[204] Moreover, despite US shuttle diplomacy between Addis Ababa and Asmara, State Department officials failed to assist their new breed partners in averting the 1998–2000 Ethiopia-Eritrea border war. Indeed, some evidence suggests that US diplomatic efforts exacerbated tensions between the states on the eve of the conflict.[205]

Meanwhile, Clinton's antiracist bona fides were beset from without and within. By early 1999 the Kosovo conflict began to consume the White House's attention, overshadowing humanitarian crises in the Congo, the Horn of Africa, and the Mano River Region. Black Clinton officials and international human rights advocates noted a clear double standard in the US decision to come to the aid of civilians in the Balkans while vacillating on similar action in Africa. Reverend Jesse Jackson privately deemed the disparity "absolutely racist."[206]

It was also during this period that African leaders and scholars began to expand on the notion of an African renaissance. The best of this intellectual tendency posed a stark contrast to the Clinton administration's vision. Rather than a preoccupation with economic growth and styles of leadership, it took up questions of social justice, cultural renewal, and equitable international relations.[207] But by the onset of the George W. Bush administration, these aspirations fell largely on deaf ears. Skepticism and pessimism toward Africa were ascendant in Washington, reinforced by the clear demise of Clinton's new breed discourse.

As Congo's civil war and the Ethiopia-Eritrea conflict dominated headlines, even African American leaders expressed an acute sense of betrayal toward their counterparts in the new breed. Donald Payne captured this sentiment in a 1999 congressional hearing, underscoring how "pleased" he once was with the "potential" of Meles and Afwerki, leaders who were "educated" and had "a lot of integrity." It was "very troubling and disappointing," Payne remarked, that these leaders who had once represented "the new winds blowing across Africa" were now embroiled in conflicts.[208] Indeed, a swelling tide of disappointment in Africa's new breed and the faltering African renaissance would usher in a period of apathy and disengagement among the African American foreign policy elite that stretched throughout the War on Terror.

Accordingly, scholars and diplomats have noted the declining influence of African American leaders and congressional officials in US foreign policy toward Africa.[209] A bloc of Black congressional officials with the will and power to scrutinize US security policies in Africa, the operations they facilitate, and the African leaders they often empower has not been a consistent feature of the political landscape since the turn of the twenty-first century. This type of nuanced engagement was largely supplanted by strong support among African American legislators for US efforts to confront terrorism.[210]

The dangers that US security initiatives posed to African civilians and democracy during the War on Terror evoked less outrage among African Americans than the malign consequences of US Cold War policies. Compounding this apathy was the challenge of establishing a clear picture of the sprawling, often covert US counterterror enterprise in Africa. This challenge was exacerbated by the decline of African American activist groups and media outlets that once called attention to US military operations in Africa.[211] These dynamics made it difficult for African Americans to form a coherent agenda vis-à-vis African governments that aimed to benefit from the US security agenda. Indeed, in this book's final chapter, an account of US–Uganda relations in the twenty-first century, the African American foreign policy elite, as a relatively unified bloc, plays almost no role in endorsing or criticizing the African security partners of the United States. In short, the close of the 1990s marked the swan song of the African American foreign policy elite as a corporate entity in US–Africa affairs. Their moderate transnationalism, once a powerful force in shaping and scrutinizing US policy toward Africa, would be nearly dormant by the dawn of the new millennium.

It was in this context that the Bush administration proposed cuts to US development aid in Africa and Secretary of Defense Donald Rumsfeld suggested eliminating peacekeeping training programs such as ACRI. Secretary of State Colin Powell resisted the idea, but prominent voices on Bush's National Security Council maintained that despite such programs, "there was no noticeable change in any of Africa's wars."[212] The events of 9/11 would ultimately lead to increases in funding for peace operations and US military aid to Africa. But in the immediate aftermath of the attack, as US officials grew concerned that Somalia had become a refuge for al-Qaeda fighters, the Bush administration was reluctant to tighten relations with the compromised avatars of Clinton's new breed. Prime Minister Meles publicly urged Washington to cooperate with him to confront the threat in Somalia. Nonetheless, US officials were "not eager" to partner with Ethiopia due to concerns that they would be pressured to take Meles's side in coming regional conflicts.[213]

Bush officials widely praised Museveni's government for the progress it had made in halting the spread of HIV in Uganda, but on other fronts relations were strained. This was in part because in early 2001 Uganda's troops remained in Eastern Congo and, under the direction of senior Ugandan officials, continued to loot Congolese timber and minerals.[214] Museveni's security forces were also engaging in a campaign of violence and voter intimidation in the run-up to Uganda's March 2001 presidential contest. Predictably, Museveni was reelected to extend his fifteen-year tenure in office. While Uganda's Supreme Court affirmed that the result was largely reflective of the will of the Ugandan people, it nonetheless noted that the poll was flawed by electoral irregularities.[215]

In the wake of the Ugandan election, Secretary of State Colin Powell met with Ugandan opposition leaders, including Dr. Kizza Besigye, and issued a measured call for Museveni to move toward more pluralistic electoral politics.[216] Museveni, in turn, found ways to express his mounting displeasure with Washington. In early 2001 he was one of the only African leaders to publicly side with a handful of African American members of Congress who were calling for the United States to offer reparations to African Americans, a position with which the Bush administration firmly disagreed.[217] This was a stunning reversal. Only three years earlier, when Museveni stood shoulder to shoulder with Clinton as a member of Africa's new breed, he had insisted that the American president refrain from apologizing for America's role in the transatlantic slave trade. In fact, the Ugandan president claimed that because African tribal chiefs had waged war on each other and sold captives into slavery, it was they who should be called on to apologize. Museveni was adamant that the very idea of a US apology for slavery was "rubbish."[218] At the time, Susan Rice—"as an African American"—agreed that far too much attention was being placed on the subject.[219]

In the months following 9/11, as the Bush administration solicited support for counterterrorism from a range of African states, it appeared willing to downgrade relations with Uganda. The United States sought the assistance and intelligence of Uganda's historical foe, Sudan, and aimed to expand security ties with Kenya.[220] It was roughly a year into the War on Terror before the Bush administration began to publicly embrace Museveni as an important security partner. During that time, Museveni vocally expressed his support for Bush's war in Iraq while denouncing terrorism in Uganda and signing sweeping antiterrorism legislation into law.[221] He also offered an airfield in Entebbe as a refueling hub and, later, a cooperative security location for the expanding US military operations in Africa.[222]

Meanwhile, the Bush administration was swiftly dispensing with Clinton-era visions of a new breed of African leadership amid an African renaissance. Its security agenda on the continent was informed by a set of stereotypes that coalesced at the other end of the spectrum. On scant evidence, it cast Africa as a continent of anarchy and ungoverned spaces that gave rise to terrorist threats.[223] Throughout the continent, the Bush administration saw conflicts, dysfunction, and underdevelopment as tinder for the growth of Islamist extremist groups and the proliferation of their ideas. In essence, this was a time-honored view of African primitivism granted fresh urgency by the threat of Islamist terrorism.

In this context, African militaries that were repressive but seasoned in regional conflicts and unencumbered by democratic oversight could help to advance US goals. Gone were the days of the renaissance and the convenient caricature of African leadership that ushered in a *new* era of US–Africa security partnerships. The Bush administration embraced its military ties with African leaders of the new breed and the old. It touted, for example, its intelligence sharing initiatives with both Meles's government and the moldering, authoritarian regime of Kenya's Daniel arap Moi.[224] Yet among the fallen icons of the new breed, it was Museveni whose friendship the United States would come to value most, and the Ugandan president was more than ready to capitalize on US fears around Somalia as an incubator of terrorism.

5

AN ALLY TO BE RECKONED WITH

The US–Uganda Partnership and the Power of Museveni's Pan-Africanism

In February 2007 President Yoweri Museveni and General William "Kip" Ward met to discuss the impending deployment of Ugandan troops to Somalia as the first contingent of an African Union peace force. After the meeting, in a press conference outside of the State House in Entebbe, Museveni acknowledged that the United States would be funding some of the deployment. He emphasized that Uganda was not acting as a US "policeman."[1] Museveni was adamant that his state's foreign policy was developed independently. The fight against terrorism in Somalia, he told the press, was in the mutual interest of Kampala and Washington. More important, as Museveni would later and consistently note, the Ugandan mission to Somalia was motivated by a deep commitment to Pan-Africanism.[2] The following month, the Uganda People's Defence Force (UPDF) initiated the African Union Mission in Somalia (AMISOM). AMISOM lasted for nearly fifteen years before being restructured as the African Transition Mission in Somalia (ATMIS) under a 2022 UN plan to wind down the operation.[3]

Many critics dismiss Museveni's abundant invocations of Pan-Africanism as illusory, a convenient cloak in a quest for regional power and profit. What cannot be dismissed is the effectiveness of his particular vision of Pan-Africanism in his campaign to shape the course of Uganda's security relations with Washington. This statist Pan-Africanism has found its most powerful expression in Uganda's long record of military interventions and backing for insurgencies, a record that has consistently evoked US support and deference. Indeed, for much of the past two decades, Museveni has recruited successive US administrations to *his* vision of regional order in East Africa.

Under Museveni's leadership, Uganda has deployed its military to more countries than any other African government. His forces have intervened in Sudan, the Democratic Republic of Congo, the Central African Republic, and South Sudan. They have participated in peace operations in Liberia, Cote d'Ivoire, East Timor, and Somalia and served as security guards with George W. Bush's "Coalition of the Willing" in Iraq.[4] They have conducted military training for armies in Somalia and Equatorial Guinea.[5] The Ugandan president has, furthermore, supported rebel groups in Kenya, Congo, Rwanda, and Burundi.[6] He has justified nearly all these activities through appeals to Pan-Africanism, a key principle of his National Resistance Movement (NRM) government and the Uganda People's Defence Force (UPDF).

At the same time, for the US Pentagon, Uganda has been a "frontline state," an "anchor" state, and a pivotal "security partner" in East Africa.[7] Hence, many observers suggest that Museveni is largely doing the regional bidding of his more powerful Western ally. Yet, this perspective overlooks, as one former US envoy to the Great Lakes observed, Museveni's "long history of acting against US interests."[8] Foregrounding Uganda's intervention in Somalia, this chapter traces Museveni's track record of compelling Washington to support his domestic and regional ambitions. It assesses the ebb and flow of Ugandan influence in its security relations with the United States and underscores the central role of Museveni's statist Pan-Africanism in this policy arena.

THE ORIGINS AND AIMS OF MUSEVENI'S PAN-AFRICANISM

Since the Reagan administration, US officials have looked to Museveni as a source of insights on crises and governance in East Africa, trusted his views on the motives and flaws of African leaders, and relied on him as a peace broker in regional conflicts. During the War on Terror, the Ugandan military's regional interventions and coalition operations with US forces afforded Museveni even greater clout in Washington. Indeed, before Ugandan forces ever stepped foot in Somalia, Museveni had begun to use the prospect of a UPDF deployment as a source of influence in his state's diplomatic relations with the United States.

As a result, the George W. Bush administration was more willing to back Museveni's bellicose approach to settling Uganda's conflict with the Lord's Resistance Army (LRA) as well as his drive to establish Uganda as a regional military power under the auspices of his unique Pan-African vision. During the Somalia intervention, the NRM government has consistently capitalized on US concerns about Somalia as a flashpoint for al-Shabaab, al-Qaeda, and ISIS. In exchange for the "stabilizing" presence of Ugandan troops in Somalia and their active collaborations with the United States in coalition operations, Uganda has received unprecedented increases in US security assistance.[9] This assistance, largely in the form of military training and equipment, has enhanced the capacity of the UPDF while helping to maintain the force as a pretorian guard, network of patronage, and mechanism of regional rent-seeking for the Museveni administration. Yet, Museveni's rewards have been both fiscal and political. The UPDF presence in Somalia has also softened US criticisms of the Ugandan president as his regime suppresses civil liberties, brutalizes and detains political opponents, and undermines judicial and parliamentary independence.[10]

My analysis foregrounds Uganda's bilateral relations with the United States. Still, it is worth noting that the Ugandan deployment to Somalia was supported by other East African states and legitimized by international organizations. A peacekeeping force for Somalia was initially proposed as early as 2005 by the Inter-Governmental Authority on Development. In the wake of this abortive effort, AMISOM was created by the African Union and authorized by the United Nations.[11] Additionally, under pressure from the United States, the European Union pledged $19 million to support the force, though it did not begin to disperse these funds until more than a year after Ugandan troops entered Somalia.[12] The Uganda deployment was also directly supported by

Burundi, which sent two hundred troops to join the Ugandan contingent of seventeen hundred soldiers at the end of 2007.[13] Just as critically, Ethiopian troops sporadically clashed with extremists in Somalia and intermittently offered protection to the Somali transitional government during the first two years of AMISOM.

Despite this ostensible outpouring of multilateralism, AMISOM served to rapidly consolidate the bilateral security partnership between Uganda and the United States. In addition to the Bush administration initially pledging $10 million to the force, the strategic planning and initial implementation of AMISOM were almost exclusively Ugandan and American efforts.[14] As Bush's former assistant secretary of state for African affairs put it, rather than following the "AU process," with AMISOM "we really took a big lead position."[15] Likewise, in the words of one Ugandan opposition parliamentarian, "Even before the AU and the UN had sanctioned the deployment, Uganda was already warming up."[16] This remains a point of contention among senior AU officials who complain that the multilateral institution often serves as a rubber stamp for the narrow, bilateral aims of African states and their Western allies.[17]

The Ugandan and American collaboration around AMISOM also reflects long-standing US attempts to tether Pan-Africanism in military affairs to Washington's security agenda. In the immediate wake of the Cold War, US security interests in Africa briefly declined, and a host of civil conflicts emerged. In this context, Washington placed greater emphasis on supporting African regional integration in security affairs, training African peacekeepers, and encouraging regional economic communities to adopt security protocols.[18] The aim, after US failures in Somalia and Rwanda, was to forestall humanitarian crisis in which the United States might become embroiled. In short, the goal was stability on the cheap with "African solutions for African problems."[19]

This impulse was apparent in the fraught roll-out of the African Crisis Response Initiative. The initiative, as noted, gave rise to widespread African concerns about US self-interest and short-sighted policy experimentation. Similar concerns have accompanied subsequent, more expansive peacekeeping training programs, such as Washington's

Global Peace Operations Initiative, which has offered training to tens of thousands of African soldiers.[20] Ugandan forces have put this training to use not only in regional peace operations but also to suppress domestic dissent and insurgencies. The training has also been vital for the Ugandans as they executed joint operations with US forces in Somalia.[21]

Early in the War on Terror, Bush officials searched for ways to solicit more active support from Africa's regional bodies for Washington's security agenda.[22] African multilateral institutions could grant legitimacy to US counterterrorism initiatives and put an "African face" on Western solutions to the continent's conflicts.[23] Pan-African security cooperation, in other words, held fresh promise for Washington's new campaign against terrorism. To help realize this promise and advance US strategic aims in Africa, few leaders were as important as Museveni, the most vocal proponent of Pan-Africanism among twenty-first-century African heads of state.

Pan-Africanism is a core principle of Museveni's National Resistance Movement Government, celebrated alongside patriotism, democracy, and socioeconomic transformation.[24] The substance of Museveni's Pan-African vision is nonetheless the subject of considerable debate. His rise to power is deeply intertwined with currents of Pan-African thought and practice that swept the continent in the second half of the twentieth century. While training as a political scientist at the University of Dar Es Salaam in the 1960s, Museveni led a Pan-African study group in which Walter Rodney was an influential lecturer and Stokely Carmichael a notable guest speaker.[25] At the time, under Julius Nyerere, Tanzania was the headquarters of the OAU's African Liberation Committee and an epicenter of support for independence movements throughout Southern Africa. It was in this staging ground for armed struggle, as an exile in Dar Es Salaam, that Museveni established the Front for National Salvation in 1971. His aim was to unseat Idi Amin, who had seized power in Uganda the same year.

Museveni embraced Nyerere's Pan-African platform and even led a delegation to meet with Samora Machel's Front for the Liberation of Mozambique as it fought to end Portuguese colonialism. Machel would later provide the Front for National Salvation financial support and military training as it struggled to overthrow Amin throughout the 1970s.[26] Museveni and Milton Obote's rebel forces would ultimately wrest power from Amin as a direct result of Tanzania's 1979 invasion of Uganda. Nyerere justified the invasion as both a strategic and Pan-African imperative due to Amin's despotism and brief occupation of Tanzania territory.[27] Museveni would then launch a rebellion against the Obote government, which came to power in Amin's wake, and in the process fight Nyerere's troops, who remained in Uganda to reinforce Obote's writ. Some five years after Museveni succeeded in taking power from Obote, Nyerere would write the introduction to the Ugandan president's book *What Is Africa's Problem*? Nyerere stopped far short of offering fulsome praise for Museveni's government, but he nevertheless identified the Ugandan president as a "committed pan-Africanist."[28]

Notably, one of Museveni's oldest ideological disagreements with Nyerere stemmed from his critiques of the Tanzanian president's program of Ujamaa African socialism. Museveni saw Ujamaa as an attempt to impose the idealized, communalistic values of Nyerere's small Zanaki ethnic group throughout Tanzania. It was thus, Museveni argued, a misguided, tribalistic project.[29] An espoused revulsion to tribalism and neocolonialism have long been central themes of Museveni's Pan-Africanism. In this regard, his rhetoric aligns closely with two of the ideology's most persistent, if pluralistically conceived, concerns: African unity and anti-imperialism.[30] However, Museveni's has taken a far more fluid and tactical approach to Pan-Africanism as a vehicle for opposing anti-Black racism and stoking global solidarity among people of African descent.[31]

In 1994, for example, he hosted the 7th Pan-African Congress in Kampala, an event attended by an array of African leaders and African American foreign policy elites. During the affair he was lauded by many of these elites but downplayed discussions of racial solidarity, opting instead to emphasize themes of African self-reliance.[32] His rhetoric of self-reliance quickly earned Museveni a reputation in the West as a teller of hard truths to recalcitrant African leaders. During his early years in power, he rarely let his fellow African leaders forget that most of them had stood silent while Idi Amin ravaged Uganda. In doing so, according to Museveni, they had countenanced Black despotism while at the same time condemning white minority rule.[33] When Museveni has prioritized expressions of racial solidarity, it has typically been in the interest of consolidating his power, amid periods of tension with his Western allies, or as a means of advancing his unswerving campaign against a perceived "Arab chauvinism." Not long after South Sudanese independence, Museveni proclaimed, "The word Sudan means 'land of black people.' . . . Sudan is an Afro-Arab country," he continued, "the mistake of the Khartoum government was to manage it as an Arab country."[34]

For Museveni's critics, his Pan-Africanism is little more than hollow sloganeering. Under his leadership, in their view, Uganda's foreign policy has been one of "military adventurism and grand dreams of empire couched in the bark cloth of Pan-Africanism."[35] His numerous military interventions belie the ideology's ideals and obscure self-interested calculations to reshape the region in accordance with his government's security goals and economic interests. These interventions either serve or coincide with American and European aims in Africa and have thus driven "Western powers into a conspiracy of silence about his tyrannical record."[36] For these critics, even Museveni's numerous efforts as a peace broker from Burundi to Congo to South Sudan are tarnished by his government's role in stoking or exacerbating regional conflicts in the first place.

An alternative position can be found among some of Uganda's longstanding domestic opposition leaders. This view often approaches Museveni's numerous military interventions with ambivalence but does not casually dismiss the ideological moorings of his Pan-Africanism. There remains a deep admiration for the NRM government's investment in regional affairs and its efforts to use Pan-African initiatives to "stand up" to the West.[37] Indeed, despite Museveni's track record of "state terrorism" some opposition figures fear that a new Ugandan administration, coming to power amid Western pressure for a democratic transition, would be more subservient to American and European aims.[38]

This perspective holds that despite its contradictions Museveni's Pan-Africanism falls well within the ideology's traditions and remains a meaningful rampart against Western hegemony in Africa.

In few areas of Ugandan foreign policy do competing views of Museveni's Pan-Africanism collide as fiercely as on the question of the UPDF mission in Somalia. The operation is not a brazen attempt to expand Uganda's access to regional markets, a motive often cited for Museveni's occupation and meddling in South Sudan.[39] Nor does Somalia offer the UPDF's patronage network a ready supply of natural resources for plunder, as was the case in the DRC.[40] Somalia's Islamist militants are broadly reviled among Ugandans, and there is no shortage of pride in the sacrifices the UPDF has made to confront them. But views of Museveni's motives for the Somalia mission stretch across a vast continuum, casting the Ugandan president as everything from a foe of neocolonialism and a Pan-African champion of regional interests to an "African imperialist" and a mercenary for the West.[41]

This chapter does not frame Museveni as an imperialist or anti-imperialist, nor does it cast him as a pliant handmaiden for Western interests. It suggests that his Pan-African project is Africa's most powerful contemporary manifestation of statist Pan-Africanism.[42] Rather than seeking broad popular participation, this Pan-Africanism prioritizes the role of government in shaping the transnational commitments and allegiances of the Ugandan people. Its rituals and rhetoric blur the boundaries between an elitist Pan-Africanism intertwined with the strategic imperatives of the state and a mass Pan-Africanism grounded in humanist ideals. Much like historical variants of statist Pan-Africanism, its approach to antiracism and Black racial solidarity is largely pragmatic.

What most distinguishes Museveni's Pan-Africanism is its militarism, which outstrips even that of earlier US security allies such as Ethiopia, Liberia, and Zaire. Moreover, since early in the War on Terror, Museveni's Pan-African project has displayed an almost complete disregard for the African American foreign policy elite as an influential force in US foreign policymaking. This approach not only reflected Museveni's ties with the American right. It was also a response to the apathy around US security policies in Africa that has taken hold among the African American foreign policy elite throughout the twenty-first century. Museveni's statist Pan-Africanism has helped both to advance US strategic aims in East Africa and to undermine US power in its relations with his government. This dynamic offers Kampala and Washington tremendous benefits—some mutual, others zero-sum. The costs of this bargain have been borne most heavily by Ugandan proponents of democracy as well as Somali civilians caught in the web of Islamist militancy and the US–Uganda counterterror agenda.

PEACE TALKS AND INTERVENTION PLANS

By the fall of 2006, when US and Ugandan officials began planning the UPDF deployment to Somalia, Ugandan incursions into the DRC and Sudan had become a prominent source of regional tension. In 2005 the International Court of Justice ruled that Uganda owed the DRC reparations for human rights violations committed by Ugandan troops during their occupation of northeastern Congo from 1998 to 2003.[43] Despite the ruling, in early 2006 Museveni made clear that he intended to send Ugandan troops back into the Congo "with or without approval" in pursuit of the Lord's Resistance Army (LRA).[44]

The LRA, a militia spawned in Northern Uganda by a synergy of fundamentalist Christianity and ethnic Acholi nationalism—notorious for massacring, mutilating, and abducting civilians—had largely retreated to the DRC in late 2005. Museveni's government had been fighting the LRA since the group's founding in 1987. The Ugandan president had long viewed the force and its leader, Joseph Kony, as pawns of their primary backer, the Sudanese government. Museveni would later say, "I hear people talking about 20 years of conflict with Kony. I don't want a narrow understanding of this affair. Our fight was not with Kony but with the Arabs of Khartoum. . . . This was an invitation to stand by the black people in Sudan."[45] In keeping with his view of the LRA as Sudanese lackeys, before Washington's War on Terror, Museveni largely referred to the group as criminals, looters, and bandits. After the conflict began, his choice moniker became "terrorists."[46]

In April 2006 US military officials met with Museveni to the lay the groundwork for a new spate of training programs aimed at improving the UPDF's capacity to combat terrorism and engage the LRA.[47] At this point, while Museveni strongly favored a military approach to ending the conflict with the LRA, the US State Department largely advocated a negotiated, political settlement. US preferences aside, by the end of that month, UPDF troops entered eastern DRC, without Kinshasa's authorization, ostensibly in pursuit of the LRA. Instead, Ugandan forces encountered and briefly clashed with the Congolese Army.[48]

Museveni's willingness to violate the DRC's sovereignty and inflame regional tensions was clear.[49] Pentagon officials, nonetheless, continued to prepare major increases in security assistance to the UPDF throughout 2006, as Ugandan diplomats reiterated a commitment to sending troops to Somalia. In fact, that summer the United States held a major multilateral military training exercise in Uganda.[50] Meanwhile, both Sudanese and Southern Sudanese officials began to express mounting opposition to the presence of Ugandan troops fighting LRA forces in Southern Sudan. Despite providing support to the LRA for more than a decade, in 2002 the Sudanese government publicly changed course and established a protocol with the Ugandan government that allowed UPDF troops to engage the LRA in Southern Sudan.[51] Even after this protocol expired in early 2006, Ugandan troops maintained a presence in Sudan with the informal approval of the recently autonomous government of Southern Sudan and its Sudanese People's Liberation Army (SPLA).[52]

The SPLA had been fighting the LRA with Ugandan guidance and assistance since 1991. But in 2006, following a comprehensive peace agreement with Khartoum, Southern Sudanese officials sought a diplomatic solution to the instability wrought by the LRA and proposed to mediate negotiations between LRA leaders and the Ugandan government. The US State Department publicly urged Uganda to participate in the peace talks, but senior NRM ministers disparaged the talks as a ploy on the part of the LRA and its supporters in the Southern

Sudanese government. Despite State Department pressure, Ugandan ministers were adamant that they "were not going to accept dictates from outside on what we are going to do about this, because we mean business."[53]

While the Ugandan government ultimately agreed to peace talks, Museveni was skeptical from the very outset and pressured the Southern Sudanese and DRC governments to collaborate with Uganda in a military initiative to dismantle the LRA. A UPDF spokesman would later assert that Uganda only agreed to the talks because it "lacked regional allies" that were competent and determined to apprehend the LRA's commanders.[54] When describing his motives for serving as the chief mediator for the peace talks, Vice-President Riek Machar of Southern Sudan remarked that he was uncomfortable being "under the foreign invasion" of UPDF troops.[55] In short, Machar wanted the Ugandans out of Southern Sudan. Museveni held deep antipathy toward Machar, whom he considered an LRA sympathizer with dangerously close ties to Khartoum.[56]

As peace talks began in the Southern Sudanese capital of Juba in 2006, the Bush administration expressed its full support for this attempt to rein in the LRA.[57] Museveni remained pessimistic about the fate of the negotiations and inconsistent about the terms of the ceasefire and amnesty he proposed to the LRA. Uganda's negotiating team evinced clear divisions between the Ugandan minister of internal affairs, who was interested in pursuing a comprehensive political solution, and the UPDF's representative, who was determined to secure the LRA's military "surrender."[58] Some observers suggest that the Ugandan president primarily agreed to the peace talks to lure LRA forces into Southern Sudan, where he intended to dismantle the militia through a military campaign.[59] There was also little commitment to peace on the part of the LRA, which continued to resupply its forces and commit attacks while negotiations were ongoing.

Museveni, nonetheless, created a major roadblock to the success of the Juba talks by sending more UPDF troops to Southern Sudan. This deployment violated a cessation of hostilities agreement between Uganda and the LRA. Once negotiations were underway, these troops effectively surrounded designated LRA assembly points, stoking anxiety among the already distrustful LRA leadership. Recognizing this stumbling block as the peace talks floundered, the Sudanese National Assembly called for an end to the 2002 protocol that allowed Ugandan troops to maintain a presence in Southern Sudan.[60] Machar also became increasingly convinced that Uganda was committed to resuming hostilities with the LRA and asked the US envoy to Sudan to "convince Museveni that there is no military solution."[61]

Instead of counseling restraint, State Department officials became more supportive of the bellicose impulses of the Museveni administration as the US desire to get Ugandan troops into Somalia grew in urgency. In October 2006 Museveni met with LRA negotiators in South Sudan for the first time. Though his visit was meant to showcase a commitment to the peace process, it reportedly resulted in a "bitter, five-minute exchange."[62] International relief organizations accused the United States of maintaining a "position of total silence" as the Juba talks continued to deteriorate in late 2006.[63]

Even as reports of the UPDF's abuses against Southern Sudanese civilians began to emerge, US officials offered little criticism of the force and prepared to expanded military aid to Uganda. During a fall 2006 meeting, Jendayi Frazer, the US assistant secretary of state for Africa, "welcomed" Museveni's "long-standing offer" to send troops to Somalia. She also garnered the Ugandan leader's appreciation by informing him that the Bush administration was raising Kony's status on the US specially designated terrorist list.[64] This heightened designation, during a delicate moment in the Juba negotiations when LRA activities had subsided, only served to buttress Museveni's underlying inclination toward military action against the militia.

Moreover, after this meeting, in keeping with Museveni's suggestion, US officials began to more forcefully advance the position that the Juba talks should be time-bound. If the LRA did not accede to the Uganda government's timeline for negotiations, State Department officials claimed, it should be prepared to face military consequences.[65] Bush's assistant secretary of state for African affairs, in fact, made this point at a press conference in Kampala during which she emphasized that the international community owed "a great deal of gratitude to Uganda" for its contribution to AMISOM.[66]

Despite the lull in LRA activities in the fall of 2006, the militia did engage in attacks against civilians. It also routinely threatened to abandon the Juba talks, stalled the negotiations with inconsistent demands, and reneged on agreements to assemble in designated camps.[67] Moreover, Kony himself refused to appear in person to sign the final Juba peace accord, despite repeated promises from his negotiating team that he would do so. This has largely been attributed to fears that he would be transported to The Hague to face trial under an ICC indictment. But Kony also had reason to be distrustful of NRM government assurances that it would call for the indictment's suspension and offer him an impartial trial on Ugandan soil. As one Ugandan official later admitted, "we were pretending. We knew [Kony] would never sign any peace document."[68]

By early 2008 the Juba talks had collapsed, and the Kabila administration in the Congo agreed to allow Ugandan troops to enter its territory to execute joint operations with the Congolese Army aimed at dismantling the LRA. This was clearly Museveni's preferred course of action, especially because the fighting would take place beyond Uganda's borders. Religious leaders and parliamentarians from Gulu, the Northern Uganda district that had been a key site of the LRA's atrocities, protested the Ugandan government's preparations for renewed military action. They decried the "warmongering" of "trigger-happy elements in the Ugandan government."[69] They warned that in response to Ugandan attacks, the LRA would likely increase its strikes against civilians, citing massacres that took place in the wake of Operation Iron Fist, the UPDF's failed 2002 military offensive against Kony's forces. Likewise, US congressional officials pressed the Bush administration to take substantive measures to help restart the peace process. Senator Russ Feingold, one of the body's experts on African affairs, lamented that "rather than intensify efforts to engage and pressure Kony to accept the agreement, the United States and others have downscaled our efforts."[70]

These appeals went unheeded by the Bush administration. By the end of 2008 it fully supported Uganda's plan to collaborate with DRC and Southern Sudan in a joint military operation against the LRA.[71] This offensive, codenamed Operation Lightening Thunder, was launched in December 2008. At the time, LRA attacks and abductions in the region triggered broad support for Operation Lightening Thunder among human rights groups, the UN, and the Bush administration. While it was billed as a joint operation, Ugandan forces led most of the initial fighting while troops from the DRC and Southern Sudan played marginal roles.[72] Uganda's closest collaborator in launching Operation Lightening Thunder was the United States. The Pentagon sent a military planning team to Uganda to review and strengthen the UPDF's plans for the operation. Moreover, the United States provided the Ugandans intelligence support and covered the cost of fuel for the mission.[73]

Operation Lightening Thunder began with Ugandan airstrikes on LRA camps in Congo's Garamba National Park followed by a ground assault by roughly 2,000 UPDF troops. However, the LRA camps had been evacuated by Kony at least a day before the operation started. Over the course of the four months that it lasted, Operation Lightening Thunder did not achieve its stated goals of crippling the LRA and capturing Kony and his top commanders. According to Ugandan government estimates, it did produce roughly 150 LRA casualties and lead to the rescue of some 300 abductees.[74] Yet, throughout the operation the UPDF established few provisions for civilian protection. Much as the peace proponents in Northern Uganda predicted, Operation Lightening Thunder gave rise to a spate of reprisal attacks by the LRA against civilians in the DRC and Southern Sudan, leading to at least 1,000 deaths and displacing roughly 200,000 people.[75] In short, it was a humanitarian disaster abetted by the Bush administration at Museveni's behest.

The Bush administration would have maintained a commitment to a negotiated settlement with the LRA for longer and been more willing to criticize Museveni's interventions in Congo and Sudan had it not been for Uganda's decision to deploy troops to Somalia. While US and Ugandan officials were mapping out the Somalia intervention, Museveni made it clear that he fully expected US support in a military campaign to crush the LRA.[76] The Bush administration proved increasingly willing to meet these expectations and to allow the Juba talks to collapse in exchange for Uganda's allegiance to the aims of the War on Terror in Somalia.

State Department officials saw Museveni's commitment to a military solution to the challenges posed by both the LRA and Islamic extremists in Somalia as closely related. This penchant for bellicosity, according to US policymakers, reflected Museveni's strong belief in "Clausewitz's conviction that war is the extension of diplomacy by other means."[77] As a result, US support for these Ugandan military campaigns took on a synergistic quality, and Uganda's willingness to face "mind-blowing" sacrifices in Somalia helped to fuel US support for Museveni's military efforts against the LRA.[78]

UNDERWRITING AN INTERVENTION

On the eve of the UPDF's 2007 deployment to Somalia, Museveni told US officials that because Uganda was a "pan-African" state, it would serve as an ideal "bridge" between the "Niger-Congo" polities of West and Central Africa and the feuding "Nilo-Saharan" factions in the Horn of Africa. According to Museveni, his government was guided by an inclusive vision of African ethnic groups and only drew distinctions between "Africans and non-Africans."[79] Museveni's depiction of the ethnic composition of Africa's regions is a brazen oversimplification. Further, Ugandan opposition leaders certainly take issue with his disavowal of the salience of ethnicity in NRM government politics.[80] But even many of these leaders would come to embrace the UPDF mission in Somalia as a Pan-African project. One of Museveni's political opponents observed: "I was so proud that of all the African states that talked about going to Somalia, Uganda was the only one to act on its Pan-Africanism."[81]

From a practical standpoint, Museveni's remarks were meant to underscore to US officials his commitment to the impending peace operation in Somalia. The idea that Uganda is engaged in a "Pan-African venture" in Somalia has been one of the Ugandan president's favorite themes over the course of the UPDF's eighteen-year operation in the country.[82] This Pan-African venture has been remarkably profitable for the Museveni administration, primarily due to the unprecedented increases in US military aid to Uganda it has yielded. At every stage of the intervention, Ugandan officials have called on the United States to fortify and upgrade Ugandan military capacity. Their demands have been met routinely. Uganda has been the largest recipient of US security assistance for AMISOM, which totals more than $2 billion.[83] On top of this, since 2007 Uganda has received more than $470 million in assistance from the Pentagon alone.[84]

This aid has helped to shore up the Museveni administration at home and abroad. Prior to the Somalia intervention, Museveni was under increasing international and domestic pressure to reduce Ugandan defense spending and to rein in corruption that had long plagued the UPDF.[85] The military itself was overstretched and undersupplied and dedicated marginal expenditures to training.[86] Given these deficiencies, Museveni had been lobbying for increases in US security assistance to Uganda since the earliest days of the Bush administration. From 1998 to early 2003, US military aid to Uganda was suspended due to UPDF participation in the second multistate conflict that engulfed the Democratic Republic of Congo after the collapse of the Mobutu regime. During their occupation of provinces in northeastern Congo, Ugandan troops engaged in illegal logging and mining as well as human rights abuses against Congolese civilians.

Once the UPDF withdrew from Congo, the Bush administration began to reinvigorate the US security partnership with Uganda, in large measure due to Museveni's vocal support for the US invasion of Iraq and the War on Terror. The initial US security aid program was relatively modest in scale, providing UPDF troops roughly $2 million worth of training and logistics support to confront the LRA.[87] The limited scale of the assistance was a reflection of lingering reservations among US officials regarding the human rights record of the UPDF as well as Museveni's penchant for regional adventurism.

In 2004 the security partnership slowly grew as Uganda became the site of a US cooperative security location at Entebbe and received roughly $5 million in military aid from Washington.[88] The United States continued this pattern of assistance in 2005 primarily by donating trucks and communications equipment to the UPDF as it attempted to push the LRA out of Northern Uganda. In the fall of 2006, however, Ugandan officials recognized a prime opportunity to dramatically reorient the scale and scope of US assistance to the UPDF.

As the Islamic Courts Union threatened to overthrow the newly established Somali transitional government, the United States perceived a small window of opportunity to constrain the militia. Both the US secretary of state and the president reportedly called Museveni to encourage him to deploy UPDF troops to shore up the Somali government.[89] The Museveni administration was explicit that increases in US security assistance to Uganda would have to underwrite the UPDF deployment. As the Ugandan president told the press on the eve of the intervention, "We have the courage but not the money. So the American government put forward the money through the African Union."[90]

Just days before the UPDF was scheduled to enter Somalia in March 2007, Ugandan defense officials thanked their US counterparts for the Pentagon's "logistics support."[91] They also requested that the United States coordinate its naval patrols of Somalia's coast with the Ugandan deployment in order to interdict terrorists who might enter Mogadishu by sea. Even more important, the Ugandan officials wanted a clear timeline for when the "funds for sustaining the contingent would be available" and when US training for the next UPDF battalion slated for deployment would begin.[92] The United States responded with a funding package of $2 million to transport the UPDF to Somalia and $8 million to equip the force, in one stroke effectively doubling US military aid to Uganda.[93]

Within months, US programs to train and equip Ugandan troops surged. Between 2007 and 2010 Washington contributed more than $341 million to the support of AMISOM, much of it directly to the Ugandan government through "equipment, logistics support, advice and training."[94] The United States funded large part of this training through the African Contingency Operations Training and Assistance program. This program provided "more muscular" training than its predecessor, ACRI, "in the skills needed for African troops to perform peacekeeping in hostile environments, including force protection, light infantry operations and small unit tactics."[95] Ugandan soldiers routinely top the list of US training recipients in Africa. Between 2020 and 2021, for example, the United States provided military training to more than five thousand Ugandan troops, more than twice as many as any other African state.[96]

In 2008 the European Union would begin paying salaries for the AMISOM troops. EU donations to the African Union funded salaries of $500 per month for each AMISOM soldier deployed to Somalia. Each Ugandan troop that participated in the mission received $400 dollars of this allotment, while the Museveni administration collected the remaining $100.[97] These salaries would grow to $1,028 per month by 2009, of which the Ugandan government would take 20 percent.[98] These wages were more than double the average monthly salary of UPDF personnel and offered a strong incentive for Ugandan troops to participate in the mission to Somalia, despite the barrage of attacks they faced from the day they entered Mogadishu.[99] In fact, in 2014 more than a dozen Ugandan officers were suspended for selling slots in AMISOM to UPDF troops enticed by the higher pay.[100]

While these salaries decreased short-term pressures on the Museveni administration's military budget, the implications of US training and equipment programs have been more far-reaching. In the run-up to the UPDF's intervention in Somalia, Ugandan defense officials openly expressed concerns regarding insufficiencies in the training of most Ugandan troops. As the Chief of Defense Forces Aronda Nyakairima put it, "Because of the continuous insurgency arising from rebel activity in the northern and western parts of the country, our military budget has always been channeled to combat, leaving little for training."[101] Also hindering the ability of the UPDF to train its troops was a general malaise of corruption in Ugandan defense spending. The most notable manifestations of this graft were salaries paid to thousands of nonexistent "ghost soldiers" and pocketed by the UPDF brass.[102]

From 2005 to 2007 the Museveni administration pressured the United States to expand its support for the UPDF not only in diplomatic exchanges, but also by hiring a Washington lobbying firm, Scribe

Strategies and Advisors.[103] The UPDF intervention in Somalia provided unprecedented leverage for these efforts. As a result of the surge in US training programs for the UPDF that accompanied the intervention, since 2007 more than 65,000 Ugandan military personnel have received US military training.[104] This extensive training for deployments to Mogadishu enhanced the UPDF's capacity for urban warfare and crowd and riot control.[105] These capabilities have been applied to suppressing demonstrations in Kampala. Soldiers of the Ugandan Special Forces Command, which oversees the elite Presidential Brigade, have received the most extensive US training and the most sophisticated military hardware, including small surveillance drones. In 2007 President Museveni's own son, Muhoozi Kainerugaba, completed a training program at the US Army Command and General Staff College at Fort Leavenworth Kansas. He was appointed commander of Uganda's Special Forces in 2012 and commander of UPDF Land Forces in 2021.[106]

Once the UPDF intervened in Somalia, State Department officials soft-pedaled their public attempts to pressure the Museveni administration to exhibit greater transparency in its defense spending. In 2004, when the Bush administration was providing Uganda limited military aid to target the LRA, the US ambassador to Uganda, Jimmy Kolker, openly expressed concerns that donors "need to know where the money is going." Kolker complained to the Ugandan press that the "defense budget is not presented in a way which allows us to judge whether expenditures are for the war in the north or something else."[107]

Increasingly larger portions of the Ugandan military budget became classified as the UPDF's intervention in Somalia and, later, South Sudan expanded, a move that privately evoked fears among US officials concerned about corruption and illegal arms trading.[108] In 2012 roughly 20 percent of the Ugandan military budget was classified—in 2019 it was over 50 percent.[109] Meanwhile, by 2014 roughly 17 percent of Uganda's entire defense budget was derived from donations to AMISOM.[110] State Department officials have, however, largely avoided criticisms of Uganda's defense spending. For their part, Ugandan officials have used the UPDF's role in peace operations to justify increases in the military budget. According to the Ugandan Ministry of Defense these increases are a clear indication of the Museveni government keeping faith with its Pan-African principles.[111]

In 2009 the NRM government would further cultivate US dependence on the UPDF in Somalia and receive even greater rewards in US military aid. In the summer of that year, under a US initiative to support the Somali transitional government, Ugandan troops provided 40 tons of arms and ammunition to Somali soldiers. Uganda was, in turn, resupplied by the United States in order to replace the matériel it provided the Somali forces. On the heels of this exchange, Uganda received another infusion of US funding by agreeing to begin military training programs for Somali soldiers.[112] Lucrative logistics and supply contracts in support of these training programs were consistently awarded to members of Museveni's inner circle, including his half-brother, General Salim Saleh.[113]

In the fall of 2009, Museveni emphasized to US officials that he thought AMISOM should begin to take more aggressive measures to force extremists out of Somalia's major towns. He suggested that the alternatives for AMISOM were to "either move forward or get out."[114] Uganda would supply more troops, but in order for the mission to truly make progress, Museveni made clear that the United States should increase the funding and equipment it was donating to AMISOM. The United States once again acceded to Museveni's request by further expanding its training and equipment assistance to the UPDF the following year.

Throughout AMISOM's tenure, the lion's share of US aid for the mission has gone to Uganda. Ugandan officials have not been passive actors in this process. They have instead actively negotiated the terms, timing, and amount of aid Uganda has received from the United States. All the while, the Ugandans have emphasized their government's commitment to deploying and maintaining troops in Somalia in support of the War on Terror. The US security assistance that has resulted from this bilateral bargaining has indeed been abundant. It can be argued, however, that US political concessions regarding the increasingly authoritarian nature of the Museveni regime have been even more consequential for the Ugandan people.

HOPE, CHANGE, AND CONTINUITY

On March 1, 2007, the same day the first UPDF troops entered Somalia, a heavily armed unit of Ugandan police and military operatives stormed the High Court in Kampala.[115] The unit, known as the Ugandan Joint Terrorism Taskforce, sealed off the high court's premises, then beat and rearrested five men who had been granted bail after fifteen months of detention. These men, including leading opposition figure Dr. Kizza Besigye, had been charged with treason due to their alleged links to the People's Redemption Army (PRA), a force many observers contend was concocted by the Museveni administration in a ruse to discredit the opposition.[116] Ugandan courts had ordered the release of the PRA suspects on three prior occasions since they had first been arrested in the run-up to Uganda's presidential election in 2006. Yet each time Ugandan security forces, under the direction of the Museveni administration, undermined the will of the judiciary and returned these suspects to detention. A similar raid on the High Court had been used to achieve this purpose just one year earlier.

Opposition MPs had been absent from Parliament, staging a walkout to protest the detention of the PRA suspects, when the body unanimously approved the UPDF deployment to Somalia in February 2007. The following month, on the heels of the High Court siege, the Ugandan judiciary initiated a strike that shut down the country's court system for more than a week.[117] While the strike was happening, the US Embassy in Kampala played host to a delegation of US National Security Council and State Department officials. In fact, US diplomats lauded the "wonderful" partnership between the United States and Uganda during a breakfast at the US ambassador's residence—even as several members of the striking Ugandan judiciary sat in the audience.[118] Despite their presence, US officials refused to issue a public statement regarding the judicial strike or the High Court siege.

Independent outlets in the Ugandan press immediately linked the lack of US criticism for Museveni to the UPDF's recent deployment to Somalia. The US silence was even more striking because only months earlier, the US ambassador to Uganda, Steven Browning, had ardently emphasized the importance of judicial independence in the East African state. At a two-day seminar organized by a local human rights organization for Ugandan judges, Ambassador Browning had delivered the keynote address. After condemning widespread corruption in government healthcare and defense spending, he emphasized the need for a courageous and independent judiciary, declaring, "It does not serve the judiciary or the public interest when courts are on the receiving ends of political threats."[119]

By March 2007, however, Browning had abandoned such pronouncements. As he suggested in a cable to the State Department that month, the embassy in Kampala maintained an interest in democratic governance in Uganda, but more recently the "UPDF deployment to Somalia has become the focus of our attention."[120] The UPDF's intervention in Somalia would continue to dominate US attention during the remaining years of Browning's tenure. Accordingly, US efforts to publicly criticize the Ugandan government would reach a virtual standstill, even as the Museveni administration ramped up detentions of politicians and journalists, shuttered TV and radio stations, and violently cracked down on public demonstrations.[121] In fact, as the United States expanded its security partnership with Uganda, US Embassy officials in Kampala fully expected the Museveni administration to grow increasingly repressive during the waning years of the Bush administration.[122] When Browning was asked by the Ugandan press about the muted US response to this trend in Museveni's policies, the US ambassador replied, "Do not confuse lack of open criticism for lack of it. I am not going to stand at some corner like these street evangelists and start pointing fingers."[123] Internal State Department correspondence suggests, however, that there was very little US effort—either publicly or behind closed doors—to challenge the Museveni administration's campaign against civil liberties and democratic participation.

At the start of the Obama administration's first term, Museveni deployed two new battalions to Somalia, bringing the total number of Ugandan troops in AMISOM to 2,750 and further solidifying the UPDF's role as the backbone of the mission.[124] Despite the presence of two Burundian battalions, composed of roughly 1,600 soldiers, Ugandan officers retained firm command of AMISOM. Attacks on the peacekeepers and the feeble Somali transitional government surged in late 2009 and early 2010, rousing US fears that the successor to the Islamic Courts Union, al-Shabaab, was closely coordinating with al-Qaeda.

It appeared, nevertheless, that the US posture toward the Ugandan government was poised for meaningful change. In a February 2010 roundtable with Ugandan journalists, the new US ambassador to Uganda, Jerry Lanier, applauded President Museveni's achievements but also suggested that the Obama administration had some concerns about the health of Uganda's democracy. "Twenty-four years is a long time," Lanier remarked, referencing the length of Museveni's tenure.[125] Lanier's statements drew a swift rebuke from the Museveni administration, whose spokesman demanded that the US diplomat "leave the internal management of Uganda to Ugandans."[126]

The Museveni administration was facing pressure on other fronts as well. Uganda had come under intense scrutiny from US and European donors due to a bill that was being debated in Parliament that proposed to make homosexuality a capital offense. President Obama called the piece of legislation "odious," and international protests led to widespread condemnation of what came to be known as the "Kill the Gays Bill."[127] During this international outcry, Museveni met with Assistant Secretary of State for Africa Johnnie Carson and reassured him that no Ugandans would be killed because they were gay. Museveni was adamant, however, that homosexuality was a "deformity" that was contrary to African family values and issued Carson a curt warning: "Don't push it . . . I'll handle it."[128] The Ugandan president also reminded the US diplomat of AMISOM's successful efforts to impede al-Shabaab's operations, in an effort to allay Carson's concerns that Somalia remained a regional epicenter of Islamist extremism.

By April 2010, Museveni had advised Uganda's ruling party legislators to stall the antigay bill in Parliament, momentarily averting further international condemnation. The following month, in response to a US congressional directive to closely monitor Uganda's electoral process, Secretary of State Hillary Clinton issued the first in a series of reports criticizing the Museveni administration.[129] In the run-up to the country's 2011 presidential poll, US diplomats encouraged Museveni to reform Uganda's electoral commission and to allow opposition candidates to campaign without threat of violence or detention.[130] Museveni was resistant to these entreaties from the start and refused to change the composition of the electoral commission, despite the fact that its leading members were the same ruling-party acolytes who many claim delivered him the election in 2006. Moreover, in a none too subtle reminder of the UPDF's pivotal role in AMISOM, Museveni privately told US diplomats that just like "the terrorists in Somalia," the Ugandan opposition had no agenda worthy of popular support.[131]

In the face of Museveni's intransigence, US officials conveyed mixed messages, primarily emphasizing the Obama administration's appreciation for Uganda's regional leadership in Somalia. On occasion, State Department officials suggested that if Uganda did not hold free and fair elections, it might become more difficult to maintain a strong security partnership. More frequently, however, Pentagon officials emphasized that the United States stood "shoulder to shoulder" with the UPDF in Somalia and was committed to finding ways to expand assistance to AMISOM.[132]

The emphasis on US support for AMISOM rose sharply following al-Shabaab's July 2010 attack on Kampala, during which twin bombings killed seventy-four people gathered to watch telecasts of the World Cup Final. Despite some calls from the Ugandan opposition to pull out of Somalia in the wake of the bombings, President Museveni vowed to take more aggressive military action against al-Shabaab.[133] In September 2010 Secretary of State Clinton would issue another report criticizing the Ugandan electoral commission and the limited space for political organizing that the Ugandan government allowed the opposition.[134] But behind closed doors, US criticism of Uganda's electoral preparations ebbed toward the end of 2010. Diplomats from both states were working together to find ways to expand the fight against extremism in Somalia, while the FBI was collaborating with Ugandan authorities to investigate the Kampala bombing.[135]

It was in this context that President Museveni won a fourth term in office. International electoral observers regarded the Ugandan elections of February 2011 as largely peaceful and credible, despite evidence of voter intimidation and ballot stuffing. While noting "some structural issues" in the Ugandan electoral process that were a source of concern, the Obama administration congratulated Museveni on his reelection.[136] Uganda's domestic opposition parties believed that the election had been rigged and rejected the results before initiating a series of protests. The Museveni administration responded with a brutal crackdown, during which security forces killed at least ten Ugandans and imprisoned hundreds more, including Uganda's leading opposition figures.[137]

As the Museveni administration's crackdown continued throughout the summer of 2011, the Obama administration issued a handful of statements regarding the deteriorating human rights situation in Uganda. At no point, however, was there any indication that Washington was considering cutting back its security assistance to Uganda. In fact, in response to fears that the al-Qaeda presence in Somalia was growing, the Obama administration called for a $45 million increase in aid to AMSIOM and an extra $4 million donation of equipment to the UPDF.[138]

RISING TENSIONS IN THE US-UGANDA PARTNERSHIP

In October 2011 Kenya invaded the Somali state of Jubaland in response to a series of cross-border attacks by al-Shabaab. The following month, Ethiopian troops surged into Somalia in support of the Kenyans, opening a front against the Islamist militia in the country's central region.[139] In December Djibouti became the third African state to make good on its troop pledge to AMISOM, deploying 960 soldiers to Somalia. By early 2012, the 4,700 Kenyan troops in Somalia had been rehatted as AMISOM peacekeepers.[140] In coordination with the UN, AMISOM developed a new concept of operations that divided the country into four geographical sectors, each patrolled by a different national contingent. More than 7,000 Ugandan troops were responsible for peace enforcement in Mogadishu and the Lower Shabelle region and still represented the largest contingent of AMISOM's 17,000-man force.[141] A Ugandan general also remained atop AMISOM's command structure, but the operation was now more decentralized. While the UPDF comprised the mission's most numerous and seasoned fighters, US officials had to consider and balance the interests of more African states in order to influence AMISOM's direction.

Western officials expressed gratitude for the pressure that the Kenyan invasion momentarily put on al-Shabaab. In February 2012, days after al-Shabaab and al-Qaeda announced a merger, the United States began to provide Kenya military aid in direct support of its mission in Somalia.[142] Still, the UPDF remained vital to AMISOM's progress. The Kenyan military had little combat experience beyond its borders. Moreover, its impartiality as a peacekeeping force in Somalia was compromised by decades of conflict between the two states. Evidence quickly emerged of the Kenyans taking sides in Somali clan disputes, rejecting dialogue with the Somali Transitional Government, and facilitating al-Shabaab's illicit charcoal trade.[143] The wave of new participants in AMISOM also gave rise to coordination challenges among its various military contingents that would perennially dog the force.

Despite its challenges, with contributions from Burundi, Kenya, Djibouti, Ethiopia, and later Sierra Leone, AMISOM's success no longer hinged entirely on Museveni's cooperation. The tenor of relations between the United States and Uganda began to change. From the earliest days of his appointment in late 2012, the new US ambassador to Uganda, Scott DeLisi, was outspoken in his opposition to the Ugandan government's suppression of dissent. For example, in early 2013, when Uganda's military brass warned that if the opposition continued to foment protests the army would be forced to intervene, DeLisi publicly insisted that militaries should, instead, support democratic institutions.[144] Later in the year, the ambassador again reproached the Museveni administration when it temporarily shuttered the Ugandan newspaper, *The Daily Monitor*, and proposed a Public Order and Management Bill that allowed for the indefinite detention of protesters.[145]

Over the course of the next two years, DeLisi would be more forthright in his criticisms of Museveni's authoritarianism than any of his predecessors since the launch of AMISOM. While US aid to Uganda in support of the peace mission remained consistent, bilateral military aid declined from nearly $70 million in 2012 to an average of $30 million over the course of the next three years.[146] These declines and DeLisi's vocal critiques of Uganda's domestic affairs underscored the mounting acrimony in US–Uganda relations.

In early 2014 the Obama administration offered its most vocal criticisms of Museveni's ongoing quest to distinguish Uganda as a regional military power. The US administration publicly questioned the Ugandan president's decision to deploy UPDF troops to the South Sudanese capital of Juba.[147] In December 2013, when clashes between rival factions of the South Sudanese government pushed the new state to the precipice of war, Uganda intervened in support of forces that remained loyal to the South Sudanese president, Salva Kiir. Throughout December and early January, the UPDF helped to repel a series of attacks on Juba launched by ethnic Nuer rebels under the leadership of South Sudan's former vice president, Riek Machar.

After Kiir and Machar signed a cessation of hostilities agreement in late January 2014, Machar demanded that all foreign forces leave South Sudan as a precondition for further negotiations. The United States echoed this call in an attempt to persuade Uganda to withdraw its troops from Juba.[148] Museveni responded with contempt and refused to pull UPDF troops out of South Sudan until twenty-two months later.[149] One US diplomat who worked in the office of the US envoy to Sudan and South Sudan offered a clear-eyed account: "Given cooperation in other regional hotspots . . . American officials demurred from a public spat with Museveni. What signals were sent publicly were met with unflinching rebuke."[150] Though Museveni's standing in Washington was diminished, his influence was clearly far from depleted.

Museveni told the press that neither the United States nor any other country could instruct Uganda to withdraw its troops, and that the UPDF would remain in South Sudan until a peacekeeping force was deployed to the new state. The Ugandan president argued that the UPDF provided "core stability" to South Sudan and was in fact preventing the eruption of a catastrophic ethnic conflict between Salva Kiir's Dinka loyalists and Riek Machar's Nuer militias.[151] In an allusion to US ingratitude and paternalism in the wake of Uganda's success in Somalia, Museveni claimed, "Whenever there are regional conflicts, the West looks to us to help but when stability is restored, they begin talking about non-interference in the affairs of an independent state."[152]

Not long after hostilities began in Juba, the European allies of the United States, including Britain and France, called for a UN arms embargo against South Sudan. The US State Department largely supported this plan. Key members of Obama's National Security Council (NSC), however, sided with Museveni, who fiercely opposed the idea on the premise that it would prevent Salva Kiir's government from importing weapons that it could use to fend off Machar's rebels. NSC officials emphasized that an embargo would be ineffective because Uganda, South Sudan's neighbor and ally, would refuse to enforce it.[153] To retain Museveni's firm cooperation on Somalia, much to the consternation of its European allies, the Obama administration did not push for an arms embargo against South Sudan until nearly two years into the conflict.[154]

The United States was hesitant to criticize Museveni's foreign policy, but tensions did emerge around Uganda's domestic affairs. In 2014, when a bill stipulating a life sentence for "aggravated homosexuality" was introduced in the Ugandan Parliament and signed into law, President Obama suggested that the new statute would "complicate" US–Uganda relations.[155] On the heels of these remarks, the State Department publicly threatened to review all US aid to Uganda. When Museveni dismissed these threats and demanded that the United States stop attempting to impose its values on Ugandans, Ambassador DeLisi would not be cowed. "If Uganda doesn't want our assistance," the ambassador told the Ugandan press, "let the government tell us and we shall turn to another African country."[156]

Throughout this war of words, US officials maintained that the security partnership with Uganda was valuable and that the UPDF's role in Somalia was commendable. That said, in June 2014 the United States imposed sanctions on Uganda, including travel bans on several proponents of the antigay law. The sanctions also included the suspension of a small package of assistance to the Ugandan police, the cancellation of a joint air-force training exercise, and the temporary suspension of funds for a health institute.[157] This gesture was primarily symbolic, and US military aid to Uganda went largely undisrupted. In fact, a Ugandan Special Forces unit received a $12 million US aid package that year and underwent a twelve-month counterterrorism training program. Many observers reasoned that the sanctions were little more than "a shot across the bow."[158] They would have been more severe if Uganda was not playing an important role in Somalia. Even so, the very act of the Obama administration sanctioning Uganda, despite its commitment to the US security agenda, represented an important turn in the bilateral relations of these states. Moreover, the stridency of US criticisms of the NRM government's attacks on civil liberties and the rights of gay Ugandans reflected a clear shift in the tenor of relations between Washington and Kampala.

In August 2014 Uganda's Constitutional Court struck down the anti-gay statute, stilling much of the international opprobrium. The United States, despite its previous protests, also began to grudgingly admit the value of the Ugandan presence in South Sudan. Obama's diplomats asserted that while the UPDF was exacerbating the conflict by backing Kiir's forces, thus making him less likely to negotiate, its intervention probably prevented more severe ethnic violence. In a moment of candor, a White House spokesman also admitted that the UPDF's success in defending South Sudan's Bor Airport and keeping it open was a "blessing" that allowed the United States to maintain a scaled-down diplomatic presence in the country.[159]

Uganda proved indispensable in other ways as well. Early in the conflict, when a US helicopter took fire above South Sudan on its way to evacuate diplomatic personnel, the aircraft made an emergency landing at the US cooperative security location at Entebbe. "The Ugandans have been invaluable," said a US Air Force officer who worked closely with the UPDF to manage the emergency landing and a cascade of ensuing evacuations.[160] Likewise, in 2016, when Obama sent 47 soldiers to South Sudan to protect US diplomats amid renewed fighting, he prepositioned 200 more at Uganda's cooperative security location.[161]

As the civil conflict persisted in South Sudan, the United States also grew concerned with setbacks in Somalia. In the wake of the 2010

Kampala bombings, AMISOM had engaged al-Shabaab more aggressively. By August 2011 the force had largely driven the Islamists from Somalia's capital.[162] In 2012, with AMISOM's support, Somalia's transitional government asserted growing authority over Mogadishu and convened the state's first formal legislative session since 1991.[163] Al-Shabaab continued its attacks and maintained control of towns in eastern and southern Somalia. But as displaced civilians poured back into the country's capital and Mogadishu maintained relative stability, optimism began to take hold among Western donors and international organizations.

Uganda's commanders in Somalia reinforced this optimism by consistently claiming that al-Shabaab was on the verge of defeat.[164] Despite a series of al-Shabaab attacks in Kenya throughout 2014, the period from 2012 to early 2015 can be considered AMISOM's most successful years. During this time, the extremists were far from defeated but often on the defensive, particularly as they weathered a series of AMISOM military operations throughout 2014 and 2015. During these offensives, the UN Special Representative to Somalia, lauded "the biggest expansion that AMISOM has made since 2007."[165]

However, by late 2015 the fragility of AMISOM's gains became apparent and increasingly concerning for Obama officials. In September of that year, al-Shabaab car-bombed and overran a UPDF base at Janaale in Somalia's Lower Shabelle region. Ugandan casualties were the subject of great dispute, but most accounts suggest that this was the deadliest strike the UPDF faced since AMISOM's outset. Indeed, it came amid a surge in al-Shabaab attacks.[166] In January 2016 AMISOM's Kenyan contingent suffered some 170 casualties when al-Shabaab struck its base near El Adde in Somalia's Gedo region.[167] AMISOM commanders complained that they lacked reliable intelligence, combat air support, and secure communications systems. They also condemned the incompetence of the Somali National Army.[168] The peace force struggled to hold territory that it had taken, with towns often repeatedly changing hands between AMISOM and al-Shabaab.[169]

Adding to the uncertainty, Burundi's participation in AMISOM came under scrutiny in 2016. Its president, Pierre Nkurunziza, responded to an attempted coup and protests against his unconstitutional third term with a wave of violence against Burundian citizens.[170] After imposing sanctions against the Nkurunziza regime, the EU refused to pay the salaries of AMISOM's Burundi contingent.[171] Likewise, the United States suspended military training for Burundian troops slated to deploy to Somalia.[172] In a notable contrast, the Museveni government did not face the prospect of similar consequences.

Significantly, al-Shabaab's resurgence overlapped with the run-up to Uganda's February 2016 presidential poll. Few were surprised when Museveni was reelected to a fifth term. Western election observers decried widespread vote rigging and the violent suppression of opposition groups. Instead of congratulating the president as it had in 2011, the US State Department issued a condemnation of the outcome, calling the elections "deeply inconsistent with international standards and expectations for any democratic process."[173]

Secretary of State John Kerry personally called Museveni, urging him to "rein in" Ugandan security forces that were cracking down on protestors and to release opposition leaders who had been detained, including Dr. Kizza Besigye.[174] Besigye and Amama Mbabazi, prominent presidential candidates, had been subjected to "preventative arrest" and held briefly before the poll.[175] During the election, the newly appointed US ambassador, Deborah Malac, publicly criticized the Ugandan government's repressive tactics, which included curtailing its citizens access to social media.[176] Museveni was characteristically combative: "I told Kerry not to worry a lot about the internal affairs of Uganda because we know how to handle the issues, and I will call the [US] ambassador and tell her the things she does not know about Uganda."[177]

In early March 2016 the State Department announced that Uganda's ongoing abuses "could endanger" the partnership between the two states.[178] Ambassador Malac soon heightened the tensions by staging a walkout at Museveni's inauguration when the Ugandan president mocked the International Criminal Court (ICC) in the presence of Sudan's Omar al Bashir, then under ICC indictment. "I cannot allow them to give me orders about Uganda or anything in the world," Museveni declared, summoning the US ambassador to the statehouse after she levied further criticisms of his government's threats to the press and political opposition.[179]

Museveni was well aware of rising fears in Washington around a "tactical upswing" in al-Shabaab activities and the growing presence of the Islamic State in Somalia.[180] As one former US diplomat to Uganda suggested, "He knew how to read the tea leaves."[181] Pentagon officials warned that "pro-ISIL sentiment is increasing in Somalia," noting that lower-level al-Shabaab operatives were being drawn to the group while al-Shabaab's leadership remained loyal to al-Qaeda.[182] The Americans worried that AMISOM was overstretched while the Somali National Army was riddled with deficiencies.[183]

Amid the outpouring of US criticism in early 2016, Museveni's government called for a review of Ugandan participation in AMISOM. The president's allies in the UPDF High Command threatened to withdraw Ugandan troops from Somalia by the end of 2017, a year earlier than scheduled.[184] The Obama administration continued to pressure the Ugandan government, suggesting, for example, that due to its abuses, it might lose eligibility for trade benefits through the African Growth and Opportunity Act.[185] Yet it was clear that Museveni's threat registered in Washington. One Ugandan official observed: "American interests aren't necessarily defined by the State Department or the Oval Office. Defense has a lot to say. So from the Pentagon you are likely to get a completely different perspective."[186]

By the summer of 2016, Museveni began to walk back his government's proposal to withdraw from AMISOM. At the same time, AFRICOM's incoming commander acknowledged declining "initiative" among AMISOM's contributing states and pledged to get "movement back on track" in Somalia.[187] The Obama administration had taken a more aggressive military posture in Somalia since the beginning of the year, increasing airstrikes, intensifying training for the Somali National Army, and deploying more US soldiers to the country than at any point since Washington's 1993 intervention.[188] As relations with Uganda soured, the United States began to increase its assistance to AMISOM's Kenyan contingent. Nairobi was one of Washington's oldest allies in Africa and offered the United States valuable access to the port of Mombasa and reconnaissance bases in Lamu.[189] However, given its numerical supremacy and nearly a decade of combat experience in Somalia, the Ugandan contingent could not be overlooked. US Special Operations Forces continued to closely collaborate with the Ugandans in "advise and assist" missions on the front lines of the conflict with al-Shabaab.[190]

The Obama administration publicly lavished military aid on Kenya while offering Uganda similar assistance with far less fanfare.[191] In fact, after Museveni's contested reelection the US Army's Security Assistance Command delivered a new package of equipment to the UPDF and outlined the "steady stream" of matériel that had been or was scheduled to be donated to maintain the Ugandans' trust.[192] This equipment ran the gamut, including helicopters, forklifts, armored personnel carriers, mine resistant ambush protected vehicles, printers, radios, and uniforms. As a Ugandan opposition parliamentarian opined, Museveni had "blackmailed" the United States for nearly a decade. Despite momentary tensions, he had the troops and acumen to continue doing so.[193]

A STRONGMAN'S ALLIANCE QUELLS RISING TENSIONS

With the first Trump administration, Museveni traded in honey rather than vinegar. From its earliest days, the Trump White House evinced an aversion to supporting multilateral peace operations. It successfully lobbied for a nearly $600 million dollar cut to the UN's already strained $7.9 billion annual peacekeeping budget.[194] The cut was a direct blow to the UN's nine authorized peace missions in Africa, including AMISOM. Even so, in 2017 Trump officials began to raise concerns about phased withdrawals of AMISOM troops under a UN plan.[195] It was evident that without AMISOM's support, the Somali security forces remained too weak to contend with ongoing extremist activity throughout the country. Moreover, al-Shabaab had recently killed an American soldier in Somalia, the first US casualty in the country since 1993's Battle of Mogadishu.[196]

Cognizant of these concerns, rather than threaten to withdraw his forces, Museveni approached Trump officials and dangled the prospect of deploying five thousand more UPDF troops to Somalia.[197] This held considerable appeal for the Trump administration which strongly preferred bilateral arrangements and placed US security concerns at the top of its Africa agenda. It aimed to shore up ties with the NRM government after the tensions of the Obama years. In summer 2017 the commander of AFRICOM's army component met with the Ugandan chief of defense forces in Kampala and praised the Ugandan military effort in Somalia. "Uganda has been our best partner in Africa, and we must stay connected," the AFRICOM commander announced.[198]

The first Trump administration's desire to maintain AMISOM's troop levels in Somalia intensified in late 2017. In one of the decade's most lethal strikes, an October truck bombing in Mogadishu killed 587 people.[199] In the wake of the attack, Museveni did not deploy five thousand more soldiers to Somalia, but his government and the Trump administration appeared to strike a deal. In exchange for a Ugandan pledge to largely preserve its force numbers in Somalia, the United States would ease its criticisms of an ongoing effort to change Uganda's presidential age-limit so that Museveni could run for a sixth term.[200] The age-limit would have prevented Museveni, who by his own estimate was 73 at the time, from vying for reelection in 2021. In mid-2017 Museveni's NRM allies in Parliament advanced legislation to amend Article 102 (b) of the Ugandan constitution, which disqualified those under 35 years of age and over 75 years of age from assuming the presidency.[201] Ugandan police raided the office of one think tank that produced a survey finding that 85 percent of Ugandans opposed the bill.[202] Demonstrations erupted around the country, and opposition parliamentarians who filibustered the legislation were harassed, arrested, and beaten.[203]

At the time, though she was an Obama appointee, Deborah Malac retained the position of US ambassador to Uganda. Her comments on the age-limit controversy were markedly subdued compared to her criticisms of the Museveni administration during the Obama administration. Malac warned that Uganda's international image would be tarnished, calling on the government to allow debate without intimidating its opponents. "Whatever the outcome is less of the issue," she remarked.[204] These criticisms likely lacked the input of the Trump administration, whose disinterest in the fate of human rights and democracy in Africa was palpable. Given how effectively Museveni had leveraged the UPDF's presence in Somalia, one Ugandan official reckoned that Ambassador Malac's comments would never exceed certain bounds: "She talked until she got her fingers burnt."[205] Ultimately, Uganda's constitutional age-limit would be amended, opening the door for Museveni to run for reelection in 2021.

On the regional front, in late 2017 the Ugandan president was elected AMISOM's official spokesman by representatives of the force's troop contributing countries. This formalized Museveni's role as AMISOM's liaison with Western states and international organizations. Upon assuming the position, he announced immediately: "This is a Pan-African venture. We are not employees of the United Nations or Somalia."[206] Trump's State Department rushed to embrace Museveni's elevated standing, publicly affirming Uganda's leading role in AMISOM.

Meanwhile, during its first two years, the Trump administration initiated the most aggressive US military effort in Somalia since the outset of the War on Terror. It loosened Obama-era restrictions on airstrikes in the country, launching thirty-five in 2017 and a record forty-seven in 2018.[207] It ramped up "advise, assist, and accompany" operations in which US soldiers collaborated with Ugandan, Kenyan, and Somali troops to fight al-Shabaab.[208] In the second half of Trump's term, Washington more actively pursued an agenda of geo-strategic competition while slashing counterterrorism funding for Africa. Nevertheless, the lion's share of this counterterrorism aid still went to Uganda. Of the $100 million in counterterrorism assistance the Pentagon authorized for seven African states in 2018, more than $70 million went to the UPDF.[209]

The Ugandans praised the Trump administration for its support. Even after it was reported that Trump privately referred to African states as "shithole countries," Museveni hailed Trump as one of America's "best presidents," lauding him for speaking "frankly" about Africa's weaknesses.[210] The Ugandan president's rhetoric would shift slightly in 2019 when the former inspector general of the Ugandan police, Kale Kayihura, was sanctioned by the US Treasury Department for human rights abuses under the Global Magnitsky Act. Kayihura had fallen out with Museveni in 2018 and been fired and then arrested on charges of corruption. Hence, Museveni's response to the sanctions, which seized Kayihura's American investments and denied him entry into the United States, was subdued. The Ugandan president declared that the United States could pursue whatever policies it deemed appropriate, even if they lacked substance. He nonetheless questioned why a Ugandan would want to invest in any country other than his own in the first place. Museveni claimed that he might, personally, consider investing in another African country, but he would never invest in a Western country. Citing Walter Rodney, he struck a radical Pan-Africanist tone: "It is the African slave labor during 300 years of slavery, the African resources during the colonial times, and the African resources during neo-colonial times that contributed greatly to the prosperity of those countries to the detriment of Africa."[211]

The sanctions against Kayihura did nothing to stem the tide of US security assistance to Uganda, which received a record $122 million in US military aid the year they were issued.[212] The Trump administration continued to train and equip Uganda's AMISOM contingents, but its mounting aversion to directly confronting terrorism in Somalia and throughout Africa became increasingly apparent. In this context, the Ugandan role in Somalia became even more vital as the Trump administration initiated a force optimization review that led to the withdrawal from Somalia of nearly all of America's seven hundred troops by the close of 2020.[213] In August of that year, for example, Washington asked Kampala to deploy the UPDF's air assets to Somalia for the first time since 2012.[214] By this point, AMISOM was locked in a bitter stalemate with al-Shabaab, and the Somali National Army remained ineffectual. Moreover, tensions wracked relations between the Somali government and the governments of Uganda, Ethiopia, and Kenya. This state of affairs was exacerbated by the onset of the COVID-19 pandemic, which threatened funding for AMISOM as donor states dedicated their resources to tackling the global crisis.

The pandemic would likewise figure prominently in Uganda's next election. In the months before the January 2021 presidential poll,

Museveni relied on COVID-19 restrictions to harass and intimidate opposition groups. In November 2020 at least 54 Ugandans were killed and some 577 were detained during protests following the arrest of Museveni's strongest rival for the presidency, parliamentarian and musician Bobi Wine (née Robert Kyagulanyi Ssentamu). Wine, a fierce critic of the NRM government, was charged with holding a mass rally in violation of Uganda's COVID-19 regulations.[215] He had been detained on at least three occasions prior to his November arrest. In 2018, after being tortured by Ugandan security forces, Wine garnered international attention by traveling to the United States for medical treatment and appealing to the Trump administration to suspend military aid to Uganda. Museveni dismissed Wine's injuries as "fake news," and the Trump administration remained largely silent about the Ugandan president's abuses.[216]

Reflecting this indifference, for much of 2020 the post of US ambassador to Uganda remained vacant after Deborah Malac's retirement. In December of that year, Secretary of State Mike Pompeo warned of "serious consequences" for those who undermined Uganda's electoral process.[217] However, Pompeo took no further action, even in the face of congressional pressure. The secretary of state's warning was difficult for Museveni to take seriously. At the time, Trump was a lame-duck president who had been far more receptive to the Ugandan leader's bargaining than his predecessor.

THE US-UGANDA SECURITY PARTNERSHIP: ERSTWHILE OR INDISPENSABLE?

In the run-up to Uganda's January 2021 presidential poll, Natalie Brown, the newly appointed US ambassador, signaled the more critical stance the incoming Biden administration would take toward Museveni's government. She implored the Ugandan administration to end its harassment of human rights proponents and civil society groups. When Uganda's electoral commission refused to offer accreditation to most election observers from the United States, Brown canceled the embassy's entire electoral observation mission. When UN, EU, and local civil society missions were also refused accreditation, she declared that the presidential contest would lack transparency and accountability.[218]

After Museveni was elected to a sixth term in yet another poll marked by irregularities, violent crackdowns, and a government shutdown of social media access, Brown stoked his ire by attempting to visit Bobi Wine, who had been placed under house arrest. She was turned back by police and denounced Wine's detainment, noting a "worrying trend" in Uganda's democracy.[219] NRM spokesmen countered that Brown was aiming to subvert Uganda's election and thwart the will of its people. Museveni would later contend that many of the Ugandans responsible for the election unrest were "terrorists," some of whom were rightfully killed by UPDF Special Forces units that had also fought in Somalia.[220] It was these Special Forces that had been the primary recipients of US training and equipment. The extent of Museveni's repression during the 2021 election and Wine's international profile catalyzed a growing outcry among human rights groups and legislators in the UK and the United States.

Shortly after Museveni's victory, amid the diplomatic row, the UPDF announced that it had raided al-Shabaab hideouts in Somalia and killed 189 militants in AMISOM's single most lethal attack.[221] The announcement was celebrated throughout the region and quickly became international news. But a handful observers noted that its claims were unconfirmed by credible sources and came at a time when the Ugandan government was anxious to underscore its value as a US security partner.[222] Within days, Uganda's permanent representative to the UN began to refute reports of the UPDF's stunning success, claiming, against clear evidence to the contrary, that the military had never released an official statement about the alleged attack.[223] This staged military "triumph" was a new tactic in Ugandan security diplomacy with the United States and an apparent response to the sharp downturn in its relations with Washington.

Administrators in the Ugandan Ministry of Finance anticipated deep cuts in US foreign aid, privately asserting, "We can survive without them.

It would hurt but it would not kill us."[224] Rather than slashing aid, in April 2021 the US State Department imposed visa restrictions on unspecified Ugandan officials alleged to have undermined the free and fair conduct of the January elections. Then, in December, Washington imposed financial sanctions on Uganda's chief of military intelligence, Major General Abel Kandiho, charging grave violations of human rights.[225] These individual sanctions were a far cry from the comprehensive review of US aid to Uganda that Museveni's harshest critics demand. They did, however, reflect clear strains in US–Uganda relations—strains unmatched in nearly two decades.

Despite the tensions, Biden administration officials continued to assert that the Museveni government was a critical counterterrorism partner in Africa, though they rarely failed to note their concerns around the Ugandan security forces' abuses. Sizing up this dynamic, a Ugandan military official observed, "The State Department says human rights, blah, blah, blah, but our operations with the Pentagon have never stopped."[226] While US bilateral military aid to Uganda declined under the Biden administration, US training programs for the UPDF continued under the GPOI, ACOTA, and the African Peacekeeping Rapid Response Partnership (APRRP). Ugandan forces applied skills acquired through these initiatives far beyond the battlefields of Somalia as the Museveni government maintained an iron grip on power at home.

Not only did Museveni prove the depths of his regime's entrenchment domestically, but he also continued to position Uganda as an indispensable actor in Washington's agenda for Central and East Africa. In April 2023 AFRICOM's commander strongly recommended that Washington continue its support for AMISOM, given al-Shabaab advances in Somalia that could threaten US interests. AFRICOM also confirmed that preventing the rise of ISIS in Uganda and throughout Central Africa were key regional objectives.[227] These concerns were discernable as early as 2021, when the US State Department designated the Allied Democratic Forces, a Ugandan rebel group based largely in Congo, as a foreign terrorist organization.[228] This move confirmed Washington's growing fears around the ADF's ties with the Islamic State. These fears, many note, have been exaggerated by the Ugandan government and its allies among US think tanks and NGOs.[229]

The Allied Democratic Forces is a rebel group formed in 1995 in Uganda's Rwenzori region by ethnic Bakonzo separatists, Muslim extremists, disaffected UPDF troops, former Interahamwe fighters, and loyalists of the late Idi Amin.[230] Given its complex history and composition, the ADF has espoused a fluid and pragmatic mélange of Islamist aims and local grievances. Since 2013 it has intensified attacks in Congo and Uganda, most notably claiming joint responsibility with ISIS for a string of bombings in Kampala throughout October and November 2021. Earlier that year, Museveni attempted to solicit US support for a joint Ugandan and Congolese military offensive against the ADF in the Congo. The Biden administration was noncommittal.[231]

Instead, the United States opted to direct most of its military assistance to Congolese forces once the joint operation began in November 2021. Still, it had little choice but to aid Museveni's military. Under the auspices of a State Department contract, the Bridgeway Foundation, a militarized NGO that established ties with Museveni as it helped the UPDF fight the LRA, was paid to coordinate cooperation and intelligence sharing between the Ugandan and Congolese forces.[232] Driven by concerns around ISIS's growing presence in Central Africa—concerns stoked by the Ugandans themselves—the Biden administration could not avoid the UPDF's significance as a regional fighting force. It thus sought to outsource its fraught security relations with Uganda. In so doing, it continued a trend that had intensified under the first Trump administration, which paid a host of US military contractors to train UPDF units and accompany them on missions in Somalia.[233]

STATIST PAN-AFRICANISM AND A RETURN TO GEOSTRATEGIC COMPETITION

China and Russia's expanding influence in Africa has also served to strengthen Museveni's hand in his diplomacy with Washington. In 2006 recoverable oil reserves of at least 1.4 billion barrels were discovered in Uganda.[234] This portended an economic windfall for Museveni's government and complemented its regional military might as a bulwark against Western edicts and aid conditionality. China led the way in the competition for contracts to oversee Uganda's oil extraction initiatives. But American firms were determined to get in on the action. US diplomats appealed consistently to Museveni on their behalf, ultimately helping a consortium led by American companies to win a contract to build Uganda's first oil refinery.[235]

Similarly, although the Biden administration attempted to publicly distance itself from Museveni, in the wake of Russia's 2022 invasion of Ukraine, it dispatched its ambassador to the UN, Linda Thomas-Greenfield, to Kampala. The highest-ranking US diplomat to visit Uganda during Biden's term, Thomas-Greenfield met with Museveni just days after Foreign Minister Sergey Lavrov of Russia sat down with the Ugandan president.[236] Thomas-Greenfield disavowed any effort to recruit Uganda to the US cause against Russia, but the specter of new Cold War politics hung heavily over her visit to Kampala. She announced an additional $20 million in US development aid to Uganda and refuted Lavrov's claims that growing food insecurity in Africa was the result of US sanctions against Russia.[237] Thomas-Greenfield noted that African countries that purchased sanctioned Russian commodities might face consequences but insisted that Washington was not opposed to these countries purchasing Russian agricultural products. The visit itself was an affirmation of Museveni's regional influence, and Thomas-Greenfield expressed her appreciation for Uganda's leading role in Somalia.

Museveni has made it clear that he has little interest in taking sides in the conflict between NATO and Russia.[238] Uganda was one of sixteen African nations to abstain from US-led UN resolution ES-11/1 condemning the Russian invasion of Ukraine. This is in part because security cooperation between Moscow and Kampala has grown in recent decades. In fact, in the months before Museveni met with Lavrov, the NRM Party and Putin's United Russia Party signed a memorandum of understanding aimed at increasing dialogue and cooperation. Likewise, Museveni himself held a virtual call with United Russia Party Chairman Dmitry Medvedev and during Lavrov's visit celebrated the history of cordial relations between Kampala and Moscow.[239]

Amid the obvious tumult in US–Uganda relations, Museveni's public stance on NATO's conflict with Russia has been consistent: "We want to make our own enemies, not fight other people's enemies."[240] His son, Lt. General Muhoozi Kainerugaba, whom Museveni appears to be grooming for the presidency, has offered full-throated support for the Russian invasion, tweeting, "The majority of mankind (that are non-white) support Russia's stand in Ukraine . . . Putin is absolutely right!"[241] Much like his father, Kainerugaba's expressions of racial solidarity emerged in the context of heightened tensions between Uganda and the West. While he overstates the extent of support for Russia, Kainerugaba's claims cannot be easily dismissed. Throughout Africa and Asia, the ambivalent response to the Russian invasion and Washington's opposition to it reflects not only the breadth of economic and strategic ties to Moscow but also an enduring skepticism toward American hegemony. It is precisely this hegemony that Museveni claims he has confronted with an ardent commitment to Pan-Africanism.

To be sure, Museveni's Pan-African project—its inherent militarism and the interventions it has overseen—has granted Uganda a louder voice and more consistent influence in its relations with the United States than that of any other African country of similar size and resource endowments. It is clear that this Pan-Africanism is a Pan-Africanism from above—a Pan-Africanism of the state—that has been mobilized largely to advance the NRM government's domestic and regional designs. Museveni's Pan-Africanism is, at best, ambivalent and, at worst, brazenly opportunistic on the question of transnational Black solidarity. But the Ugandan intervention in Somalia that has become the centerpiece of Museveni's Pan-African project, under the auspices of the African Union peace mission, may soon come to an end. It is not likely that the peace mission will conclude within the two-year timeline put forward by the newly established African Union Transition Mission in Somalia (ATMIS). Nonetheless, AMISOM's replacement by ATMIS reflects mounting pessimism within the AU, the UN, Western capitals, and the Somali government itself about the long-term efficacy of the Ugandan-led peace force. Moreover, the Biden administration revived Obama-era efforts to maintain a US military and intelligence presence in Somalia, rendering the United States marginally less dependent on coalition operations in the country with Uganda, Kenya, and other African security partners.

In short, the future of the US–Uganda security partnership is as uncertain as it has been since the outset of the War on Terror. This moment of uncertainty offers an opportunity to take stock. Such a reckoning is not only a matter of assessing Museveni's record of influence in his relations with Washington. Museveni's Pan-African project—its militarism, regional reach, and history of US investment—offers a window into a broader political reality. It alerts us to the profound chasm between Pan-Africanism as a popular ideology of liberation and Pan-Africanism as a statist mechanism of influence in contemporary world politics.

CONCLUSION

In January 1983 President Reagan's National Security Council requested a secret review of recent negotiations with states that hosted major US military facilities. The review found that the negotiations had preserved US access to these facilities and largely advanced the White House's broader geostrategic agenda. The distribution of "quids"—primarily security and economic aid—had been instrumental in achieving these goals.[1] Yet, this approach to securing the cooperation of allies was a delicate matter. The official US position was that the military aid programs provided to these states were not quids but rather a response to common strategic objectives.

"The payment of a quid publicly recognized by the US as such," the NSC study noted, "would dilute the fundamental basis of a mutual security relationship and in time perhaps even sour it as quids rather than shared security interests became the focus of the relationship."[2] Historically, this challenge has been persistent and at times insurmountable for US administrations that valued security partnerships with African governments. As illustrated, Washington's loss in this regard has been the gain of Monrovia, Addis Ababa, Kinshasa, and Kampala. The military aid and political backing that these governments received sprang from more than simply the calculus of US officials who coveted strategic assets in Africa. Likewise, bargaining between the United States and its African security partners was more than a matter of careful negotiations underpinned by power asymmetries among states.

Realist imperatives certainly constrained American and African leaders, but within these constraints bargaining was often a matter of anticipation and experimentation. It was a political process, an "art" even, laced with candor and deceit, resourcefulness and ineptitude, cold calculations and racial allegiances.[3] In this context African governments amassed the influence to press for concessions and, more broadly, to shape the political consequences of security relations with the United States. This dynamic and the discord that it sowed has animated my analysis.

From the cautious bartering of Ethiopia and Liberia to the extortionate schemes of Zaire and Uganda, the bargaining acumen of the African security partners of the United States has been critical to their influence in Washington. It was this acumen that helped them to navigate persistent currents of racism in twentieth-century US foreign policy. It was also this acumen that led them to size up the American political landscape and look beyond the administrations in power. In doing so, Selassie and Tubman largely sought the support of the African American foreign policy elite. Later, Mobutu and Museveni would take a similar tack while also pursuing profitable ties with white conservatives. Such was the stock-in-trade of a statist Pan-Africanism—indeed, a mercenary Pan-Africanism—that came to characterize US allies in Africa. An aptitude for leveraging security partnerships with the United States often strengthened the hand of statist Pan-African regimes with little interest in peace and democratic reforms.

This dynamic came under threat at the close of the Cold War as African American elites, led by the likes of Ron Dellums and Randall Robinson, condemned US military ties with Liberia and Zaire. But Clinton's "new breed" of African leaders would soon emerge with an even sharper capacity for capitalizing on security partnerships with the United States. Meles and Museveni, bellicose avatars of the new breed, received a warm reception from the African American foreign policy elite. African American leaders rarely noted their role as opportunistic allies in Clinton's emerging campaign against terrorism in Africa. Instead, they framed

Meles and Museveni as leaders in whom the Black world could take pride. These men were armed humanitarians poised to bring stability and development to the continent, which might serve the economic interests of both Africans and African Americans. With these aspirations in mind, Clinton's African American allies were all too willing to downplay new breed leaders' suspect commitments to democracy and skepticism toward the peaceful resolution of disputes.

The new breed's timing was ideal. In the 1990s a vogue for armed humanitarianism overlapped with the emergence of counterterrorism as a guiding US concern in Africa. Clinton's new breed leaders managed to benefit from both developments until their militaries, bolstered by US aid, went to war in the Congo and the Horn of Africa at the end of the decade. Nonetheless, the George W. Bush administration would soon restore the US–Uganda partnership and readily meet Museveni's demands for military aid. Much to Museveni's benefit, Bush would broadly institutionalize counterterrorism and armed humanitarianism as conjoined facets of US foreign policy in Africa. In 2003, for example, Bush positioned US warships off the coast of Liberia during that country's second civil war. The American president was under pressure to help allay mounting civilian casualties in Liberia, but he was also motivated by sparsely documented claims that Charles Taylor's regime had ties to al-Qaeda.[4] As liberal African American leaders pressured Bush to intervene more forcefully in Liberia, proposals for a new US combatant command for Africa gained traction in Washington.[5]

Congresswoman Sheila Jackson Lee looked back on this moment proudly in 2023 as she and Congressman Gregory Meeks strongly opposed a resolution to withdraw US forces from Somalia. "It was members of the Congressional Black Caucus who organized to say how important it was under the George W. Bush Administration that the Africa Command be set up," Jackson Lee remarked. "It was crucial in the bloody fight in Liberia for that command to be set up, and only without shooting one gun were they able to begin to bring peace."[6]

While well intentioned, Jackson Lee's comments reflect a support for the militarization of US policy in Africa that has deep roots in Black moderate transnationalism. The congresswoman overstates the case by suggesting that US Joint Task Force for Liberia deployment brought peace to the West African state. It did, however, contribute to ECOWAS's efforts to end the second Liberian civil war. More obliquely, the deployment offered a glimpse of the opportunistic mixture of hard power and espoused humanitarianism that would become US Africa Command's hallmark upon its founding in 2007. For the following decade and a half, these often contradictory impulses would fuel AFRICOM's aid to and collaborations with Uganda's troops in Somalia. Indeed, this relationship has been so beneficial for Museveni's government that the same month that Jackson Lee championed the US presence in Somalia, Ugandan dissidents decried the fact that nearly a quarter of their country's soldiers were deployed to Somalia and the DRC.[7]

Notably, the 2023 resolution to withdraw AFRICOM's forces from Somalia was introduced by far-right Congressman Matt Gaetz, a prominent supporter of the Trump administration's attacks against diversity, equity, and inclusion initiatives. In addition to Black lawmakers' qualms about the wording of the resolution, Gaetz's partisan and racial politics likely figured into their opposition to his legislative effort. Their stance strongly resonated with that of midcentury Black liberals who opposed the efforts of racist, white politicians to deny African countries military aid. Gaetz's resolution did, however, gain the support of Democratic Representative Ilhan Omar, the only Somali-American member of Congress.

As AFRICOM was being formed in 2007, Congressman Kendrick Meek exemplified Black liberal support for the command by arguing that it was "well positioned to build relationships with our African allies, protect Africa's natural resources, and play a vital role in offering humanitarian assistance."[8] It should come as little surprise that Africa Command's track record suggests otherwise. As US–Uganda relations demonstrate, counterterrorism has been far more intrinsic to AFRICOM's mission than humanitarian assistance. Moreover, US security partnerships in Africa that grew under the command's guidance have been largely unstable. Worse still, these partnerships have often undermined peace and democracy in Africa by offering support to authoritarian leaders such as Museveni, Ismail Guelleh in Djibouti, and former president Mahamadou Issoufou in Niger.[9] Despite these hazards, the malign consequences of the War on Terror in Africa began to slip from sight in the late 2010s as the United States turned its attention to geostrategic competition.

It is thus worth recalling that during the first two decades of the War on Terror, US troops conducted more missions in Africa's lands and waters than at any point since World War II.[10] In addition to a permanent forward operating base in Djibouti and an expeditionary sea base in the Gulf of Guinea, the United States maintained a dense web of more than two dozen lily-pad bases in over a dozen African states.[11] From these sites it initiated combat operations, conducted reconnaissance and drone strikes, and ran training programs for African militaries. In 2019 there were more US Special Operations troops deployed to Africa than to any other region except for the Middle East.[12] Supporting roughly $2 billion in operations, the annual expenditures of the US Africa Command (AFRICOM) far exceed the defense budgets of every sub-Saharan African state except regional giants Nigeria and South Africa.[13] The command's deployments and footprint can be downplayed only in comparison to massive US defense outlays in other regions. Since September 11, 2001, the United States has spent some $355 billion to pursue its counterterrorism agenda in Africa.[14]

The specter of failure, nonetheless, stalks US security policy across the continent. Extremist networks stretch from the Sahel to the West African coast, ISIS franchises have emerged in the Great Lakes region and Mozambique, and al-Shabaab has displayed remarkable staying power in Somalia. There have been record increases in terrorist strikes in Africa over the course of the last decade alongside a clear shift in US strategy from confronting to containing the threat.[15] US government investigations have revealed that the Pentagon cannot produce accurate inventories of the arms transferred to African governments, nor does it conduct effective oversight to determine how these arms are used.[16] AFRICOM has a long-standing "personnel accountability" problem and on any given day cannot determine the status and whereabouts of the numerous military contractors it deploys to the continent.[17]

Some US regional security assistance programs are so disorderly that no agency in Washington can account for the number of individual military initiatives that fall within their auspices or whether these initiatives actually serve US or African interests.[18] For example, in 2020 a government audit of the Trans-Sahara Counterterrorism Partnership (TSCP) found that the program was deeply flawed. The TSCP is a US security initiative that has provided hundreds of millions of dollars in military aid to illiberal governments in Mauritania, Burkina Faso, and Niger.[19] Yet, in one of many examples of ineptitude, State Department officials had no systematic means of verifying how the matériel donated to African militaries through the program was actually being put to use. This posed the risk that the military equipment could be turned against African civilians or fall into the hands of extremist groups.

Similarly, during the War on Terror the US military used Congolese bases such as Kitona and Kisangani to execute a number of training programs for the Armed Forces of the Democratic Republic of the Congo (FARDC). Some of these programs featured anodyne courses on military justice and combat medicine, others trained and equipped Congolese brigades that subsequently engaged in gross humanitarian abuses.[20] Even in the wake of these abuses, the first Trump administration secretly supplied arms to the Congolese military in contravention of a UN embargo.[21] The Biden administration likewise took steps to expand US military aid to DRC's armed forces.[22] The United States justified these efforts as attempts to help the DRC government defeat local insurgents and subvert their ties with organizations such as the Islamic State.[23] In 2019 security officials I interviewed at the African Union scoffed at these claims. They argued that the United States largely maintained ties with the Congolese military in a rear-guard effort to combat Chinese influence. According to this logic, DRC's strategic location in the heart of Central Africa, its cobalt reserves, and other mineral resources were far too valuable for US policymakers to ignore.[24]

Indeed, by 2024 the logic of a new Cold War was pervasive in Washington. Amid the growing US rivalry with China and Russia for spheres of influence in Africa, many of Washington's security partnerships with African governments were unraveling. Running tensions with Uganda and Rwanda threatened the halting efforts of the United States to contain violent extremism in East Africa. US security ties with Ethiopia hung by a thread despite its legacy of support for the War on Terror in Africa. In the Sahel, US counterterror partnerships with Mali, Niger, and Burkina Faso were in various stages of collapse.

Some US officials cited coups, civil conflicts, and human rights abuses across Africa as the causes for this malaise in security relations.[25] Others argued that China, Russia, and the Gulf States offered a new devil's bargain and aimed to control African governments by providing support that allowed them to dispense with Washington's demands.[26] While this argument emphasizes the self-interest of the world's rising powers, it tends to underestimate the agency of African officials. African states are not the world's children, easily lured east with "white elephants," usurious loans, and vague promises of patronage. The history of US–Africa security partnerships reminds us that African governments will fight to advance their own agendas, often at the expense of their allies and citizens.

NOTES

INTRODUCTION

1. Author interview, senior official 1, African Union Commission Peace and Security Department, July 10, 2018.
2. Author interview, former senior US diplomat to Uganda, April 14, 2022.
3. Author interview, brigadier general, Uganda People's Defense Force, March 17, 2022.
4. Author interview, former senior intelligence officer, US Central Intelligence Agency, March 23, 2018.
5. "U.S. Aims to Head Off Threat of Famine," *The Record*, June 4, 1994, Proquest.
6. Michael K. Frisby, "U.S. Policy on Africa Moves to Front-Burner During Clinton Trip, but Will the Flame Cool?," *Wall Street Journal*, April 3, 1998, https://www.proquest.com/newspapers/u-s-policy-on-africa-moves-front-burner-during/docview/398751707/se-2.
7. Susan Rice, *Tough Love: My Story of the Things Worth Fighting For* (New York: Simon & Schuster, 2019), 159–60.

1. THE MAKING OF US-AFRICA SECURITY RELATIONS

1. US Department of State, *Foreign Relations of the United States (FRUS), 1969–1976, Volume XXVIII, Southern Africa* (Washington, DC: US Government Printing Office, 2011), doc. 182, https://history.state.gov/historicaldocuments/frus1969-76v28.
2. Dick Clark, "An Alternative U.S. Policy," *Africa Report* 21, no. 1 (1976): 16–17; "The Kissinger Thesis," *Africa Report* 21, no. 1 (1976): 13–15.
3. *FRUS, 1969–1976, Volume XXVIII*, doc. 182.

4. "Liberia Recongizes [*sic*] MPLA as Legitimate Government of Angola," Wikileaks, Public Library of US Diplomacy (Liberia, Monrovia, February 14, 1976), https://wikileaks.org/plusd/cables/1976MONROV01134_b.html.
5. Piero Gleijeses, *Conflicting Missions: Havana, Washington, and Africa, 1959–1976* (Chapel Hill: University of North Carolina Press, 2002), 339–46.
6. "Liberia Recongizes [*sic*] MPLA."
7. *FRUS, 1969–1976, Volume XXVIII*, doc. 182.
8. *FRUS*, doc. 182.
9. For analyses of militarization in Africa as a process abetted by foreign powers, see Robin Luckham, "The Military, Militarization and Democratization in Africa: A Survey of Literature and Issues," *African Studies Review* 37, no. 2 (1994): 13–75, https://doi.org/10.2307/524766; Rita Abrahamsen, "Return of the Generals? Global Militarism in Africa from the Cold War to the Present," *Security Dialogue* 49, no. 1–2 (2018): 19–31.
10. D. Elwood Dunn, *Liberia and the United States During the Cold War: Limits of Reciprocity* (New York: Palgrave Macmillan, 2009), 194–96.
11. US Central Intelligence Agency, "Postcoup Prospects in Liberia," Interagency Intelligence Memorandum, December 1980.
12. For assessments of shifts in the conceptualization of and nomenclature around security cooperation, see Bruno Tertrais, "The Changing Nature of Military Alliances," *Washington Quarterly* 27, no. 2 (March 1, 2004): 133–50, https://doi.org/10.1162/016366004773097759; Thomas S. Wilkins, "'Alignment,' Not 'Alliance'—the Shifting Paradigm of International Security Cooperation: Toward a Conceptual Taxonomy of Alignment," *Review of International Studies* 38, no. 1 (January 2012): 53–76, https://doi.org/10.1017/S0260210511000209.
13. African states with which the United States maintained security partnerships of varied durations and cohesiveness during the twentieth and twenty-first centuries: Burkina Faso, Chad, Djibouti, Ethiopia, Kenya, Liberia, Mali, Mauritania, Niger, Somalia, South Africa, Sudan, Uganda, Zaire.
14. US Department of State, *United States Treaties and Other International Agreements*, vol. 2, part 1 (US Government Printing Office, 1952), 1, https://tile.loc.gov/storage-services/service/ll/lltreaties//lltreaties-2-1/lltreaties-2-1.pdf#page=9; vol. 4, part 1 (1955), 421, https://tile.loc.gov/storage-services/service/ll/lltreaties//lltreaties-4-1/lltreaties-4-1.pdf#page=429.
15. Steven R. David, "Explaining Third World Alignment," *World Politics* 43, no. 2 (January 1991): 246; Dunn, *Liberia and the United States*, 154.
16. Alexander Cooley, *Contracting States: Sovereign Transfers in International Relations* (Princeton: Princeton University Press, 2009), 106.
17. Tom Masland, "Fighting for Africa," *Newsweek*, March 30, 1998, Lexis/Nexis.
18. Carl Patrick Burrowes, *Power and Press Freedom in Liberia, 1830–1970: The Impact of Globalization and Civil Society on Media-Government Relations* (Trenton, NJ: Africa World Press, 2004), 250. Burrowes applies these descriptors to styles of presidential

leadership in Liberia's domestic context. I contend that they also hold salience in Liberia's foreign relations with the United States.

19. *FRUS, 1977–1980, Volume XVII, Part 2, Sub-Saharan Africa* (US Government Printing Office, 2018), doc. 52, https://history.state.gov/historicaldocuments/frus1977-80v17p2/d52.
20. Bas Arts and Piet Verschuren, "Assessing Political Influence in Complex Decision-Making: An Instrument Based on Triangulation," *International Political Science Review* 20, no. 4 (October 1, 1999): 413, https://doi.org/10.1177/0192512199204006.
21. Arts and Verschuren, 413.
22. US Central Intelligence Agency, "Memorandum for National Foreign Intelligence Board Principals," October 7, 1983.
23. Moses K. Tesi, "Economic Relations and Political Behavior: A Study of the Political Economy of Cameroon's Relations with France Since 1960" (PhD diss., Vanderbilt University, 1985), 57.
24. Tesi, 54.
25. Christer Jönsson and Jonas Tallberg, "Compliance and Post-Agreement Bargaining," *European Journal of International Relations* 4, no. 4 (December 1, 1998): 371–408, https://doi.org/10.1177/1354066198004004001.
26. Jönsson and Tallberg, 388.
27. Jeffrey L. Pressman and Aaron Wildavsky, *Implementation: How Great Expectations in Washington Are Dashed in Oakland; Or, Why It's Amazing That Federal Programs Work at All, This Being a Saga of the Economic Development Administration as Told by Two Sympathetic Observers Who Seek to Build Morals on a Foundation* (Berkeley: University of California Press, 1984), 107, 49, 132, 136–42, 144.
28. Rayford Whittingham Logan, *The Diplomatic Relations of the United States with Haiti, 1776–1891* (Chapel Hill: University of North Carolina Press, 1941).
29. Rayford W. Logan, "No Peace for the Pacifists," ed. Merze Tate, *Journal of Negro Education* 12, no. 1 (1943): 92–93, https://doi.org/10.2307/2292432.
30. Rayford W. Logan, "Discrimination: Weakness of Our African Policy," *Current History* 42, no. 245 (1962): 28.
31. Logan, *Diplomatic Relations of the United States with Haiti*, 411.
32. Rayford W. Logan, "The U.S. 'Colonial Experiment' in Haiti," *World Today* 17, no. 10 (1961): 439.
33. Rayford W. Logan, "Introduction," in Frederick Douglass, *The Life and Times of Frederick Douglass* (London: Collier Books, 1962), 21.
34. Logan, *Diplomatic Relations of the United States with Haiti*, 426.
35. Logan, "The U.S. 'Colonial Experiment' in Haiti," 437.
36. Rayford W. Logan, "Ethiopia's Troubled Future," *Current History* 44, no. 257 (1963): 50.
37. Brenda Gayle Plummer, *Haiti and the Great Powers, 1902–1915* (Baton Rouge: Louisiana State University Press, 1988).
38. Plummer, 117.

39. Charles Lockhart, *Bargaining in International Conflicts* (New York: Columbia University Press, 1979), 97. See also Tesi, "Economic Relations and Political Behavior," 55.
40. Lockhart, *Bargaining in International Conflicts*, 97.
41. Lockhart, 98.
42. US Department of State, "Liberia: Background to Revolt," August 12, 1980, https://foia.state.gov/FOIALIBRARY/SearchResults.aspx?searchText=%22background%20to%20revolt%22.
43. William A. Shack, "Ethiopia and Afro-Americans: Some Historical Notes, 1920–1970," *Phylon (1960–)* 35, no. 2 (1974): 142–55, https://doi.org/10.2307/274703.
44. Pearl Robinson, "Playing the Arab Card: Niger and Chad's Ambivalent Relations with Libya," in *African Security Issues: Sovereignty, Stability & Solidarity*, ed. Bruce Arlinghaus (Boulder: Westview, 1984).
45. David, "Explaining Third World Alignment"; Jean-François Bayart and Stephen Ellis, "Africa in the World: A History of Extraversion," *African Affairs* 99, no. 395 (2000): 217–67.
46. Robinson, "Playing the Arab Card," 183.
47. Robinson, 171.
48. Robinson, 172.
49. Reiland Rabaka, *Routledge Handbook of Pan-Africanism* (London: Routledge, Taylor & Francis Group, 2020), https://doi.org/10.4324/9780429020193.
50. Hakim Adi, *Pan-Africanism: A History* (London: Bloomsbury Academic, 2018), 230–73.
51. For incisive treatments of state-centered or top-down Pan-Africanism, see Issa G. Shivji, "Pan-Africanism or Imperialism? Unity and Struggle Towards a New Democratic Africa," *African Sociological Review / Revue Africaine de Sociologie* 10, no. 1 (2006): 208–20; Horace Campbell, *Pan-Africanism, Pan-Africanists, and African Liberation in the 21st Century: Two Lectures* (Washington, DC: New Academia, 2006). Seth M. Markle, *A Motorcycle on Hell Run: Tanzania, Black Power, and the Uncertain Future of Pan-Africanism, 1964–1974*, Ruth Simms Hamilton African Diaspora Series (East Lansing: Michigan State University Press, 2017); Jemima Pierre, *The Predicament of Blackness: Postcolonial Ghana and the Politics of Race* (Chicago: University of Chicago Press, 2013).
52. Susan Aurelia Gitelson, "Major Shifts in Recent Ugandan Foreign Policy," *African Affairs* 76, no. 304 (1977): 359–80; Ali A. Mazrui, "Pan-Africanism and the Intellectuals: Rise, Decline and Revival," in *African Intellectuals: Rethinking Politics, Language, Gender and Development*, ed. Thandika Mkandawire (London: Zed Books, 2005); Daniel arap Moi, *Kenya African Nationalism: Nyayo Philosophy and Principles* (London: Macmillan, 1986); Korwa G. Adar and Issac M. Munyae, "Human Rights Abuse in Kenya Under Daniel Arap Moi, 1978–2001," *African Studies Quarterly* 5, no. 1 (February 25, 2001): 1–18.
53. Julius K. Nyerere, "Julius K. Nyerere's Speech to the Congress," *Black Scholar* 5, no. 10 (July 1, 1974): 20, https://doi.org/10.1080/00064246.1974.11431438; Markle, *A Motorcycle on Hell Run*, 47.

54. Kwame Nkrumah, *Africa Must Unite*, new ed. (New York: International Publishers, 1970), 214–15; Thomas Tieku, "Collectivist Worldview: Its Challenge to International Relations," in *Africa and International Relations in the 21st Century*, ed. Scarlett Cornelissen, Fantu Cheru, and Timothy M. Shaw (New York: Palgrave Macmillan, 2012), 46.
55. Thomas Turner, "Zaire: Flying High Above the Toads: Mobutu and Stalemated Democracy," in *Political Reform in Francophone Africa*, ed. John F. Clark and David E. Gardinier (Boulder: Westview, 1997), 252; Yoweri Museveni, Remarks, Maureen Reagan Memorial Service, August 18, 2001, CSPAN, https://www.c-span.org/program/public-affairs-event/maureen-reagan-memorial-service/107110.
56. US Central Intelligence Agency, "The Probable Interrelationships of the Independent African States," National Intelligence Estimate, August 31, 1961, https://www.cia.gov/readingroom/docs/DOC_0000746173.pdf; Jendayi Frazer, "Sustaining Civilian Control: Armed Counterweights in Regime Stability in Africa" (PhD diss., Stanford University, 1994), 82, https://www.proquest.com/docview/304105730.
57. J. Wayne Fredericks Papers 1907–2010, Box 50, Folder 5, Notes, Schomburg Center for Research in Black Culture, Manuscripts, Archives and Rare Books Division, New York Public Library.
58. US Department of State, "African Political Cooperation," March 12, 1964, https://link.gale.com/apps/doc/CK2349383318/GDCS?u=uclosangeles&sid=bookmark-GDCS&xid=b6519f08&pg=2.
59. For a summary of key debates on this question, see Elizabeth N. Saunders, "Elites in the Making and Breaking of Foreign Policy," *Annual Review of Political Science* 25 (May 12, 2022): 219–40, https://doi.org/10.1146/annurev-polisci-041719-103330.
60. Desmond King, "The Racial Bureaucracy: African Americans and the Federal Government in the Era of Segregated Race Relations," *Governance* 12, no. 4 (1999): 354, https://doi.org/10.1111/0952-1895.00109; Michael L. Krenn, *Black Diplomacy: African Americans and the State Department, 1945–1969* (Armonk, NY: M. E. Sharpe, 1999), 63–64, 81, 145, 164.
61. For leading works chronicling this dynamic, see Robin D. G. Kelley, "'But a Local Phase of a World Problem': Black History's Global Vision, 1883–1950," *Journal of American History* 86, no. 3 (December 1, 1999): 1045–77, https://doi.org/10.2307/2568605; Penny M. Von Eschen, *Race Against Empire: Black Americans and Anticolonialism, 1937–1957* (Ithaca, NY: Cornell University Press, 1997); David Levering Lewis, *W.E.B. Du Bois: The Fight for Equality and the American Century, 1919–1963* (New York: Holt, 2000); Jeffrey C. Stewart, *The New Negro: The Life of Alain Locke* (New York: Oxford University Press, 2018).
62. Pierre, *The Predicament of Blackness*, 207–13.
63. Alphaeus Hunton, *Decision in Africa: Sources of Current Conflict* (New York: International Publishers, 1957); Barbara Ransby, *Eslanda: The Large and Unconventional Life of Mrs. Paul Robeson*, 2nd ed. (La Vergne: Haymarket Books, 2022).
64. Paul Tiyambe Zeleza, "The Perpetual Solitudes and Crises of African Studies in the United States," *Africa Today* 44, no. 2 (1997): 195; Robin D. G. Kelley, "'Western

Civilization Is Neither': Black Studies' Epistemic Revolution," *Black Scholar* 50, no. 3 (July 2, 2020): 7, https://doi.org/10.1080/00064246.2020.1780862.

65. For leading works documenting this activism, see Brenda Gayle Plummer, *Rising Wind: Black Americans and U.S. Foreign Affairs, 1935–1960* (Chapel Hill: University of North Carolina Press, 1996); Brenda Gayle Plummer, *Window on Freedom: Race, Civil Rights, and Foreign Affairs, 1945–1988*, new ed. 1 (Chapel Hill: University of North Carolina Press, 2003); James Hunter Meriwether, *Proudly We Can Be Africans: Black Americans and Africa, 1935–1961*, John Hope Franklin Series in African American History and Culture (Chapel Hill: University of North Carolina Press, 2002); Carol Anderson, *Eyes Off the Prize: The United Nations and the African American Struggle for Human Rights, 1944–1955* (Cambridge: Cambridge University Press, 2003).
66. Adolph L. Reed, *The Jesse Jackson Phenomenon: The Crisis of Purpose in Afro-American Politics* (New Haven: Yale University Press, 1986), 4.
67. Robert C. Smith, *We Have No Leaders: African Americans in the Post-Civil Rights Era*, SUNY Series in Afro-American Studies (Albany: State University of New York Press, 1996); Cedric Johnson, *Revolutionaries to Race Leaders: Black Power and the Making of African American Politics* (Minneapolis: University of Minnesota Press, 2007); Reed, *The Jesse Jackson Phenomenon*.
68. For surveys of the role of Black official elites in US policy toward Africa, see Elliott P. Skinner, *African Americans and U.S. Policy Toward Africa, 1850–1924: In Defense of Black Nationality* (Washington, DC: Howard University Press, 1992); Michael L. Clemons, *African Americans in Global Affairs: Contemporary Perspectives* (Boston: Northeastern University Press, 2010); Linda M. Heywood et al., *African Americans in U.S. Foreign Policy: From the Era of Frederick Douglass to the Age of Obama* (Urbana: University of Illinois Press, 2015); Michael L. Krenn, *The African American Voice in U.S. Foreign Policy Since World War II*, Race and U.S. Foreign Policy from the Colonial Period to the Present (New York: Routledge, 2019), https://doi.org/10.4324/9781315785189.
69. Susan Curtis, *Colored Memories: A Biographer's Quest for the Elusive Lester A. Walton* (Columbia: University of Missouri Press, 2008).
70. Celestine Tutt, "Ambassador William Beverly Carter, Jr.," interview, Foreign Affairs Oral History Project, Association for Diplomatic Studies and Training, April 30, 1981.
71. Michael C. Dawson, *Black Visions: The Roots of Contemporary African-American Political Ideologies* (Chicago: University of Chicago Press, 2001), 252–55.
72. Curtis, *Colored Memories*, 109.
73. Herbert Aptheker, ed., *The Correspondence of W.E.B. Du Bois*, vol. 3 (Amherst: University of Massachusetts Press, 1973), 20.
74. W. E. Burghardt Du Bois, "Liberia, the League and the United States," *Foreign Affairs* 11, no. 4 (1933): 684, https://doi.org/10.2307/20030546.
75. Dawson, *Black Visions*, 17.
76. For an analysis of this in the US domestic context, see Cornel West, "Demystifying the New Black Conservatism," *PRAXIS International* 7, no. 2 (1987): 150–51.
77. Curtis, *Colored Memories*, 223–24; Tutt, "Ambassador William Beverly Carter, Jr."

78. "Our Correspondence Letter from Wm. Whipper to Miss. Griffiths Columbia, Pa.," *Frederick Douglass' Paper*, February 18, 1859, no. 10, Readex: African American Newspapers.
79. Paul Cuffe, *Memoir of Captain Paul Cuffee: A Man of Colour: To Which Is Subjoined The Epistle of the Society of Sierra Leone, in Africa, &c.*, Sabin Americana: History of the Americas, 1500–1926 (York: C. Peacock, 1812); Niger Valley Exploring Party and Martin Robison Delany, *Official Report of the Niger Valley Exploring Party* (Rhistoric Publications, 1861).
80. Dawson, *Black Visions*, 21.
81. For Padmore's views on capitalism and imperialism, see George Padmore, *The Life and Struggles of Negro Toilers*, African Diaspora, 1860–Present (Hollywood, CA: Sun Dance Press, 1971).
82. For comprehensive accounts of these ideologies and their tenets, see Padmore; and Eddie S. Glaude, *Is It Nation Time? Contemporary Essays on Black Power and Black Nationalism* (Chicago: University of Chicago Press, 2002).
83. For a concise biography of Straker, see Glenn O. Phillips, "The Response of a West Indian Activist: D. A. Straker, 1842–1908," *Journal of Negro History* 66, no. 2 (July 1981): 128–39, https://doi.org/10.2307/2717282.
84. D. Augustus Straker, "The Land of Our Fathers. Interest in the Congo Region. Why Are the European Powers Grasping African Territory," *New York Freeman*, January 23, 1886, Readex: African American Newspapers; "World Congress of Colored Race," *Wisconsin Weekly Advocate*, July 19, 1900, Readex: African American Newspapers.
85. Straker, "The Land of Our Fathers."
86. Straker, "The Land of Our Fathers. Interest in the Congo Region. Why Are the European Powers Grasping African Territory?," *New York Freeman*, January 30, 1886, Readex: African American Newspapers.
87. Straker.
88. Elliott P. Skinner, *African Americans and U.S. Policy Toward Africa, 1850–1924: In Defense of Black Nationality* (Washington, DC: Howard University Press, 1992), 69, 90, 81, 97.
89. Khary Oronde Polk, *Contagions of Empire: Scientific Racism, Sexuality, and Black Military Workers Abroad, 1898–1948*, North Carolina Scholarship Online (Chapel Hill: University of North Carolina Press, 2021).
90. David P. Kilroy, "Alone at West Point: The Military Education of Charles Young, 1884–1889," *Historian*, June 1, 2002, 589, https://www.tandfonline.com/doi/abs/10.1111/1540-6563.00006.
91. Polk, *Contagions of Empire*, 108
92. Praeger Kilroy, *For Race and Country: The Life and Career of Colonel Charles Young* (New York: Praeger, 2003), 86, 88.
93. "Along the Color Line," *Crisis*, March 1, 1913, 220, The Internet Archive.
94. "Men of the Month," *Crisis*, April 1, 1917, 283, The Internet Archive.
95. "Along the Color Line."

96. For a sampling of the preoccupation with Ethiopia's military might, see "King Menelik of Abyssinia," *Washington Bee*, March 16, 1901, Readex: African American Newspapers; "Menelik a Real Monarch: Abyssinian Ruler's Chief Interest Lies in Military Affairs," *Appeal*, February 13, 1904, Readex: African American Newspapers; "Was in Favor of Peace but King Menelik Knew All About the Fighting Game," *Plaindealer*, April 18, 1913, Readex: African American Newspapers.
97. M. B. Akpan, "Liberia and the Universal Negro Improvement Association: The Background to the Abortion of Garvey's Scheme for African Colonization," *Journal of African History* 14, no. 1 (January 1973): 106, https://doi.org/10.1017/S0021853700012196.
98. I. K. Sundiata, *Brothers and Strangers: Black Zion, Black Slavery, 1914–1940* (Durham: Duke University Press, 2003), 77.
99. Harry Haywood, "The Road to Negro Liberation: The Tasks of the Communist Party in Winning Working Class Leadership of the Negro Liberation Struggles, and the Fight Against Reactionary Nationalist-Reformist Movements Among the Negro People," *PRISM: Political & Rights Issues & Social Movements* (June 1934): 31–34, https://stars.library.ucf.edu/cgi/viewcontent.cgi?article=1389&context=prism; Padmore, *The Life and Struggles of Negro Toilers*, 64, 69.
100. Sundiata, *Brothers and Strangers*, 219.
101. Du Bois, "Liberia, the League and the United States," 684.
102. Dunn, *Liberia and the United States*, 83.
103. I. K. Sundiata, *Black Scandal, America and the Liberian Labor Crisis, 1929–1936* (Philadelphia: Institute for the Study of Human Issues, 1980), 150.
104. W.E.B. Du Bois, "Postscript," *Crisis*, December 1, 1932.
105. Sundiata, *Black Scandal*, 57–68.
106. W.E.B. Du Bois, "Letter from W.E.B. Du Bois to Edwin Barclay," August 18, 1931, W.E.B. Du Bois Papers (MS 312), Special Collections and University Archives, University of Massachusetts Amherst Libraries, http://credo.library.umass.edu/view/full/mums312-b189-i093.
107. Herbert Aptheker, ed., *The Correspondence of W.E.B. Du Bois*, vol. 3 (Amherst: University of Massachusetts Press, 1973), 134, 144, 287–89.
108. Curtis, *Colored Memories*, 108.
109. Sundiata, *Brothers and Strangers*, 210.
110. "Lester A. Walton to US Secretary of State Cordell Hull," May 22, 1941, Box 8, Folder 8, Lester Walton Papers Sc MG 183, Schomburg Center for Research in Black Culture, Manuscripts, Archives and Rare Books Division, New York Public Library.
111. Lester A. Walton, "Liberia's New Industrial Development," *Current History (1916–1940)* 30, no. 1 (1929): 114.
112. Polk, *Contagions of Empire*, 13–47, 77–123.
113. Sundiata, *Black Scandal*, 161.
114. Cedric J. Robinson, "The African Diaspora and the Italo-Ethiopian Crisis," *Race & Class* 27, no. 2 (October 1, 1985): 60, 59, https://doi.org/10.1177/030639688502700204.
115. Jeffrey C. Stewart, "A New Negro Foreign Policy: The Critical Vision of Alain Locke and Ralph Bunche," in *African Americans in U.S. Foreign Policy: From the Era of*

Frederick Douglass to the Age of Obama, ed. Linda M. Heywood et al. (Urbana: University of Illinois Press, 2015), 32.

116. Stewart, 32, 33.
117. Carol Anderson, *Bourgeois Radicals: The NAACP and the Struggle for Colonial Liberation, 1941–1960* (New York: Cambridge University Press, 2015), 48–49, 80–81.
118. Straker, "The Land of Our Fathers."
119. Stewart, "A New Negro Foreign Policy," 54.
120. Alvin B. Tillery, *Between Homeland and Motherland: Africa, U.S. Foreign Policy, and Black Leadership in America* (Ithaca: Cornell University Press, 2011), 8, https://doi.org/10.7591/9780801461019.
121. Tillery, 150.
122. Anderson, *Bourgeois Radicals*, 163.
123. "Grafting Is Real Art in Liberia, Says Schuyler, Home from Abroad: Forced Labor Still Exists in Liberia Schuyler, Just Back from Republic, Describes Conditions. Grafters Rule Barclay Swells 15,000 Voters to 200,000," *Afro-American*, June 27, 1931, Proquest; George S. Schuyler, "Views and Reviews," *Pittsburgh Courier*, August 2, 1947, Proquest; George S. Schuyler, "Views and Reviews," *Pittsburgh Courier*, June 4, 1949, Proquest; George S. Schuyler, *The Reminiscences of George S. Schuyler, 1962*, ed. William T. Ingersoll (Alexandria: Alexander Street Press, 2003), 263, 264, 271. Schuyler notes that when he traveled to Liberia in 1931 to expose the abuses of the country's elite, he used the maps that Major Charles Young had drawn during his tours in the West African state.
124. "Rep. Powell Rips U.S. Snub of Afro-Asians," *Los Angeles Sentinel*, April 21, 1955; "Bev Carter Defends Kissinger on Angola," *Afro-American*, February 21, 1976; "Diggs Urges Better U. S. Attitude Toward Africa," *Daily Defender*, December 23, 1958.
125. For a sampling, see "State Dept. Hears Yergan on Plans to Help Africa," *Daily Worker*, March 28, 1944; "Progress in Liberia," *Negro History Bulletin* 15, no. 4 (1952): 79–79; Chatwood Hall, "As Good Will Gesture: Ethiopia Bids for Colored Personnel in Pact Plan," *Afro-American*, June 27, 1953, Proquest.
126. Tillery, *Between Homeland and Motherland*, 133, 148.
127. Jim McGee, "Rep. Dymally's Contacts Raise Issue of Public Trust, Private Interests," *Washington Post*, January 2, 1990, Proquest; Tommie Hill, "Gray's African Harvest: $150 Million in Deals," *Philadelphia Tribune*, August 28, 1984, Proquest.
128. Hon. Charles C. Diggs, Jr., Michigan, Chairman et al., "Report of the Special Study Mission to Africa November 27–December 14, 1965" (Committee on Foreign Affairs, House of Representatives, March 17, 1966), Congressional.ProQuest.
129. Carter Woodson, "Dr. Johnson Sees No Hope in Liberia Under Present Regime: History Association Hears That Government in Liberia Has Failed," *Afro-American*, November 28, 1931, Proquest.
130. Robert Pear, "Congress Gives African Leaders the Human Rights Test," *New York Times*, July 2, 1989, Proquest.
131. Robinson, "The African Diaspora and the Italo-Ethiopian Crisis," 60; Tillery, *Between Homeland and Motherland*, 4, 66.

132. For notable examples, see House Committee on Foreign Affairs, Subcommittee on Africa, "Foreign Assistance Legislation for FY80–FY81 Part 6: Economic and Military Assistance Programs in Africa," March 13, 1979, Congressional.ProQuest; House Committee on Foreign Affairs, Subcommittee on Human Rights and International Organizations, "Human Rights Situation in South Africa, Zaire, the Horn of Africa, and Uganda," August 21, 1984, Congressional.ProQuest.
133. Don Rojas, "African and African-American Leaders Hold Summit in W. Africa," *New York Amsterdam News*, April 27, 1991, Proquest; George B. N. Ayittey, "A Summit to Legitimize a Corrupt Regime? Africa: American Participants in Gabon Should Ask Hard Questions About Human Rights," *Los Angeles Times*, May 25, 1993; Proquest; Simon Barber, "Taking a Leading Role on the African Stage," *Sunday Times*, April 27, 1997.
134. Pear, "Congress Gives African Leaders the Human Rights Test."
135. W.E.B. Du Bois, "The African Roots of War," *Atlantic*, May 1915, https://www.theatlantic.com/magazine/archive/1915/05/the-african-roots-of-war/528897/.
136. Errol Anthony Henderson, *African Realism? International Relations Theory and Africa's Wars in the Postcolonial Era* (Lanham, MD: Rowman & Littlefield, 2015), 83.
137. Robert Vitalis, *White World Order, Black Power Politics: The Birth of American International Relations*, The United States in the World (Ithaca: Cornell University Press, 2015), ix, x, https://doi.org/10.7591/9781501701887.
138. W.E.B. Du Bois, *The Souls of Black Folk* (Oxford: Oxford University Press, 2007), 15.
139. Merze Tate, *The Disarmament Illusion: The Movement for a Limitation of Armaments to 1907* (New York: Macmillan, 1942), 11.
140. W.E.B. Du Bois, "Worlds of Color," *Foreign Affairs* 3, no. 3 (1925): 423, https://doi.org/10.2307/20028386.
141. Tate, *The Disarmament Illusion*, 351.
142. W.E.B. Du Bois, "Scholarly Delusion: Review of The Disarmament Illusion: The Movement for a Limitation of Armaments to 1907, by Merze Tate," *Phylon (1940–1956)* 4, no. 2 (1943): 189–91, https://doi.org/10.2307/271896.
143. Tate, *The Disarmament Illusion*, 161.
144. Tate, 358–59, 330.
145. Michael H. Hunt, *Ideology and U.S. Foreign Policy* (New Haven: Yale University Press, 2009), 80.
146. Tate, *The Disarmament Illusion*, 330, 359.
147. Merze Tate, *The United States and Armaments* (Cambridge, MA: Harvard University Press, 1948), 265.
148. Tate, 264.
149. Merze Tate, "The War Aims of World War I and World War II and Their Relation to the Darker Peoples of the World," *Journal of Negro Education* 12, no. 3 (1943): 523, https://doi.org/10.2307/2293070.
150. "General Bolte Sent to Ethiopia by U.S.," *New York Times*, June 12, 1951, Proquest; "General Bolte Sent to Ethiopia by U.S.," *New York Times*, June 12, 1951, Proquest; "President's Letter to Congress on U.N.: Acted Without Hesitation Lauds Troops

of Other Nations No Double Standard Cites Acheson's Speech U.N. Intensifies Activities No One Nation Can Have Its Way," *New York Times*, July 27, 1951, Proquest.

151. "Text of President's Address in Tennessee at Dedication of Air Research Center: A Welcome by the President in Tennessee," *New York Times*, June 26, 1951, Proquest; "Negus for U.S. Ideals, Collective Security," *New York Herald Tribune*, May 28, 1954, International Herald Tribune Historical Archive, 1887–2013, https://link.gale.com/apps/doc/XSGECV640708733/GDCS?u=uclosangeles&sid=bookmark-GDCS&xid=ea47c44c.
152. Norman E. Fiske, "Report of Military Observer with Italian Armies in East Africa Part 1," Military Intelligence Division, US War Department General Staff, March 25, 1936; J. M. Pittman, "Italo-Abyssinian War, 1935: Organization of Theatre Operations and Strategical Conduct of Campaign," US Army Infantry School, Regular Course, 1936–1937.
153. *Ethiopia in the Free World* (US Information Services, Periscope Film LLC, 1951).
154. *FRUS, 1950, The Near East, South Asia, and Africa, Volume V* (US Government Printing Office, 1978), doc. 914, https://history.state.gov/historicaldocuments/frus1950v05/d914.
155. Robinson, "The African Diaspora and the Italo-Ethiopian Crisis," 60.
156. "Ethiopia Gives, Doesn't Get: Great Powers Helped, Not Helping in Korea," *Afro-American*, December 30, 1950, Proquest.
157. "U. S. Asked to Give 100 Ships to Ethiopia," *New Journal and Guide*, May 19, 1951, Proquest.
158. Marcus Garvey, "Why Support a Lost Cause?," *Philadelphia Tribune*, January 21, 1937, Proques.
159. *FRUS, 1951, The Near East and Africa, Volume V* (US Government Printing Office, 1982), doc. 698, https://history.state.gov/historicaldocuments/frus1951v05/d698.
160. *FRUS, 1952–1954, Africa and South Asia, Volume XI, Part 1* (US Government Printing Office, 1983), doc. 196, https://history.state.gov/historicaldocuments/frus1952-54v11p1/d196.
161. Dagmawi Abebe, *The Emperor's Own: The History of the Ethiopian Imperial Bodyguard Battalion in the Korean War 1950–53*, Asia@War, no. 10 (Warwick, UK: Helion, 2019), 16.
162. *FRUS, 1948, Western Europe, Volume III* (US Government Printing Office, 1974), doc. 602, https://history.state.gov/historicaldocuments/frus1948v03/d602.
163. *FRUS, 1952–1954, Africa and South Asia, Volume XI, Part 1* (US Government Printing Office, 1983), doc. 188, https://history.state.gov/historicaldocuments/frus1952-54v11p1/d188.
164. John H. Spencer, *Ethiopia at Bay: A Personal Account of the Haile Selassie Years* (Hollywood, CA: Tsehai Publishers, 2006), 117.
165. Spencer, 263.
166. US Department of State, *United States Treaties and Other International Agreements, Volume 4, Part 1* (Washington, DC: US Government Printing Office, 1955), 421, https://tile.loc.gov/storage-services/service/ll/lltreaties//lltreaties-4-1/lltreaties-4-1.pdf

#page=429; *Volume 5, Part 1*, 749, https://tile.loc.gov/storage-services/service/ll/lltreaties//lltreaties-5-1/lltreaties-5-1.pdf#page=759.

167. Tekeda Alemu, "The Unmaking of Ethio-American Military Relations: U.S. Foreign Policy Toward the Ethiopian Revolution" (PhD diss., The Claremont Graduate School, 1983), 72, Proquest.
168. Edmond Joseph Keller, *Revolutionary Ethiopia: From Empire to People's Republic* (Bloomington: Indiana University Press, 1991), 79–80.
169. *FRUS, 1955–1957, Africa, Volume XVIII* (US Government Printing Office, 1989), doc. 109, https://history.state.gov/historicaldocuments/frus1955-57v18/d109.
170. *FRUS, 1955–1957*, doc. 110, https://history.state.gov/historicaldocuments/frus1955-57v18/d110.
171. *FRUS, 1952–1954, Africa and South Asia, Volume XI, Part 1* (US Government Printing Office, 1983), doc. 212, https://history.state.gov/historicaldocuments/frus1952-54v11p1/d212.
172. Homer Bigart, "Selassie Charges Egyptians Try Subversion in Ethiopia: Mistreatment Charged Selassie Charges Egyptians Try to Subvert Ethiopian Moslems Ethiopia to Get Fleet Nucleus," *New York Times*, February 16, 1957, Proquest.
173. Spencer, *Ethiopia at Bay*, 291–92.
174. Homer Bigart, "U.S. Is Regaining Ethiopia's Favor: Selassie, Angered by Slights, Mollified by Dulles Shift U.S. Is Regaining Ethiopia's Favor Soviet Followers Move In," *New York Times*, February 18, 1957, Proquest.
175. Bigart; Abebe, *The Emperor's Own*, 69
176. Bigart.
177. *FRUS, 1955–1957, Africa, Volume XVIII* (US Government Printing Office, 1989), doc. 120, https://history.state.gov/historicaldocuments/frus1955-57v18/d120; Bigart, "Selassie Charges Egyptians Try Subversion in Ethiopia."
178. Alemu, "The Unmaking of Ethio-American Military Relations," 68.
179. *FRUS, 1955–1957, Africa, Volume XVIII* (US Government Printing Office, 1989), doc. 117, https://history.state.gov/historicaldocuments/frus1955-57v18/d117.
180. Jay Walz, "U.S. Radio Station in Ethiopia Becomes Issue at African Parley," *New York Times*, May 15, 1963, Proquest.
181. *FRUS, 1964–1968, Volume XXIV, Africa* (US Government Printing Office, 1999), doc. 322, https://history.state.gov/historicaldocuments/frus1964-68v24/d322; doc. 327, https://history.state.gov/historicaldocuments/frus1964-68v24/d327.
182. *FRUS, 1969–1976, Volume E-6, Documents on Africa, 1973–1976* (US Government Printing Office, 2006), doc. 166, https://history.state.gov/historicaldocuments/frus1969-76ve06/d166.
183. Keller, *Revolutionary Ethiopia*, 79.
184. Edmond J. Keller, "The Revolutionary Transformation of Ethiopia's Twentieth-Century Bureaucratic Empire," *Journal of Modern African Studies* 19, no. 2 (June 1981): 322, https://doi.org/10.1017/S0022278X00016955.
185. Keller, 323.

186. Hon. Adam C. Powell, Jr., "Congressional Record-Appendix," vol. 102 (House of Representatives, Session 84–2, May 3, 1956), Congressional.ProQuest.
187. Hon. Charles C. Diggs Jr., "Congressional Record-Extension of Remarks," vol. 118 (House of Representatives, Session 92–2, July 27, 1972), Congressional.ProQuest.
188. Bernard Lemelin, "The Isolationist Sentiment in North Dakota During the Truman-Eisenhower Years," *Canadian Review of American Studies* 33, no. 1 (April 2003): 63, https://doi.org/10.3138/CRAS-s033-01-04.
189. Hon. William Langer, "Congressional Record-Appendix," vol. 100 (Senate, Session 83–2, June 23, 1954), Congressional.ProQuest.
190. Hon. Brad Gentry, "Congressional Record-Appendix," vol. 100 (House of Representatives, Session 83–2, March 22, 1954), Congressional.ProQuest.
191. Hon. Mike Mansfield, "Congressional Record," vol. 106 (Senate, Session 86–2, August 29, 1960).
192. Louis Lautier, "Five African Nations on Brink of Freedom," *Cleveland Call and Post*, June 18, 1960, Proquest.
193. Carl T. Rowan, "A Formula for Enemies," *Minneapolis Star*, August 28, 1970, Proquest.
194. Alan Joseph Ellender, "A Report on United States Foreign Operations" (Senate Committee on Appropriations, March 15, 1961), Congressional.ProQuest.
195. Miriam Alburn, "Senator's Reaction to Africa Doesn't Set Well Any Place," *Minneapolis Morning Tribune*, August 14, 1963, Proquest.
196. "Africans Protest Slur by Ellender: 20 Nations' Envoys Object to Charge of 'Inability,'" *New York Times*, June 20, 1963, Proquest.
197. Stanley Meisler, "State Department Uses Kid Gloves for Solons," *Austin Statesman*, January 2, 1963, Proquest.
198. "Repudiated Ellender Somewhere in Africa," *Atlanta Daily World*, December 16, 1962, Proquest.
199. Norman G. Cornish, "Rep. O'Hara Defends Gift of Flagship to Ethiopia," *Chicago Daily Defender*, April 24, 1962, Proquest.
200. "Thousands of Years: Self-Government in Ethiopia Refutes Slur," *Afro-American*, October 12, 1963, Proquest.
201. "Urges U. S. End All Arms Aid to African Nations," *Chicago Daily Defender*, March 18, 1963, Proquest.
202. Hendrick Smith, "Kennedy and Haile Selassie Agree on African Objectives," *St. Louis Post-Dispatch*, October 3, 1963, Proquest; "African Unity Is Foreseen: United States-Like Set-Up Predicted by Selassie," *Baltimore Sun*, October 4, 1963, Proquest.
203. Max Harrelson, "The Deepening Crisis: Racial Troubles Hurting U.S. Image Abroad," *Pittsburgh Post-Gazette*, August 8, 1963, Proquest.
204. Extract from Resolutions Adopted by the Summit Conference of Independent African States, May 22–25, 1963, "Congressional Hearing" (House Committee on Appropriations-Subcomittee on Foreign Operations, Export Financing, and Related Programs, July 5, 1963), Congressional.ProQuest.

205. Hon. Silvio Conte, "Congressional Hearing" (House Committee on Appropriations-Subcomittee on Foreign Operations, Export Financing, and Related Programs, July 5, 1963), Congressional.ProQuest.
206. Takele Merid and Alexander Meckelburg, "Abolitionist Decrees in Ethiopia: The Evolution of Anti-Slavery Legal Strategies from Menilek to Haile Selassie, 1889–1942," *Law and History Review* 42, no. 1 (February 2024): 99, 116, https://doi.org/10.1017/S073824802300055X.
207. W. Alphaeus Hunton, *Decision in Africa: Sources of Current Conflict* (New York: International Publishers, 1957), 113–14; "Interview with Kwame Ture, All-African People's Revolutionary Party," *Breakthrough: Political Journal of Prairie Fire Organizing Committee* 12, no. 1 (Summer 1988): 16, https://www.freedomarchives.org/Documents/Finder/DOC501_scans/Break/501.break.16.sum.88.pdf; author interview with chair of the Education Committee, New York chapter of the All African People's Revolutionary Party, 1972–1977, March 18, 2025.
208. "Rocky Sounds Alarm," *Afro-American*, July 27, 1963, Proquest.
209. Hon. William S. Broomfield, "Congressional Hearing: U.S.-South African Relations" (House Committee on Foreign Affairs, Subcommittee on Africa, May 26, 1966), Congressional.ProQuest.
210. "Resolutions Adopted by the Forty-Fourth Annual Convention of the NAACP at St. Louis, Missouri June 27, 1953," *Crisis*, August 1, 1953, Internet Archive.

2. "UNCLE TOM'S" AIR BASE?

1. Elliott P. Skinner, *African Americans and U.S. Policy Toward Africa, 1850–1924: In Defense of Black Nationality* (Washington, DC: Howard University Press, 1992), 36.
2. "The Avalon Project : The Federalist Papers: No. 14," https://avalon.law.yale.edu/18th_century/fed14.asp.
3. William V. S. Tubman, *The Official Papers of William V. S. Tubman, President of the Republic of Liberia: Covering Addresses, Messages, Speeches and Statements 1960–1967* (Monrovia, Liberia: Department of Information and Cultural Affairs, 1968), 342.
4. D. Elwood Dunn, *Liberia and the United States During the Cold War: Limits of Reciprocity* (New York: Palgrave Macmillan, 2009), 21–24.
5. I. K. Sundiata, *Black Scandal, America and The Liberian Labor Crisis, 1929–1936* (Philadelphia: Institute for the Study of Human Issues, 1980), 91–92, 109; Charles Spurgeon Johnson, *Bitter Canaan: The Story of the Negro Republic*, Black Classics of Social Science (New Brunswick, NJ: Transaction Books, 1987), lix.
6. Ronald W. Davis, "The Liberian Struggle for Authority on the Kru Coast," *International Journal of African Historical Studies* 8, no. 2 (1975): 222–65, https://doi.org/10.2307/216649; Harrison Ola Abingbade, "The Settler-African Conflicts: The Case of the Maryland Colonists and the Grebo 1840–1900," *Journal of Negro History* 66, no. 2 (July 1981): 93–109, https://doi.org/10.2307/2717280; Carl Patrick Burrowes, *Power and*

Press Freedom in Liberia, 1830–1970: The Impact of Globalization and Civil Society on Media-Government Relations (Trenton: Africa World Press, 2004), 112–13.

7. Dunn, *Liberia and the United States*, 194.
8. Hon. Homer D. Angell, "Congressional Record-Appendix," vol. 92 (House of Representatives, Session 79–2, July 26, 1946), Congressional.ProQuest.
9. Dunn, *Liberia and the United States*, 28.
10. Lester A. Walton, "The Importance of American Air Terminals in Liberia," Lester Walton Papers Sc MG 183, Schomburg Center for Research in Black Culture, Manuscripts, Archives and Rare Books Division, New York Public Library.
11. US Department of State, *Foreign Relations of the United States (FRUS) Diplomatic Papers, 1939, Volume IV, The Far East; The Near East and Africa* (US Government Printing Office, 1955), doc. 631, https://history.state.gov/historicaldocuments/frus1939v04/pg_565.
12. *FRUS Diplomatic Papers, 1939*, docs. 647, 648, 653.
13. *FRUS Diplomatic Papers, 1939*, doc. 669.
14. *FRUS Diplomatic Papers, 1939*, doc. 674.
15. Dunn, *Liberia and the United States*, 27.
16. "Roosevelt Visits Liberia: President Pays Respects to Race Troops, Barclay Fierce African Fighters Sail to Thick of Battle," *Atlanta Daily World*, January 29, 1943, Proquest.
17. "War Dept. Says Race Soldiers in Liberia: Important Base for Operations by Air and Sea Two Airports Constructed by Negroes," *Atlanta Daily World*, November 4, 1942, Proquest.
18. George S. Schuyler, "Views and Reviews," *Pittsburgh Courier*, October 31, 1942, Proquest.
19. Marjorie McKenzie, "Pursuit of Democracy: Roosevelt Studies Three Plans to Aid Negro Morale," *Pittsburgh Courier*, June 6, 1942, Proquest.
20. Charley Cherokee, "National Grapevine," *Chicago Defender*, December 5, 1942, Proquest.
21. "Push Lanier for Post of Minister to Liberia," *Pittsburgh Courier*, July 7, 1945, Proquest.
22. Alfred E. Smith, "GI Howl on Liberia Ousted Diplomat: Negro Named by Truman as Successor New Appointee Gets Approval by Dawson, Mrs. Bethune," *Chicago Defender*, June 16, 1945, Proquest.
23. George Padmore, "Padmore Sees Wall St. Invasion of Liberia," *Chicago Defender*, November 18, 1944, Proquest.
24. *FRUS Diplomatic Papers, 1939*, doc. 622, https://history.state.gov/historicaldocuments/frus1939v04/pg_558.
25. C. G. Woodson, "An Advance in Diplomacy," *Negro History Bulletin* 9, no. 5 (1946): 102.
26. "Patterson Urged to Maintain Base in Liberia," *Atlanta Daily World*, February 27, 1947, Proquest.
27. "Liberia's Lone Airport May Close," *Atlanta Daily World*, March 6, 1947, Proquest.
28. "Dawson Challenges U. S. to Give Tangible Recognition to Liberia," *New Journal and Guide*, June 14, 1947, Proquest.

29. "Truman Sees Closer Link with Liberia: . . . Commemorating the 100th Anniversary of Republic Unveiled," *Pittsburgh Courier*, August 2, 1947, Proquest.
30. "Stettinius's Aide Gets Fat Air Base Contract: Firm Owned by Illinois Politician Paid $300,000 Yearly to Run Roberts Field," *Afro-American*, April 30, 1949, Proquest.
31. It is worth noting, given his pleas to keep Roberts Field open, that Dr. Channing Tobias held a seat on the Liberia Company's board of directors.
32. "Liberian Renaissance: Sweeping Challenge," *New Journal and Guide*, July 3, 1948, Proquest.
33. Présence Africaine, Alioune Diop, and John A. Davis, *Africa from the Point of View of American Negro Scholars* (Paris: Présence Africaine, 1958), 358–59.
34. "Feel Barclay Visit Means Rubber Aid to U.S.," *Pittsburgh Courier*, June 5, 1943, Proquest.
35. *FRUS, 1952–1954, Africa and South Asia, Volume XI, Part 1* (US Government Printing Office, 1983), doc. 237, https://history.state.gov/historicaldocuments/frus1952-54v11p1/d237.
36. *FRUS, 1952–1954*, doc. 233, https://history.state.gov/historicaldocuments/frus1952-54v11p1/d233.
37. *FRUS, 1952–1954*, doc. 233.
38. "Liberian Renaissance: Sweeping Challenge," *New Journal and Guide*, July 3, 1948.
39. *FRUS, 1952–1954*, doc. 237, https://history.state.gov/historicaldocuments/frus1952-54v11p1/d237; doc. 238, https://history.state.gov/historicaldocuments/frus1952-54v11p1/d238.
40. *FRUS, 1952–1954*, doc. 239.
41. *FRUS, 1952–1954*, doc. 242.
42. Thomas Borstelmann, *The Cold War and the Color Line: American Race Relations in the Global Arena* (Cambridge: Harvard University Press, 2009), 88–90, https://doi.org/10.4159/9780674028548.
43. *FRUS, 1952–1954*, doc. 219.
44. *FRUS, 1952–1954*, doc. 243.
45. *FRUS, 1952–1954*, doc. 243.
46. James L. Hicks, "Tubman Gets Big Ovation: 500,000 Turn Out for Ticker Tape Welcome to Visitor," *The Call*, November 5, 1954, Proquest.
47. "They're Everybody's President and Vice President," *Los Angeles Sentinel*, November 1, 1956.
48. Burrowes, *Power and Press Freedom in Liberia*, 265.
49. For estimates of Liberia's indigenous population and "Americo-Liberian" population, see Joseph S. Roucek, "Liberia," *Journal of Geography* 54, no. 8 (November 1955): 407–13, https://doi.org/10.1080/00221345508982911.
50. Rayford W. Logan, "Liberia in the Family of Nations," *Phylon (1940–1956)* 7, no. 1 (1946): 10, https://doi.org/10.2307/271276.
51. Charles H. Wesley, "Liberia Begins Its Second Century," *Negro History Bulletin* 12, no. 3 (December 1, 1948): 57.
52. Burrowes, *Power and Press Freedom in Liberia*, 217.

53. Burrowes, 243.
54. Defense Intelligence Agency, "Liberia," National Intelligence Survey, December 1973.
55. "The Enhanced Strategic Importance of Liberia," *New Journal and Guide*, January 20, 1951, Proquest.
56. *FRUS, 1952–1954*, doc. 239; US Department of State Fourth Interdepartmental Survey Group, "Report for the President on Liberia and Tunisia," April 1, 1963, US Declassified Documents Online.
57. US Department of State, "Analysis of DOD Memorandum on Military Assistance Program," November 1966, Gale.com.
58. US White House, "Semi-Final Draft for U.S. Operations Plan for Liberia," November 26, 1958, US Declassified Documents Online; US National Security Council, "NSC Report #6005/1: U.S. Policy Toward West Africa," April 9, 1960, US Declassified Documents Online.
59. Dunn, *Liberia and the United States*, 204.
60. US Department of State, *FRUS, 1951, The Near East and Africa, Volume 5* (US Government Printing Office, 1982), doc. 713, https://history.state.gov/historicaldocuments/frus1951v05/d713.
61. "Liberian President Walter White, Duel: International Controversy Rages Over Barring of Two from Ballot," *Afro-American*, July 21, 1951, Proquest.
62. Akpojevbe Omasanjuwa and Junisa Phebean, "Acrimony in Colonial Liberia," *Journal of Universal History Studies* 3, no. 1 (June 6, 2020): 12, https://doi.org/10.38000/juhis.689657.
63. Jesse Walker, "Hunted by Government: Vows Return to Liberia to Face Sedition Charge," *Afro-American*, April 26, 1952, Proquest.
64. W. A. Hunton, "Liberia's Exploiters Hail Tubman's Inauguration," *Freedom*, February 1952, Tamiment Library & Robert F. Wagner Labor Archives, https://mc.dlib.nyu.edu/files/books/tamwag_fdm000014/tamwag_fdm000014_hi.pdf.
65. "Liberian President Tells Walter White to Mind Business," *Philadelphia Tribune*, June 3, 1951, Proquest.
66. Walter White, "A Suggestion for Change in the Name of the NAACP," *Chicago Defender*, September 3, 1949, Proquest; "NAACP Official Answers Tubman's Denunciation," *Atlanta Daily World*, July 18, 1951, Proquest.
67. "NAACP Official Answers Tubman's Denunciation."
68. Celestine Tutt, "Ambassador Edward Richard Dudley," interview, Foreign Affairs Oral History Project (Association for Diplomatic Studies and Training, April 3, 1981), https://tile.loc.gov/storage-services/service/mss/mfdip/2010/2010dud01/2010dud01.pdf.
69. Burrowes, *Power and Press Freedom in Liberia*, 112.
70. "Half Million Hail Tubman: NYC Ticker Tape Greets President," *Afro-American*, November 6, 1954, Proquest; Ralph J. Bunche, "Guest Column for Walter White," November 2, 1954, Box 395 Folder 18, Ralph J. Bunche Papers UCLA Library Special Collections, Charles E. Young Research Library.
71. Burrowes, *Power and Press Freedom in Liberia*, 238.
72. Burrowes, 256.

73. George S. Schuyler, *Slaves Today: A Story of Liberia* (New York: Brewer, Warren & Putnam, 1931).
74. For an early firsthand account of Firestone's practices, see Arthur I. Hayman, *Lighting Up Liberia* (New York: Creative Age Press, 1943).
75. George S. Schuyler, "Views and Reviews: Republicans Surprising Victory Saves Nation from Socialism," *Pittsburgh Courier*, November 15, 1952, Proquest.
76. George S. Schuyler, "The World Today," *New Pittsburgh Courier*, October 28, 1961, Proquest.
77. Carl Murphy, "Tubman Has Memory like Jim Farley's," *Afro-American*, February 9, 1952, Proquest.
78. "State Dept. Hears Yergan on Plans to Help Africa," *Daily Worker*, March 28, 1944.
79. "Yergan in Final Blast at Reds as He Leaves for Paris," *The Call*, October 29, 1948, Proquest; Max Yergan, "The American Negro and Mr. Robeson," *New York Herald Tribune*, April 27, 1949, International Herald Tribune Historical Archive, 1887–2013, https://link.gale.com/apps/doc/IHKFCZ711583894/GDCS?u=uclosangeles&sid=bookmark-GDCS&xid=d4e719ed.
80. Senate Hearing, "Nomination of Channing H. Tobias" (Senate Committee on Foreign Relations Subcommittee on Nominations, October 18, 1951), Congressional. ProQuest.
81. Joseph V. Baker, "Africa Council Ousts Robeson," *Philadelphia Inquirer Public Ledger*, May 2, 1948, Proquest; Gerald Horne, *Black and Red: W.E.B. Du Bois and the Afro-American Response to the Cold War, 1944–1963* (Albany: SUNY Press, 1986), 188–89.
82. Mary McLeod Bethune, "Mrs. Bethune Describes Liberia as 'Land of Opportunity' for All," *Chicago Defender*, February 2, 1952, Proquest.
83. "Rep. Dawson Calls Ballot 'Safeguard,'" *Afro-American*, February 14, 1953, Proquest.
84. "Robeson Me-Too's Commies," *Philadelphia Tribune*, April 23, 1949, Proquest.
85. "Robeson Scores Use of Guns on Africans," *St. Louis American*, February 23, 1950, Proquest.
86. Barbara Ransby, *Eslanda: The Large and Unconventional Life of Mrs. Paul Robeson*, 2nd ed. (La Vergne: Haymarket Books, 2022), 161.
87. Alphaeus Hunton, "Today's Guest Column," *Daily Worker*, November 16, 1944, Proquest; Hunton, "Liberia's Exploiters Hail Tubman's Inauguration."
88. See Alphaeus Hunton, *Decision in Africa: Sources of Current Conflict* (New York: International Publishers, 1957), chap. 8.
89. Lillian Scott, "U.S. Company to Exploit Liberian Resources in Deal with Government," *Chicago Defender*, October 4, 1947, Proquest.
90. Burrowes, *Power and Press Freedom in Liberia*, 242.
91. Paul McStallworth, "The Impact of West African Political Resurgence," *Negro History Bulletin* 20, no. 5 (1957): 100.
92. Rosalyn Higgins, "The International Court and South West Africa: The Implications of the Judgment," *International Affairs* 42, no. 4 (1966): 575–77.
93. Charles Loeb, "Back to Africa . . . This Time for Leadership," *Cleveland Call and Post*, May 2, 1959, Proquest.

94. Martin Luther King Jr., "'The Birth of a New Nation,' Sermon Delivered at Dexter Avenue Baptist Church," Martin Luther King, Jr. Research and Education Institute, April 7, 1957, https://kinginstitute.stanford.edu/king-papers/documents/birth-new-nation-sermon-delivered-dexter-avenue-baptist-church; James H. Meriwether, "The American Negro Leadership Conference on Africa and Its Arden House Conference: Politicizing & Institutionalizing the Relationship with Africa," *Afro-Americans in New York Life and History* 21, no. 2 (July 31, 1997): 14, Proquest.
95. Hon. Robert N. C. Nix, "Congressional Record-House," 88–1 (House of Representatives, July 29, 1963), Congressional.ProQuest.
96. Hon. Adam C. Powell Jr., "Congressional Record–House," vol. 101 (House of Representatives, Session 84–1, July 27, 1955), Congressional.ProQuest.
97. "Castro Is Defended by Powell," *Afro-American*, January 31, 1959, Proquest.
98. Powell Jr., "Congressional Record–House," July 27, 1955.
99. Robert S. McNamara, "Robert S. McNamara Statements as Secretary of Defense, February 5–March 15, 1962," March 15, 1962, ProQuest: Public Statements by the Secretaries of Defense, 1961–1969, the Kennedy and Johnson Administrations; 1960–1963.
100. "Tubman Comes to Call: New Look in Liberia," *Afro-American*, October 28, 1961, Proquest.
101. Roy Wilkins, "Wilkins Speaks: Nigerian War Saddens All Blacks," *Afro-American*, January 4, 1969, Proquest.
102. Roy Wilkins, "An Insult to Liberians," *Austin Statesman*, August 9, 1971, Proquest.
103. Dunn, *Liberia and the United States*, 83.
104. Dunn, 84.
105. Willie Givens, "Liberia's Tolbert Making Big Changes as President," *Afro-American*, January 22, 1972, Proquest; Julius Emeka Okolo, "Liberia: The Military Coup and Its Aftermath," *World Today* 37, no. 4 (1981): 152, http://www.jstor.org/stable/40395282.
106. Dunn, *Liberia and the United States*, 88.
107. J. Hughes, "William R. Tolbert, President of Liberia," *Africa Report* 24, no. 4 (July 1, 1979): 4.
108. Albert Porte, "The Enigma of a One-Party State," *Daily Observer*, July 12, 1982, East View Global Press Archive, https://gpa.eastview.com/crl/doda/newspapers/lodo19820712-01.1.4.
109. Stephen S. Hlophe, "Ruling Families and Power Struggles in Liberia," *Journal of African Studies* 6, no. 2 (Summer 1979): 80, Proquest; Godpower O. Okereke, "Crime and Punishment in Liberia," *International Journal of Comparative and Applied Criminal Justice* 37, no. 1 (February 1, 2013): 72, https://doi.org/10.1080/01924036.2011.571832.
110. Eric Werker and Lant Pritchett, "Deals and Development in a Resource-Dependent, Fragile State: The Political Economy of Growth in Liberia, 1960–2014," in *Deals and Development: The Political Dynamics of Growth Episodes*, ed. Lant Pritchett, Sen Kunal, and Eric Werker (Oxford: Oxford University Press, 2018), 51.
111. Stephen Ellis, "Liberia 1989–1994: A Study of Ethnic and Spiritual Violence," *African Affairs* 94, no. 375 (1995): 51.

112. "Liberian President Slain in Sergeant-Led Coup," *Atlanta Constitution*, April 13, 1980, Proquest.
113. Dunn, *Liberia and the United States*, 116, 120.
114. Hughes, "William R. Tolbert, President of Liberia," 7.
115. Louis Martin, "Attack S. African 'Dialogs," *Chicago Defender*, July 9, 1975, Proquest.
116. Dunn, *Liberia and the United States*, 132.
117. U.S. Central Intelligence Agency, "Africa Review," February 16, 1979, CIA FOIA Reading Room, https://www.cia.gov/readingroom/home.
118. U.S. Central Intelligence Agency, February 16, 1979.
119. "Freedom Fight Watched in Africa," *Afro-American*, January 3, 1961, Proquest.
120. Dunn, *Liberia and the United States*, 195.
121. US Department of State, "Secretary's Remarks in Monrovia," April 30, 1976, US Department of State FOIA Library.
122. U.S. Central Intelligence Agency, "Liberia: Difficult Passage Ahead," Intelligence Assessment, June 1983, https://www.cia.gov/readingroom/home.
123. "Thomas W. M. Smith to James J. Blake," January 15, 1976, W. Beverly Carter Papers, Manuscript Division, Library of Congress, Box 4, Folder 5.
124. US Department of State, "MAAG Requirement Study," May 19, 1976, US Department of State FOIA Library.
125. Dunn, *Liberia and the United States*, 118.
126. "Thomas W. M. Smith to James J. Blake"; US Department of State, *FRUS, 1977–1980, Volume XVII, Part 2, Sub-Saharan Africa* (US Government Printing Office, 2018), doc. 52, https://history.state.gov/historicaldocuments/frus1977-80v17p2/d52.
127. US Department of State, "MAAG Requirement Study," May 19, 1976.
128. Dunn, *Liberia and the United States*, 204.
129. Celestine Tutt, "Ambassador William Beverly Carter Jr.," interview, Foreign Affairs Oral History Project (Association for Diplomatic Studies and Training, April 30, 1981), https://tile.loc.gov/storage-services/service/mss/mfdip/2010/2010car01/2010car01.pdf.
130. "W. Beverly Carter to Mr. Jesse Dixon," November 29, 1973, W. Beverly Carter Papers, Manuscript Division, Library of Congress, Box 5, Folder 11.
131. "Jackson Holds Fruitful Talks in Liberia," *Afro-American*, December 2, 1972, Proquest."
132. "Congressmen Seek Facts on Current African Tour," *New York Amsterdam News*, July 9, 1975, Proquest.
133. "Alpha Phi Alpha Convenes in Liberia," *Chicago Defender*, September 2, 1976, Proquest.
134. "A. B. Tolbert Receives Key," *Los Angeles Sentinel*, January 5, 1978, Proquest.
135. "NAACP Lauded for Africa Focus," *New York Amsterdam News*, June 17, 1978, Proquest.
136. "Another Baptist President with Ties to Georgia," *San Francisco Examiner*, April 3, 1978, Proquest; Tolbert White, "The Brothers Tolbert," *Financial Times*, November 14, 1974, Financial Times Historical Archive, https://link.gale.com/apps/doc/HS230

2954213/GDCS?u=uclosangeles&sid=bookmark-GDCS&xid=8af9cfae; Henry Bolma Fahnbulleh, Sr., "The Nature of Our New Society," *Daily Observer*, April 15, 1981, East View Global Press Archive, https://gpa.eastview.com/crl/doda/newspapers/lodo19810415-01.1.9.

137. Julius Emeka Okolo, "Liberia: The Military Coup and Its Aftermath," *World Today* 37, no. 4 (1981): 152, http://www.jstor.org/stable/40395282.
138. "World News Briefs: U.S. Officials Visit Uganda to Weigh End of Embargo Liberia Suspends Rights in Aftermath of Riots Soviet Said to 'Blockade' Wife of Freed Dissident Bombs Explode in Paris; Anarchists Are Suspected," *New York Times*, May 3, 1979, Proquest.
139. Okolo, "Liberia: The Military Coup and Its Aftermath," 153.
140. Simon Anekwe, "20 Liberian Students Arrested After Sit-In," *New York Amsterdam News*, May 12, 1979, Proquest.
141. "Politics, Economics Highlight Visit of President Tolbert," *Afro-American*, October 13, 1979, Proquest.
142. US Department of State, *Foreign Relations of the United States, 1977–1980, Volume XVII, Part 2, Sub-Saharan Africa* (Washington, DC: US Government Printing Office, 2018), doc. 49, https://history.state.gov/historicaldocuments/frus1977-80v17p2/d49.
143. *FRUS, 1977–1980.*
144. "Thomas W. M. Smith to Mr. Moose," May 21, 1979, W. Beverly Carter Papers. Manuscript Division, Library of Congress, Box 5, Folder 2.
145. Graham Hovey, "U.S. Is Sending First Mission to Liberia Since Coup," *New York Times*, June 1, 1980, Proquest.
146. *FRUS, 1977–1980, Volume XVII, Part 2, Sub-Saharan Africa*, doc. 59, https://history.state.gov/historicaldocuments/frus1977-80v17p2/d59.
147. *FRUS, 1977–1980*, doc. 60, https://history.state.gov/historicaldocuments/frus1977-80v17p2/d60.
148. US Central Intelligence Agency, "Postcoup Prospects in Liberia," Interagency Intelligence Memorandum, December 1980.
149. *FRUS, 1977–1980*, doc. 60.
150. *FRUS, 1977–1980*, doc. 61, https://history.state.gov/historicaldocuments/frus1977-80v17p2/d61.
151. William Gray, "Why Blacks Must Get Involved in Shaping U.S. Foreign Policy," *Philadelphia Tribune*, June 27, 1980, Proquest.
152. Gray.
153. William Raspberry, "Liberia Brutality Erodes Coup's Moral Basis," *Austin American Statesman*, May 2, 1980, Proquest.
154. Burrowes, *Power and Press Freedom in Liberia*, 2.
155. US Central Intelligence Agency, "Liberia: Doe's Expectations," September 21, 1983, CIA FOIA Reading Room, https://www.cia.gov/readingroom/.
156. Dunn, *Liberia and the United States*, 154.
157. Dunn, 174–75.

158. US Department of State Senior Interagency Group No. 36, "NSSD 4–83: U.S. Strategy Towards Liberia," June 16, 1983, CIA FOIA Reading Room, https://www.cia.gov/readingroom/.
159. J. Zamgba Browne, "Black Caucus to Doe: Shape Up or Ship Out," *New York Amsterdam News*, June 22, 1985, Proquest.
160. J. Zamgba Browne, "Doe's Goons to Kill Dissidents?," *New York Amsterdam News*, August 31, 1985, Proquest.
161. Browne, "Doe's Goons."
162. Hon. George Crockett Jr., "Congressional Hearing-Liberia: Recent Developments and U.S. Foreign Policy" (House Committee on Foreign Affairs, Subcommittee on Human Rights and International Organizations, January 23, 1986), Congressional.ProQuest.
163. Ethel Payne, "Behind the Scenes: Ask Release of Ellen Sirleaf, Liberian Women Seek End to Repression," *Afro-American*, March 29, 1986, Proquest.
164. Robert Pear, "Congress Gives African Leaders the Human Rights Test," *New York Times*, July 2, 1989, Proquest; Michael K. Frisby, "Black Leaders Get South Africa Pledge: Baker Says US Sanctions Won't Be Lifted Until Dismantling of Apartheid Begins," *Boston Globe*, March 13, 1990, Proquest.
165. Michael Getler, "Hill May Block Somalian Base Pact," *Washington Post*, September 18, 1980, Proquest; Pear, "Congress Gives African Leaders the Human Rights Test"; Frank McCoy, "TransAfrica Explores New Challenges," *Black Enterprise*, August 1992, Proquest.
166. See, for example, *FRUS, 1961–1963, Volume XXI, Africa* (US Government Printing Office, 1995), doc. 367, https://history.state.gov/historicaldocuments/frus1961-63v21/d367.
167. "Bishop, Housewife Testify Against Atlantic Pact: Walls Says Arms Could Be Used Against Oppressed Colonials: Red Label Pointed Out," *Afro-American*, May 28, 1949, Proquest.
168. "Liberating Liberia," *Afro-American*, July 20, 1929; "Stop Backing Tshombe, Urges Negro Leaders," *Call and Post*, December 5, 1964, Proquest; "Group Labels Amin Traitor to Continent," *Afro-American*, February 20, 1971, Proquest.
169. Bernard Weinraub, "U.S. Is Sending African Nations More Arms Aid: U.S. Is Doubling Arms Aid to African Nations," *New York Times*, July 3, 1983, Proquest.
170. "Hill May Block Somalian Base Pact," *Washington Post*, September 18, 1980; "Washington to Raise Military Aid to Sudan," *Ethiopian Herald*, June 10, 1984; Pear, "Congress Gives African Leaders the Human Rights Test."
171. See, for example, Raymond Bonner, "African Dictators, American Silence," *New York Times*, June 30, 1989, Proquest; Stephen Chapman, "Africans Have Been Forced to Skip Democracy's Party," *Chicago Tribune*, April 15, 1990, Proquest; William Raspberry, "Africans Oppressing Africans," *Washington Post*, May 21, 1990, Proquest.
172. Crockett, "Congressional Hearing-Liberia."
173. Chester Crocker, "On U.S.'s Actions Towards Apartheid," *Chicago Defender*, March 11, 1985, Proquest.
174. "U.S. Is Sending African Nations More Arms Aid," *New York Times*, July 3, 1983.

175. Tim Naftali, "Ronald Reagan's Long-Hidden Racist Conversation with Richard Nixon," *Atlantic*, July 30, 2019, https://www.theatlantic.com/ideas/archive/2019/07/ronald-reagans-racist-conversation-richard-nixon/595102/.
176. Jon Nordheimer, "Reagan Attacks Kissinger for His Stand on Rhodesia," *New York Times*, May 1, 1976, Proquest.
177. Noel C. Koch, "Memorandum for the Secretary of Defense: My Visit to Africa and Europe" (Department of Defense International Security Affairs, March 15, 1983), Office of the Secretary of Defense and Joint Staff (OSD/JS) FOIA Reading Room, https://www.esd.whs.mil/FOID/Reading-Room/.
178. US Department of State, "An Assessment of Reagan Administration Political Strategy in Africa from 1981 Through 1984," May 31, 2025, US Declassified Documents Online.
179. Siba N. Grovogui, "Come to Africa: A Hermeneutics of Race in International Theory," *Alternatives* 26, no. 4 (October 1, 2001): 440, https://doi.org/10.1177/030437540102600404.
180. Darren C. Brunk, "Curing the Somalia Syndrome: Analogy, Foreign Policy Decision Making, and the Rwandan Genocide," *Foreign Policy Analysis* 4, no. 3 (July 1, 2008): 304, https://doi.org/10.1111/j.1743-8594.2008.00071.x.
181. *President Ronald Reagan's Meeting with President Mohammed Siad Barre of Somalia*, video, March 11, 1982, https://catalog.archives.gov/id/66383776; Helen Winternitz, "U.S. Backs Mobutu in Spite of Repressions," *Sun*, February 15, 1984, Proquest; "Reagan Praises Liberian Leader," *Boston Globe*, August 18, 1982, Proquest.
182. "U.S. Aims to Head Off Threat of Famine," *Record*, June 4, 1994, Proquest.

3. THE HEART OF DARK OPERATIONS

1. Hon. Ronald Dellums, "Congressional Record Daily-Extension of Remarks," Volume 133 (House of Representatives, Session 100–1, February 27, 1987), Congressional. ProQuest.
2. James Brooke, "The CIA Said to Send Weapons Via Zaire to Angolan Rebels," *New York Times*, February 1, 1987, Proquest.
3. "Conyers Vows to Seek Aid Cutoff for Zaire," *Associated Press*, December 10, 1986, LexisNexis.
4. Lise A. Namikas, *Battleground Africa: Cold War in the Congo, 1960–1965*, Cold War International History Project Series (Washington, DC: Woodrow Wilson Center Press, 2013), 189; Piero Gleijeses, *Conflicting Missions: Havana, Washington, and Africa, 1959–1976* (Chapel Hill: University of North Carolina Press, 2002), 361.
5. Chester A. Crocker, *High Noon in Southern Africa: Making Peace in a Rough Neighborhood* (New York: Norton, 1992), 280.
6. "Summary of Secretary of Defense Caspar Weinberger's meeting with Zairian President Mobutu Sese Seko regarding US military assistance to Zaire," November 2, 1985, National Security Council, US Declassified Documents Online.

7. "Background information on a disagreement between the Departments of State and Defense regarding a Defense agreement with Zairian President Mobutu Sese Seko" (1987), US Declassified Documents Online.
8. National Security Briefing, July 25, 1960, *Foreign Relations of the United States (FRUS), 1964–1968, Volume 23: Congo, 1960–1968*, doc. 7, https://history.state.gov/historicaldocuments/frus1964-68v23/d7.
9. Chairman of the Joint Chiefs of Staff memorandum to Gates, *FRUS, 1958–1960, Volume 14: Africa*, doc. 181, https://history. state.gov/historicaldocuments/frus1958-60v14/d181.
10. Captain Giles K. Van Nederveen, "USAF Airlift Into the Heart of Darkness, the Congo 1960–1978, Implications for Modern Air Mobility Planners," Research Paper, 5, LexisNexis.
11. Ebere Nwaubani, "Eisenhower, Nkrumah and the Congo Crisis," *Journal of Contemporary History* 36, no. 4 (2001): 607.
12. Chairman of the Joint Chiefs of Staff memorandum to Gates, *FRUS*, August 18, 1960.
13. Memorandum to Gates.
14. Memorandum to Gates.
15. United States Mission [UN] telegram to State Department, July 14, 1960, *FRUS, 1958–1960, Volume 14*, doc. 123, https://history.state.gov/historicaldocuments/frus1958-60v14/d123. See also State Department telegram to American Embassy [Brussels], August 2, 1960, *FRUS, 1958–1960, Volume 14*, doc. 160; State Department telegram United States Mission [UN], December 8, 1960, *FRUS, 1958–1960, Volume 14*, doc. 279.
16. David Gibbs, "The United Nations, International Peacekeeping and the Question of 'Impartiality': Revisiting the Congo Operation of 1960," *Journal of Modern African Studies* 38, no. 3 (2000): 359–82.
17. Stephen Weissman, "CIA Covert Action in Zaire and Angola: Patterns and Consequences," *Political Science Quarterly* 94, no. 2 (1979): 263–82; Ludo De Witte, *The Assassination of Lumumba* (London: Verso, 2001), 113–24; Namikas, *Battleground Africa*, 125–26.
18. Walter Dorn, "The UN's First Air Force: Peacekeepers in Combat, Congo 1960–64," *Journal of Military History* 77, no. 4 (2013): 1412.
19. Namikas, *Battleground Africa*, 208.
20. "Six Leaders Ask US Withdrawal from Congo Strife," *Philadelphia Tribune*, December 1, 1964.
21. "Malcolm X Off to Smethwick," *Times* (London), February 12, 1965.
22. James H. Meriwether, *Proudly We Can Be Africans: Black Americans and Africa, 1935–1961* (Chapel Hill: University of North Carolina Press, 2002), 224–28; Alvin B. Tillery Jr., *Between Homeland and Motherland: Africa, US Foreign Policy, and Black Leadership in America* (Ithaca: Cornell University Press, 2011), 117–18.
23. Alvin C. Adams "Chicagoans Blast Tshombe as an 'Uncle Tom': Lumumba Slaying May Hurt West in Africa," *Chicago Daily Defender*, February 14, 1961.

24. Edward Reeves, "Richard Wright Hits U.S. Racial Hypocrisy: Country Is Rapped," *Chicago Daily Defender*, November 28, 1960.
25. Peter Kihss, "Tshombe Support Rises in Congress: Legislators in Both Parties Assail US Congo Role," *New York Times*, December 15, 1961.
26. Walter Shapiro, "The US Senate's Oldest Office Building Honors a Racist: Richard Russell Was a Segregationist and a Fervent Opponent of Civil Rights. So Why Does His Name Still Adorn the Russell Senate Office Building?," *New Republic*, April 26, 2021.
27. "Proposed US Assistance to Moise Tshombe," Congressional Record—Senate, Congress Session 90–1, July 21, 1967, Congressional.ProQuest.
28. "Negro Leaders Visit Senate, Hear Rights Bill Heartbeat," *St.Petersburg Times*, March 27, 1964, Proquest.
29. "Amendment No. 1399, Purpose: To Provide Assistance to the National Union for the Total Independence of Angola," Congressional Record Bound—Congressional Record, CR-1985-1210, Congress Session 99–1, December 10, 1985, Congressional ProQuest; "The Regional Conflict in Angola and Soviet Relations," Congressional Record Daily Edition—Senate, 134 Cong Rec S 7045, Congress Session 100–2, Congressional.ProQuest; Sanford J. Ungar, "Washington: The New Conservatives," *Atlantic*, February 1979; Lois Romano, "Playing it Zaire," *Washington Post*, October 22, 1985.
30. "Army Strongman Joseph Mobutu Key Figure in Congo's Recovery," *Chicago Daily Defender*, May 23, 1963, Proquest; "General Mobutu Visits Mt. Kisco," *New York Amsterdam News*, June 8, 1963, Proquest.
31. "Soviets Gamble on Wrong Man in Congo, and Lose," *Chicago Daily Defender*, July 6, 1961, Proquest.
32. Hon. Charles C. Diggs, Jr., Michigan, Chairman et al., "Report of the Special Study Mission to Africa November 27–December 14, 1965," Committee on Foreign Affairs, House of Representatives, March 17, 1966, Congressional.ProQuest.
33. Phil Newsom, "Mobutu Remained Silent Too Long," *Chicago Daily Defender*, December 2, 1965, Proquest.
34. Gleijeses, *Conflicting Missions*, 262.
35. Richard D. Mahoney, *JFK: Ordeal in Africa* (New York: Oxford University Press, 1983), 22–23.
36. Central Intelligence Memorandum, Subject: Holden Roberto, 11 October 1961, Central Intelligence Agency [CREST, FOIA Reading Room], https://www.cia.gov/library/readingroom/docs/CIA-RDP79S00427A000500020020-1.pdf; William Minter, *Apartheid's Contras: An Inquiry Into the Roots of War in Angola and Mozambique* (London: Zed Books, 1994).
37. J. E. Davies, *Constructive Engagement? Chester Crocker and American Policy in South Africa, Namibia & Angola 1981–8* (Athens: Ohio University Press, 2007), 13. For early indications of Savimbi's collaboration with the Portuguese, see Colin Legum, "What Really Happened at Mogadishu?" *Africa Report* 19, no. 4 (1974): 42–44.
38. Gleijeses, *Conflicting Missions*, 243–44.
39. Minter, *Apartheid's Contras*, 20.

40. Gleijeses, *Conflicting Missions*, 282.
41. Piero Gleijeses, "Interview with Robert W. Hultslander, Last CIA Station Chief in Luanda, Angola" (1998), Electronic Briefing Book #67, Wilson Center National Security Archive.
42. "Opening Address by Mobutu Sese-Seko at a Conference of African and American Representatives at the Palais de la Nation, Kinshasa, Zaire, 21 January 1975," *Africa Report* (March–April 1975), 4.
43. Crawford Young and Thomas Turner, *The Rise and Decline of the Zairian State* (Madison: University of Wisconsin Press, 2013), 326.
44. Russell Rickford, *We Are an African People: Independent Education, Black Power, and the Radical Imagination* (Oxford: Oxford University Press, 2016), 151.
45. Kevin C. Dunn, "Imagining Mobutu's Zaire: The Production and Consumption of Identity in International Relations," *Millennium* 30, no. 2 (2001): 251–52.
46. "Opening Address by Mobutu Sese-Seko."
47. *FRUS, 1969–1976, Volume E-6, Documents on Africa, 1973–1976*, doc. 267, Office of the Historian, https://history.state.gov/historicaldocuments/frus1969-76ve06/d267.
48. *FRUS, 1969–1976*, doc. 23, https://history.state.gov/historicaldocuments/frus1969-76ve06/d23.
49. Gleijeses, *Conflicting Missions*, 293.
50. Leslie Gelb, "US, Soviet, China Reported Aiding Portugal, Angola," *New York Times*, September 25, 1975.
51. Senator Edward Kennedy, "What America Should Do," *Africa Report*, November–December 1975, 46.
52. Gleijeses, *Conflicting Missions*, 289.
53. "Black Caucus Demands End to US Angola Intervention," *Oakland Post*, December 25, 1987.
54. Senator Dick Clark, "An Alternative U.S. Policy," *Africa Report*, January–February 1976, 16.
55. It was this legislative effort that Kissinger had aimed to overcome with his abortive smuggling operation at Roberts Field.
56. Charles C. Diggs, "America Should Help Southern Africa Remove Chains of White Rule," *Los Angeles Times*, April 19, 1976, Proquest.
57. "Interview: Jimmy Carter on Africa," *Africa Report*, May–June 1976, 19.
58. Michael G. Schatzberg, *Mobutu or Chaos: The United States and Zaire, 1960-1990* (Lanham: University Press of America, 1991), 67.
59. Van Nederveen, "USAF Airlift."
60. Don Oberdorfer, "Hill Panel Moves to Reorient U.S. Policies in Africa," *Washington Post*, May 3, 1977, Proquest.
61. Brandon Grove, *Behind Embassy Walls: The Life and Times of an American Diplomat* (Columbia: University of Missouri Press, 2005), 272.
62. "Governor Ronald Reagan's Southern Africa Policy," *Africa Report*, July–August 1976, 15.

63. Tim Naftali, "Ronald Reagan's Long-Hidden Racist Conversation with Richard Nixon," *Atlantic*, July 30, 2019; Daniel S. Lucus, *Reconsidering Reagan: Racism, Republicans, and the Road to Trump* (Boston: Beacon Press, 2020), 198.
64. Gerald Horne, *From the Barrel of a Gun: The United States and the War Against Zimbabwe, 1965–1980* (Chapel Hill: University of North Carolina Press, 2001), 84; Kyle Burke, *Revolutionaries for the Right: Anti-communist Internationalism and Paramilitary Warfare in the Cold War* (Chapel Hill: University of North Carolina Press, 2018), 47, 60, 78; Jeremiah Denton, "The Role of the Senate Subcommittee on Security and Terrorism in the Development of U.S. Policy against Terrorism," *Ohio Northern University Law Review* 13, no. 1 (1986): 19.
65. Andrew DeRoache, *Black, White, and Chrome: The United States and Zimbabwe, 1953–1998* (Trenton: Africa World Press, 2002), 266; "Voting Rights Act and the South African Connection," *Philadelphia Tribune*, May 22, 1981; William Darity Jr., M'Balou Camara, and Nancy MacLean, "Setting the Record Straight on the Libertarian South African Economist W. H. Hutt and James M. Buchanan," Institute for New Economic Thinking Working Paper, May 26, 2022, 10; "Civil Rights: No Action in '84," *MacNeil/Lehrer News Hour* transcript, October 3, 1984.
66. William Minter, "Behind the UNITA Curtain," *Africa Report*, May–June 1990, 48.
67. "Black Caucus Blasts Hatch Complaint Over TransAfrica; Senator Backs Down," *Associated Press*, October 6, 1989; "Washington News," *United Press International*, December 8, 1981; "Angola Guerrilla Leader Drawing Diverse US Support," *Associated Press*, November 25, 1985.
68. Gary Thatcher, "Activists Make US Policy Toward South Africa a Campaign Issue," *Christian Science Monitor*, April 20, 1987; Gary Silverman, "Democrats Agree to Review Angola Policy," *United Press International*, May 14, 1990.
69. Jennifer Seymour Whitaker, "Africa Beset," *Foreign Affairs*, January 1, 1984.
70. Crocker, *High Noon in Southern Africa*, 64–65.
71. Patrick E. Tyler and David B. Ottaway, "The Selling of Jonas Savimbi and a $600,000 Tab; Public Relations Firm Paved Guerrilla's Way," *Washington Post*, February 9, 1986.
72. Daniel Volman, "Africa and the New World Order," *Journal of Modern African Studies* 1, no. 31 (1993): 1–30; Brooke, "Weapons Via Zaire."
73. CIA, "Angola-Zaire and Uneasy Peace," July 1986.
74. CIA, "Angola-Zaire and Uneasy Peace."
75. US Embassy Kinshasa, "Actions Needed to Meet a Yet Quiet Crisis in Our Relations with Zaire," January 1986, US State Department Virtual FOIA Reading Room, https://foia.state.gov/Search/Search.aspx.
76. US Embassy Kinshasa, "Review of US/Zaire Relations," Ronald Reagan Presidential Library Archive, Simi Valley, CA, July 1984, National Security Council Working File.
77. William Pascoe, "Strengthening the US-Zaire Relationship," Heritage Foundation, December 1986, https://www.heritage.org/report/strengthening-the-us-zaire-relationship.

78. "The Israeli Presence in Black Africa," July 1984, NARA Central Intelligence Agency.
79. Ian Black, "US Boosts Aid to Chad as Fighting Intensifies," *Washington Post*, August 5, 1983.
80. "Zaire: A Look at a Post-Mobutu Regime," September 1983, NARA Central Intelligence Agency.
81. US Embassy in Kinshasa, "Review of US/Zaire Relations," July 1984, Reagan National Security Council Working File.
82. Trevor Parfitt and Stephen P. Riley, *The African Debt Crisis* (New York: Routledge, 2011), 85.
83. US Embassy in Kinshasa, "Review of US/Zaire Relations," July 1984.
84. Michael McFaul, "Rethinking the 'Reagan Doctrine' in Angola," *International Security* 14, no. 3 (1990): 99–135.
85. Pascoe, "US–Zaire Relationship," 3.
86. Brooke, "Weapons Via Zaire."
87. Robert M. Gates, *From the Shadows: The Ultimate Insiders Story of Five Presidents and How They Won the Cold War* (New York: Touchstone, 2007), 347.
88. McFaul, "Rethinking the 'Reagan Doctrine,'" 99–135; George Wright, *The Destruction of a Nation: United States Policy Towards Angola Since 1945* (London: Pluto Press, 1997), 120–21.
89. Gates, *From the Shadows*, 347.
90. "Official Working Visit of Zairian President Mobutu Sese Seko," December 1986, United States State Department, US Declassified Documents Online.
91. "Official Working Visit."
92. Michael Putzel, "Reagan Promises Debt Help to Zairian Leader," *Associated Press*, December 9, 1986.
93. "Conyers Vows to Seek Aid Cutoff for Zaire," December 10, 1986.
94. John Friederland, "Zaire, Brief Flirtation as Rebel Debtor Ends, Returns to IMF," *Inter-Press Service*, March 26, 1987.
95. Clyde Farnsworth, "$327 Loan Set for Egypt by IMF," *New York Times*, March 16, 1987.
96. Blaine Harden, "Seeds of Reform Grow Slowly in Zaire; Corruption Pervades Economy Despite Steps to Please Creditors," *Washington Post*, November 20, 1987.
97. Parfitt and Riley, *African Debt Crisis*, 95–96; William Reno, *Warlord Politics and African States* (Boulder: Lynne Rienner, 1999), 151; Volman, "New World Order," 1–30.
98. Wright, *Destruction of a Nation*, 127.
99. US Embassy Kinshasa, "President Mobutu Comments on Kamina and Alleged Aid to UNITA," March 1987, US Declassified Documents Online.
100. US Embassy Kinshasa, "President Mobutu's Commentary During Ambassador's Credential Presentation Ceremony," January 1988, US Declassified Documents Online.
101. Volman, "New World Order."
102. G. R. Berridge, "Diplomacy and the Angola/Namibia Accords," *International Affairs* 65, no. 3 (1989): 463–79.

103. Peter Spielmann, "US Officials Say No Diplomatic Recognition for Angola Without UNITA Talks," *Associated Press*, December 21, 1988.
104. Herman J. Cohen, *Intervening in Africa: Superpower Peacemaking in a Troubled Continent* (New York: Palgrave Macmillan, 2000), 95–96; Reed Kramer, "Lobby Gets Results for Savimbi," *Africa News* 32, no. 5–6 (November 1989).
105. Rakiya Omaar, "A Question of Human Rights," *Africa Report* (May–June 1989).
106. Ruth Sinai, "White House Wants to Keep Angolan Aid Covert Despite Peace Accord," *Associated Press*, June 12, 1991.
107. Cohen, *Intervening in Africa*, 92–93.
108. Wright, *Destruction of a Nation*, 149.
109. Samantha Sparks, "Savimbi Meets Bush as Peace Accord Crumbles," *Guardian*, October 5, 1989.
110. "Memorandum of Conversation: Meeting with Mobutu Sese Seko, President of Zaire," October 1989, George H. W. Bush Presidential Library and Archive, College Station, TX, United States National Security Council.
111. "Memorandum of Conversation."
112. US Defense Security Cooperation Agency, Data Management Division, "Foreign Military Construction Sales and Military Assistance Facts as of September 30, 1990," Washington, DC, 1990.
113. Lally Weymouth, "Endgame in Angola: Is The CIA Pulling the Plug on Savimbi?," *Washington Post*, March 25, 1990.
114. Brooke, "Weapons Via Zaire."
115. Alan George, "US Arms Boost Angolan Rebels," *Guardian*, June 25, 1990.
116. "UNITA Aid Made Conditional," *Africa News-All Africa*, November 12, 1990.
117. "US Policy Hinders Peace in Angola," *Congressional Record Daily Edition*, Extension of Remarks, 136 Cong Rec E2198, Congress Session 101–2, June 28, 1990, Congressional.ProQuest.
118. "Squaring Off on Angola," *Africa News-All Africa*, June 18, 1990.
119. Jim Drinkard, "House Panel Preserves Covert Aid Programs for Angola, Cambodia, Afghanistan," *Associated Press*, September 12, 1990; "House Proceedings," Congressional Record Bound—Congressional Record, CR 1990-1017, Congress Session 101–2, October 17, 1990, Congressional.ProQuest.
120. Jim Lobe, "Zaire: Bush Administration Defends Aid," *Inter-Press Service*, April 11, 1990.
121. "Friends to the End," *All Africa: Africa News*, October 21, 1991.
122. "Zaire: Bush Renews Pressure on Mobutu to Transfer Power," *Inter-Press Service*, December 8, 1992.

4. MAKING BLACK FRIENDS

1. Embassy of the Republic of Uganda, "News Briefs," *Uganda Newsletter*, January/February 1989.
2. Embassy of the Republic of Uganda, "News Briefs."

3. Neil Henry, "A Stranger in Africa; in the Continent of My Ancestors, Was I a Returned Son or Just Another Westerner?," *Washington Post*, August 18, 1991, Proquest.
4. Francis E. S. Katana, "A Call from Uganda," *Washington Post*, August 31, 1991.
5. Elizabeth Mundschenk, "USA and Uganda; Wherever Injustice Exists, People Die," *USA Today*, February 1, 1989, LexisNexis.
6. Henry, "A Stranger in Africa."
7. Embassy of the Republic of Uganda, "News Briefs," *Uganda Newsletter*, March/April 1989.
8. Donnie Radcliffe, "Maureen Reagan's Capital Connection," *Washington Post*, February 7, 1989, Proquest; Embassy of the Republic of Uganda, "Maureen Reagan Calls for Strengthening USA-Uganda Ties," *Uganda Newsletter*, September/October 1988.
9. Embassy of the Republic of Uganda, "President Yoweri Museveni Visits the United States of America," *Uganda Newsletter*, January/February 1989; "News Briefs," January/February 1989.
10. Hans Peter Schmitz, *Transnational Mobilization and Domestic Regime Change: Africa in Comparative Perspective*, International Political Economy Series (Basingstoke, UK: Palgrave Macmillan, 2006), 102; Jane Perlez, "Uganda After Its Years of Terror: A New Political Stability Emerges," *New York Times*, June 15, 1989, LexisNexis.
11. "Presidents Museveni and Reagan Talk for Peace, Friendship, Better Relations," *Baltimore Afro-American*, November 14, 1987, Proquest.
12. J Zamgba Browne, "Uganda President Urges Closer Ties Between Us and Africans," *New York Amsterdam News*, October 31, 1987, Proquest.
13. Charles Baillou, "Uganda Prez Attacks White Rape of Africa," *New York Amsterdam News*, October 31, 1987, Proquest.
14. Donnie Radcliffe, "Barbara Bush, at Home in the White House," *Washington Post*, January 31, 1989, Proquest.
15. Hon. George Crockett, "Human Rights Situation in South Africa, Zaire, the Horn of Africa, and Uganda," Session 98–2, US House of Representatives, Committee on Foreign Affairs, Subcommittee on Human Rights and International Organizations, August 9, 1984.
16. "U.S. Help for Uganda Police Urged," *Chicago Tribune*, August 10, 1984, Proquest.
17. Hon. George Crockett, "Foreign Assistance Legislation for FY83 (Part 7): Economic and Security Assistance Programs in Africa," US House of Representatives, Session 97–2, April 20, 1982, Congressional.ProQuest.
18. "Crockett, 21 Cosponsors Call for Release of Nelson Mandela," *Atlanta Daily World*, February 16, 1986, Proquest; Steve Goldfield and Hilton Obenzinger, "South Africa: The Isreali Connection," *American-Arab Affairs*, September 30, 1986, 106; Joanne Omang, "Focusing on Policy, Not Scandal: Dodd, Crockett Head Panels on Hemisphere," *Washington Post*, January 13, 1987, Proquest.
19. Crockett, "Human Rights Situation."
20. In a notable instance of historical resonance, the Wolverine Bar Association, Michigan's oldest organization of Black attorneys, had awarded Crockett the David Augustus Straker Outstanding Jurist Award just over a decade earlier.

21. For a spectrum of theorizing around the concept of humanitarian war, see Adam Roberts, "Humanitarian War: Military Intervention and Human Rights," *International Affairs (Royal Institute of International Affairs 1944–)* 69, no. 3 (1993): 429–49, https://doi.org/10.2307/2622308; Charles Krauthammer, "The Short, Unhappy Life of Humanitarian War," *National Interest*, no. 57 (1999): 5–8; Susan L. Woodward, "Humanitarian War: A New Consensus?," *Disasters* 25, no. 4 (2001): 331–44, https://doi.org/10.1111/1467-7717.00182; Nicholas J. Wheeler, *Saving Strangers: Humanitarian Intervention in International Society* (Oxford: University Press, 2002), 172–208; Thomas G. Weiss, *Military-Civilian Interactions: Humanitarian Crises and the Responsibility to Protect*, 2nd ed. (Lanham, MD: Rowman & Littlefield, 2004), 55–71.
22. Nincic and Nincic note that African Americans were "generally less enthusiastic" about the US intervention in Somalia than white Americans, while Burris finds that "racial differences were weak with respect" to the intervention. See Miroslav Nincic and Donna J. Nincic, "Race, Gender, and War," *Journal of Peace Research* 39, no. 5 (2002): 533. Nincic and Nincic and Burris observe that African Americans offered stronger support for the US intervention in Haiti than white Americans, with Nincic demonstrating that up to 64 percent of African Americans expressed approval of the intervention. Burris aptly notes that the military intervention in Haiti was "strongly promoted by black leaders." See Val Burris, "From Vietnam to Iraq: Continuity and Change in Between-Group Differences in Support for Military Action," *Social Problems* 55, no. 4 (November 1, 2008): 463, https://doi.org/10.1525/sp.2008.55.4.443. Barring the case of Haiti, Nincic and Nincic, Burris, and Green-Riley and Leber all find that skepticism toward US military interventions is generally more prevalent among everyday African Americans than their white counterparts. See Naima Green-Riley and Andrew Leber, "Whose War Is It Anyway? Explaining the Black-White Gap in Support for the Use of Force Abroad," *Security Studies* 32, no. 4–5 (October 20, 2023): 811–45, https://doi.org/10.1080/09636412.2023.2230881.
23. For an incisive account of this transition, see Bill Martin, "Waiting for Oprah & the New US Constituency for Africa," *Review of African Political Economy* 25, no. 75 (1998): 9–24.
24. Merida and Cooper, "Support of Black Politicians Fragments."
25. "Testimony March 24, 1994, Percy Wilson Vice Chairman the Corporate Council on Africa Senate Foreign Relations/Africa Situation in Sub-Saharan Africa," *Federal Document Clearing House Congressional Testimony*, March 24, 1994, LexisNexis.
26. "Testimony September 11, 1997, Susan Rice Nominee to Be Assistant Secretary of State for African Affairs Senate Foreign Relations Africa Ambassadorial Nominations," *Federal Document Clearing House Congressional Testimony*, September 11, 1997, LexisNexis.
27. Charles Stuart Kennedy, "Ambassador E. Michael Southwick," interview, Foreign Affairs Oral History Project (Association for Diplomatic Studies and Training,

May 4, 2004), https://www.adst.org/OH%20TOCs/Southwick,%20E.%20Michael.toc.pdf.

28. Hon. Donald M. Payne, "Congressional Hearing-Foreign Assistance Legislation for Fiscal Years 1990–91 (Part 1)," US House of Representatives, Committee on Foreign Affairs, February 21, 1989, Congressional.ProQuest.
29. James Bock, "Black Leaders Back U.S. Role in Somalia: Policy Shift Seen as Long in Coming," *Sun*, December 11, 1992, Proquest; Herb Boyd and Don Rojas, "Black Leaders Support U.S. Military Operation in Somalia: Others Doubt Washington's Stated Purpose," *New York Amsterdam News*, December 12, 1992, Proquest.
30. Boyd and Rojas, "Black Leaders Support U.S. Military Operation."
31. Bock, "Black Leaders Back U.S. Role in Somalia," December 11, 1992.
32. Rick Hampson, "Many Blacks Question Gulf War, Support the Warriors," *Philadelphia Tribune*, January 29, 1991, Proquest.
33. Jonathan Stevenson, "Hope Restored in Somalia?," *Foreign Policy*, no. 91 (1993): 138, https://doi.org/10.2307/1149064.
34. "Why Ignore Somalia?," *Miami Times*, August 13, 1992, Proquest.
35. Louis Stokes, "President Bush's Failed Foreign Policy," *Call & Post*, October 1, 1992, Proquest.
36. Jesse Jackson, "A Racist U.S. Yawns as Liberia Bleeds," *Newsday*, July 30, 1990, Proquest.
37. Donald M. Payne, "A View from the Hill: Somalia Is a Test of U.S. Commitment for Africa," *Washington Report on Middle East Affairs*, December 31, 1993, Proqeust.
38. Ola C. Akinshiju, "Panelists See Somali Operation as Beginning of Recolonization," *New York Amsterdam News*, December 26, 1992, Proquest.
39. Samori Marksman, "The White Man's Burden," *New York Amsterdam News*, January 2, 1993, Proquest; Marksman, "Somalia: Warlords, Cold Warriors and Global Warriors: Second Part of a Series," *New York Amsterdam News*, December 26, 1992, Proquest; Marksman, "Somalia: 'The White Man's Burden': Third in a Series," *New York Amsterdam News*, January 2, 1993, Proquest.
40. Marksman, "The White Man's Burden."
41. Charles Baillou, "Is Neocolonialism to Blame for Somalia's Condition?," *New York Amsterdam News*, January 2, 1993, Proquest.
42. Samori Marksman, "Why Have Black Leaders Rushed to Support Invasion of Somalia? Analysis First of Two Parts," *New York Amsterdam News*, December 19, 1992, Proquest; Akinshiju, "Panelists See Somali Operation as Beginning."
43. "Rescue Somalia?," *Nation*, December 21, 1992.
44. Boyd and Rojas, "Black Leaders Support U.S. Military Operation."
45. Frank Sesno, "Somalia—Dying for Food, Part 1," *CNN*, November 26, 1992, Lexis/Nexis.
46. Alex de Waal and Rakiya Omaar, "Disaster Pornography from Somalia," *Los Angeles Times*, December 10, 1992, Proquest.

47. "U.S. Envoy Urged Superiors Not to Send in American Troops," *Associated Press*, December 5, 1992, Lexis/Nexis.
48. Michael Gordon, "28,000 U.S. Troops: Aim Is to Safeguard Food—Peacekeepers Are to Take Over Later, U.N. Backs U.S.-Led Force to Get Aid to Somalia," *New York Times*, December 4, 1992, Proquest.
49. Boyd and Rojas, "Black Leaders Support U.S. Military Operation."
50. Gregory Gordon, "Mission to Somalia May Signal Policy Shift," *Detroit Free Press*, December 6, 1992, Proquest.
51. Dorothy Gilliam, "Watching Somalia with Hope, Angst," *Washington Post*, December 5, 1992, Proquest.
52. John Lancaster, "Powell Says Mission Duration Is Flexible: Operation Could Take 3 Months, General Says," *Washington Post*, December 5, 1992, Proquest.
53. Don Oberdorfer and John Lancaster, "U.N. Chief Weighs Use of U.S. Troops in Somalia; Security Council to Consider Options for Protecting Relief Supply Lines," *Washington Post*, November 27, 1992, Proquest.
54. "With Caution: We Support Military Action to Help Save Dying Somalians," *Michigan Chronicle*, December 2, 1992, Proquest.
55. Theo Farrell, "Sliding Into War: The Somalia Imbroglio and US Army Peace Operations Doctrine," *International Peacekeeping* 2, no. 2 (June 1, 1995): 204, https://doi.org/10.1080/13533319508413551; Walter S. Clarke and Jeffrey Ira Herbst, eds., "Foreign Military Intervention in Somalia: The Root Cause of the Shift from UN Peacekeeping to Peacemaking and Its Consequences," in *Learning from Somalia: The Lessons of Armed Humanitarian Intervention* (Boulder, CO: Westview Press, 1997), 132–33; Paul D. Williams, "United Nations Operation in Somalia II (UNOSOM II)," in *The Oxford Handbook of United Nations Peacekeeping Operations*, ed. Joachim A. Koops (Oxford Academic, 2014), 435, https://doi.org/10.1093/oxfordhb/9780199686049.013.41.
56. Kevin Merida and Kenneth Cooper, "As the Crisis Grows, the Support of Black Politicians Fragments," *Washington Post*, October 9, 1993, Proquest.
57. John O'Donnell, "Black Caucus Cautious About Furor Over Somalia," *Sun*, October 8, 1993, Proquest.
58. "Ronald V. Dellums to Bill Clinton," September 30, 1993, Ronald V. Dellums Congressional Papers, Oakland Public Library, African American Museum and Library at Oakland, Box 15, Folder 49.
59. Emory Curtis, "Another View: Present Administration Similar to Previous Administrations," *San Francisco Metro Reporter*, August 29, 1993, Proquest.
60. Ronald V. Dellums and H. Lee Halterman, *Lying Down With the Lions* (Boston: Beacon, 2000), 185–86.
61. Merida and Cooper, "Support of Black Politicians Fragments."
62. Sonya Ross, "Blacks Support Clinton on Haiti Mission," *Philadelphia Tribune*, October 19, 1993, Proquest.
63. Nathalie Baptiste, "Harkening Back to Dark Days in Haiti," *Foreign Policy in Focus*, March 11, 2014, Proquest.

64. William Raspberry, "This Far, No Farther, with Randall Robinson; He Was Right on the Haitian Refugees, but Now He's Talking War," *Washington Post*, May 18, 1994, Proquest.
65. Sonya Ross, "Blacks Support Clinton on Haiti Mission," *Philadelphia Tribune*, October 19, 1993, Proquest.
66. Joseph L. Lewis, "Black Caucus Members Support U.S. Invasion of Haiti," *Philadelphia Tribune*, September 16, 1994, Proquest.
67. Jason Vest, "Keeping the Pressure on Over Haiti: TransAfrica Honors Aristide and Roars for Randall Robinson," *Washington Post*, June 6, 1994, Proquest.
68. Richard Cohen, "Blacks Look Abroad," *Washington Post*, November 2, 1993, Proquest.
69. United States Department of State, "Letter from Strobe to Chris," April 29, 1994, US Department of State FOIA Library, https://foia.state.gov.
70. Christopher Phelps, "An Interview with Ron Daniels: Black Politics Under Clinton," *Against the Current* IX, no. 6 (February 1995): 20, Proquest.
71. United States Department of State, "Milestones in the History of U.S. Foreign Relations: Intervention in Haiti, 1994–1995," US State Department Office of the Historian, https://history.state.gov/milestones/1993-2000.
72. Rogers Worthington, "Jubilant Haiti Greets a Triumphant Aristide: A Message of Reconciliation," *Chicago Tribune*, October 16, 1994, Proquest.
73. "Ronald V. Dellums to Bill Clinton."
74. Jennifer Parmelee, "Africans Told to Expect Less from the U.S," *Washington Post*, December 16, 1994, Proquest.
75. "Africans Take Control of an Outrage: A Hopeful Moment in War-Riven Liberia," *Los Angeles Times*, March 6, 1994, Proquest.
76. Sobukwe Odinga, "'We Recommend Compliance': Bargaining and Leverage in Ethiopian–US Intelligence Cooperation," *Review of African Political Economy* 44, no. 153 (July 3, 2017): 436, https://doi.org/10.1080/03056244.2017.1368472.
77. White House, "Memorandum of a White House Working Luncheon Between President William J. Clinton, Belgian Prime Minister Jean-Luc Dehaene, and Other US and Belgian Government Officials," February 11, 1995, US Declassified Documents Online, https://www.gale.com/primary-sources.
78. "Memorandum of a White House Working Luncheon."
79. "Sudan Denies U.S. Charge That It Backs Terrorism," *Chicago Tribune*, August 19, 1993, Proquest.
80. "East Africa: Euro-American Palavers," *Indian Ocean Newsletter*, January 7, 1995, www.africanintelligence.com.
81. "The Sudan Menace," *International Herald Tribune*, December 5, 1996, https://link.gale.com/apps/doc/EEXVXX808476967/GDCS?u=uclosangeles&sid=bookmark-GDCS&xid=369d400a.
82. "South Africa Sanctions?," *MacNeil/Lehrer NewsHour*, June 16, 1986.
83. Robert Kaplan, "The Coming Anarchy: How Scarcity, Crime, Overpopulation, Tribalism, and Disease Are Rapidly Destroying the Social Fabric of Our Planet," *Atlantic Monthly*, February 1994.

84. "Cairo Talks Pit North vs. South," *Pittsburgh Post-Gazette*, September 4, 1994, Lexis/Nexis.
85. "Robert Kaplan's Coming Anarchy: Reality or Hyperbole?," June 1995, US State Department Virtual FOIA Reading Room, https://foia.state.gov.
86. "State Department Regular Briefing Briefers: George Moose, Assistant Secretary of State for African Affairs," *Federal News Service*, March 10, 1994, Lexis/Nexis.
87. Michela Wong, "Clinton Hails 'New African Renaissance,'" *Financial Times*, March 24, 1998, Financial Times Historical Archive, link.gale.com/apps/doc/HS2305929262/GDCS?u=uclosangeles&sid=bookmark-GDCS&xid=46c3eaa1.
88. Frank Wright, "White House Opens Conference on Africa," *Star Tribune*, June 27, 1994, Lexis/Nexis.
89. "US Aims to Head off Famine," *Record*, June 4, 1994.
90. "US Aims to Head off Famine"; Parmelee, "Africans Told to Expect Less from the U.S."; Gilbert M. Khadiagala, "The United States and Africa," *SAIS Review (1989–2003)* 21, no. 1 (2001): 260.
91. "Welcome to President Meles Zenawi," *Congressional Record* Daily—Extension of Remarks, 140 Congressional Record E1718, Congress Session 103–2, August 12, 1994, Congressional.ProQuest; "Ethiopia: Tough Customer," US State Department Bureau of Intelligence and Research, October 8, 1996, US State Department FOIA Virtual Reading Room, https://foia.state.gov; Bill Richardson, "A Soft Landing in Zaire?," *Newsweek*, May 20, 1997; Ted Dagne, "Africa: A New Bloc in the East and Center," *CRS Report for Congress*, April 13, 1998.
92. Philip Roessler and Harry Verhoeven, *Why Comrades Go to War: Liberation Politics and the Outbreak of Africa's Deadliest Conflict* (Oxford: Oxford University Press, 2016), 161.
93. US Department of State, "Visit of the Secretary to Africa: A New Generation of African Leaders," December 1, 1997, US Department of State FOIA Library, https://foia.state.gov.
94. "Visit of the Secretary to Africa."
95. Michael Holman and Michela Wrong, "Ethiopia Signals Start of Foreign Investment Drive," *Financial Times*, March 2, 1998; "Reformers Keep Up Fast Pace," *International Herald Tribune*, October 7, 1998.
96. Marshet Tadesse Tessema, *Prosecution of Politicide in Ethiopia: The Red Terror Trials* (Berlin: Springer, 2018), 4.
97. "White House Underscores Africa Priority with Nujoma Visit," *Agence France Presse*, June 14, 1998; Jonathan Fisher, *East Africa After Liberation: Conflict, Security and the State Since the 1980s* (Cambridge: Cambridge University Press, 2020), 126, 156–57.
98. "Testimony Susan Rice Nominee to be Assistant Secretary of State for African Affairs Senate Foreign Relations Ambassadorial Nominations," *Federal Document Clearing House*, September 11, 1997.
99. Michael Bratton, "Second Elections in Africa." *Journal of Democracy* 9, no. 3 (1998): 52.
100. Clifford Krauss, "Ethiopian Rebels Open Fire on Demonstrators in Capital," *International Herald Tribune*, May 30, 1990.

101. J. Oloka-Onyango, "New Wine or New Bottles: Movement Politics and One-partyism in Uganda," in *No-Party Democracy in Uganda: Myths and Realities*, ed. Justus Mugaju and J. Oloka-Onyango (Kampala: Fountain Publishers, 2000).
102. Louise Tunbridge, "Don't Lecture on Democracy, Uganda Leader Tells US," *Daily Telegraph*, June 20, 1995; "Ethiopia: Tough Customer," US State Department Bureau of Intelligence and Research, October 8, 1996, US State Department FOIA Virtual Reading Room, https://foia.state.gov.
103. Howard W. French, *A Continent for the Taking: The Tragedy and Hope of Africa* (New York: Knopf, 2004), 157, 242–43.
104. "US Aims to Head Off Famine," *Record*, June 4, 1994.
105. French, *A Continent for the Taking*, 247–48.
106. For pioneering analysis on the production and framing of identities in Africa's international relations, see Kevin C. Dunn, "Imagining Mobutu's Zaïre: The Production and Consumption of Identity in International Relations," *Millennium* 30, no. 2 (2001): 236–37; Jonathan Fisher, "Framing Kony: Uganda's War, Obama's Advisers and the Nature of 'Influence' in Western Foreign Policy Making," *Third World Quarterly* 35, no. 4 (2014): 687.
107. "Intelligence Memorandum Regarding the Ability of the Congolese Government to Control Ethnic Rebellions in That Country," Central Intelligence Agency, June 12, 1964, Gale Primary Sources, US Declassified Documents Online; "Brussels Meeting Between President George HW Bush, Belgian Prime Minister Wilfried Martens, and Other US and Belgian Government Officials," May 28, 1989, Gale Primary Sources, US Declassified Documents Online; Ben Barber, "US Redirects Africa Policy," *Christian Science Monitor*, May 26, 1993.
108. Jim Lobe, "Zaire-US: Washington's Confusion Mirror's Kinshasa's," *IPS-Inter Press Service*, April 10, 1997.
109. "US-Africa Relations Briefer: George Moose, Assistant Secretary of State for African Affairs," *Federal News Service*, June 2, 1994.
110. Jim Lobe, "Zaire: US Lawmakers Call for an Asset Freeze on Mobutu," *IPS-Inter Press Service*, February 23, 1993.
111. Thomas P. Odom, *Journey Into Darkness: Genocide in Rwanda* (College Station: Texas A&M University Press, 2005), 82.
112. Abbas H. Gnamo, "The Rwandan Genocide and the Collapse of Mobutu's Kleptocracy," in *The Rwanda Crisis from Uganda to Zaire*, ed. Howard Adelman and Astri Suhrke (New Brunswick: Transaction Publishers, 1999), 334.
113. René Lemarchand, "The Fire in the Great Lakes," *Current History* 98, no. 628 (1999): 198.
114. "Taoiseach Urged to Ask Clinton to Send US Military Force to Rwanda," *Irish Times*, May 26, 1994; Richard Dowden, "Don't Blame the UN for an American Mess," *Independent*, May 18, 1994; Brunk, "Curing the Somalia Syndrome," 304.
115. "Proposed Elements of USG Strategy for Bringing Long-Term Stability to Rwanda," 1995, US State Department Virtual FOIA Reading Room, https://foia.state.gov.
116. Odom, *Journey Into Darkness*, 108, 112.

117. Odom, 139.
118. "Zaire Regional Issues; The Arms Embargo," American Embassy Paris, cable, June 1994, US State Department Virtual FOIA Reading Room, https://foia.state.gov; French, *A Continent for the Taking*, 217.
119. Odom, *Journey Into Darkness*, 197.
120. "Ad Hoc Meeting at NSC Regarding Rwanda and Burundi," briefing memorandum, August 21, 1995, US State Department Virtual FOIA Reading Room, https://foia.state.gov.
121. Richard Dowden, "Mobutu Could Lose World Pariah Status," *Independent*, September 24, 1994; Lenora Fulani, "What Lies Behind the Refugee Crisis in Zaire," *New York Beacon*, December 4, 1996; "Black Caucus Head Says Administration Dawdling in African Crisis," *Associated Press*, December 4, 1996.
122. "Ad Hoc Meeting at NSC Regarding Rwanda and Burundi," Briefing Memorandum, August 21, 1995, US State Department Virtual FOIA Reading Room, https://foia.state.gov.
123. "Under Secretary Talbott Meets Kengo," telegram, October 12, 1994, US State Department Virtual FOIA Reading Room, https://foia.state.gov.
124. Howard W. French, "US Weighs Sending Ambassador to Zaire, a Dictator's Fief," *New York Times*, October 24, 1994; Steven Greenhouse, "U.S. Seeks a Balance to Save Shaky Zaire," *International Herald Tribune*, November 9, 1994.
125. "Welcome Home Update-Burundi-Rwanda-Zaire," memorandum, June 16, 1995, US State Department Virtual FOIA Reading Room, https://foia.state.gov.
126. Inigo Gilmore, "Zaire Expels 2,000 Rwanda Refugees Despite UN Appeal," *Times* (London), August 22, 1995; "Rwandan Refugee Repatriation and Ouster of the Prime Minister," information memorandum, August 30, 1995, US State Department Virtual FOIA Reading Room, https://foia.state.gov.
127. French, *A Continent for the Taking*, 217.
128. "Paris Meeting Between French President Jacques Chirac, National Security Adviser Anthony Lake, and Other US and French Government Officials," White House, November 1, 1996, Gale Primary Sources, US Declassified Documents Online.
129. "Paris Meeting."
130. Gerard Prunier, *Africa's World War: Congo, The Rwandan Genocide, and the Making of a Continental Catastrophe* (Oxford: Oxford University Press, 2009), 127; Filip Reyntjens, *The Great African War: Congo and Regional Geopolitics, 1996–2006* (Cambridge: Cambridge University Press, 2009), 75–79.
131. Prunier, *Africa's World War*, 126; US Foreign Assistance Tracker, Trends, Military Aid to Uganda, 1996–1998, https://foreignassistance.gov/aid-trends.
132. Christopher R. Cook, "American Policymaking in the Democratic Republic of the Congo 1996–1999: The Anti-Kabila Bias and the Crushing Neutrality of the Lusaka Accords," *African and Asian Studies* 9, no. 4 (2010): 400.
133. Frank Smyth, "A New Game: The Clinton Administration on Africa," *World Policy Journal* 15, no. 2 (Summer 1998): 90.
134. Smyth, 85.

135. "Madeline Albright Holds First Press Conference as Secretary of State," *CNN Special Event*, January 24, 1997; "Interview with Madeline Albright," *Federal News Service*, January 21, 1998.
136. Anthony Lake, "US and 'Afro-realism,'" *Africa Report* 40, no. 2 (1995): 22–24.
137. Bill Martin, "Waiting for Oprah & The New US Constituency for Africa," *Review of African Political Economy* 25, no. 75 (1998): 15–16.
138. James Adams, "Americans Move to Destabilize Sudanese Regime," *Sunday Times*, November 17, 1996.
139. "Sudan-AF Testimony Before HIRC Africa Subcommittee," US Secretary of State, Washington DC, telegram, March 23, 1995, US State Department FOIA Virtual Reading Room, https://foia.state.gov; "Terrorism: Bin Laden's Network," US State Department Bureau of Intelligence and Research, January 22, 1996, US State Department FOIA Virtual Reading Room, https://foia.state.gov.
140. Craig R. Whitney, "Western Nations Chart War Against Terrorism," *International Herald Tribune*, July 31, 1996; Con Coughlin, "Tempting Array of Strike Target for Pentagon," *Sunday Telegraph*, August 4, 1996; David B. Ottaway, "More Active US Policy on Terrorism Is Studied," *International Herald Tribune*, October 18, 1996.
141. Sam Kiley, "Ugandan Troops Dig in for Fight on Border," *Times* (London), February 3, 1995.
142. Jonathan Clarke and James Clad, "The American Foreign Policy Machine Has Stopped Purring," *International Herald Tribune*, June 20, 1995.
143. Sally Healy, "Seeking Peace and Security in the Horn of Africa: The Contribution of the Inter-Governmental Authority on Development," *International Affairs* 87, no. 1 (2011): 110.
144. "Sudan View from the Top," US State Department Bureau of Intelligence and Research, February 2, 1997, US State Department FOIA Virtual Reading Room, https://foia.state.gov.
145. David B. Ottaway, "U. S. Sending Aid to Foes of Sudan," *International Herald Tribune*, November 11, 1996,
146. Author interview, former senior US diplomat to Uganda, August 2022.
147. "Meeting with Museveni," telegram, January 21, 1987, 87KAMPALA184_a, Wikileaks Public Library of US Diplomacy; Tunbridge, "Don't Lecture on Democracy"; "Uganda: From Reagan to Biden, the Ebb and Flow of the US-Museveni Relationship," *Africa Report*, January 18, 2022.
148. Alan Philips, "Rebel Chief to Head Interim Government," *Daily Telegraph*, May 29, 1991.
149. "Ethiopia: Tough Customer," US State Department Bureau of Intelligence and Research.
150. Ottaway, "U.S. Sending Aid to Foes of Sudan,"
151. A. Sarjoh Bah and Kwesi Aning, "US Peace Operations Policy in Africa: From ACRI to AFRICOM," *International Peacekeeping* 15, no. 1 (2008): 121.
152. Liu Yegang, "Roundup: Africa Rejects US-Led Crisis Response Force," *Xinhua News Agency*, October 15, 1996.

153. Daniel Volman, "The Clinton Administration and the Africa Crisis Response Force," *Africa News*, March 24, 1997, Lexis/Nexis.
154. Patrick Smith, "Calculated Diplomacy," *Financial Times*, March 2, 1998; Paul Omach, "The African Crisis Response Initiative: Domestic Politics and Convergence of National Interests," *African Affairs* 99, no. 394 (2000): 89.
155. "African Crisis Response," CSPAN, July 29, 1997, https://www.c-span.org/program/news-conference/africa-crisis-response/66845.
156. Paul Omach, "The African Crisis Response Initiative: Domestic Politics and Convergence of National Interests," *African Affairs* 99, no. 394 (January 2000): 93.
157. "Even Poor Nations Must Respect Citizens' Rights," *Monitor*, August 25, 1997, https://gpa.eastview.com/crl/ean/newspapers/motr19970825-01.1.3.
158. Bah and Aning, "US Peace Operations Policy in Africa," 121.
159. "Senegal: Dakar: U.S. President Clinton Visit Update," video, April 1, 1998, AP Archive.
160. Roger Simon, "On Africa Trip, Clinton to Push Trade as a Tool for Democracy," *Chicago Tribune*, March 22, 1998, Proquest.
161. Michael K. Frisby, "U.S. Policy on Africa Moves to Front-Burner During Clinton Trip, but Will the Flame Cool?," *Wall Street Journal*, April 3, 1998, Proquest.
162. Stephen Buckley, "Authority's Changing Face in Africa; Enlightened Leaders, or Savvy Strongmen?," *Washington Post*, February 2, 1998, Proquest.
163. Roger Simon, "Clinton Will Visit the Rock of Slavery, Tour of Africa Will End on Island Where Millions Lost Their Freedom," *Chicago Tribune*," April 2, 1998.
164. James Wright and Willie Givens, "South African V.P. Attacks U.S. Policy: Mfume Joins Clinton," *Afro-American Red Star*, March 28, 1998, Proquest.
165. "Large Black Delegation with President Clinton on Historic Trip to Africa," *The Call*, March 27, 1998, Proquest.
166. US Information Agency, "United States and Africa; Susan Rice Outlines Goals of President's Africa Trip," *Africa News*, March 23, 1998, Lexis/Nexis.
167. Susan Rice, *Tough Love My Story of the Things Worth Fighting For* (New York: Simon & Schuster, 2019), 159, 160. Rice would establish such close ties with new breed leader Meles Zenawi that in 2002 she met with the Ethiopian prime minister for an "informal visit" at a Washington, DC, hospital just two hours after giving birth to her second child.
168. Charles Onyango-Obbo, "What's the Bottom Line on Clinton's Visit," *Monitor*, March 24, 1998.
169. White House, "Press Briefing by Reverend Jesse Jackson, John Prendergast, Susan Rice, & Brian Atwood," *M2 Presswire*, April 15, 1998, Lexis/Nexis.
170. Sylvia Juuko, "Jesse Jackson Calls for Corrupt Free Africa," *Monitor*, March 25, 1998.
171. "Clinton's Trip to Africa Has a Lot to Do with Respect; the Visit Aims to Show America a Different View; Expanding Global Market Is Goal," *St. Louis Post-Dispatch*, March 22, 1998, Lexis/Nexis.
172. Jim Lobe, "Trade—U.S.: Africa Trade Bill Off to Fast Start," *IPS-Inter Press Service*, February 4, 1999, Lexis/Nexis; Alvin B. Tillery, *Between Homeland and Motherland:*

Africa, U.S. Foreign Policy, and Black Leadership in America (Ithaca: Cornell University Press, 2011), 146.

173. "Clinton's Trip to Africa."
174. Charles Rangel, "It's Time to Deliver for Africa," *New York Amsterdam News*, March 5, 1998, Proquest.
175. "Africa Is Treasured Assignment for U.S. Trade Representative: Whitaker Knows Africa, Africans and Washington, Too," *Sun*, August 31, 1998, Proquest.
176. Ken Silverstein, "Former U.S. Trade Official Capitalizes on Her Connections: Public and Private Dealings with African Governments Highlight Revolving-Door Issue," *Los Angeles Times*, March 2, 2004, Proquest.
177. Elizabeth Shogren, "Trip to Africa Deeply Moves Several in U.S. Contingent," *Los Angeles Times*, April 1, 1998, Proquest.
178. James C. J. McKinley, "A New Model for Africa: Good Leaders Above All," *New York Times*, March 25, 1998, Proquest.
179. Sonya Ross, "President in Africa: Trip Puts Spotlight on 34 Million Americans' Homeland," *Los Angeles Sentinel*, April 1, 1998, Proquest.
180. James A. Joseph, "The Idea of African Renaissance: Myth or Reality?," *Vital Speeches of the Day* 64, no. 5 (1997): 133; "United States and Africa: Clinton Will Extend Hand to 'New Generations of Africans,'" *Africa News*, February 11, 1998; William J. Clinton, President of the United States, "Delivers Remarks to Peace Corps Volunteers: Ghana," *FDCH Transcripts*, March 23, 1998; "Rev. Jesse Jackson Addresses Civil Rights and Politics," *CNN Evans and Novak Transcript*, April 4, 1998.
181. Adolph L. Reed Jr., *W.E.B. Du Bois and American Political Thought: Fabianism and the Color Line* (Oxford: Oxford University Press, 1997), 82.
182. Joseph Oloka-Onyango, "'New-Breed' Leadership, Conflict, and Reconstruction in the Great Lakes Region of Africa: A Sociopolitical Biography of Uganda's Yoweri Kaguta Museveni," *Africa Today* 50, no. 3 (2004): 29.
183. Ronald Walters, "The African Growth and Opportunity Act: Changing Foreign Policy Priorities Toward Africa in a Conservative Political Culture," in *Diversity and US Foreign Policy: A Reader*, ed. Ernest J. Wilson III (New York: Routledge, 2004), 299; William G. Jones, "Congress and Africa's Constituency: The Development of the Africa Growth and Opportunity Act and the Intersection of African American and Business Interests," in *African Americans in Global Affairs: Contemporary Perspectives*, ed. Michael Clemmons (Boston: Northeastern University Press, 2010), 111–13.
184. "Holds News Conference with Other Members of the President's Delegation to Africa," *FDCH Political Transcripts*, April 3, 1998; Mimi Hall, "Trade, Not Aid in Africa to Executives, Trip Is Business and More," *USA Today*, March 10, 1998.
185. Steven Greenhouse, "US Blacks Pledge Aid for Africa," *New York Times*, May 10, 1995.
186. "The Second African-African American Summit Program," Box 301, May 24, 1993, Ronald V. Dellums Congressional Papers, Oakland Public Library, African American Museum and Library at Oakland.
187. Mark Fritz, "Young Says Clinton Hurt the Angolan Peace Talks," *Philadelphia Tribune*, June 1, 1993, Proquest.

188. Don Rojas, "African and African-American Leaders Hold Summit in W. Africa: Agree to Grant African-Americans Dual Citizenship," *New York Amsterdam News*, April 27, 1991, Proquest; Francois Ngolet, "African and American Connivance in Congo-Zaire," *Africa Today* (2000): 72; Henry J. Richardson III, "The Black International Tradition and African American Business in Africa," *North Carolina Central Law Review* 34 (2011): 170.
189. Donald Payne Papers, CBC Clinton/National Security November 18, 1992, Folder 570, Seton Hall University Archives and Special Collections.
190. "Ethiopians Protest U.S. Support to the TPLF Dictatorial Regime: As U.S. President Plans to Visit Africa," *Ethiopian Review* 8, no. 1 (March 31, 1998): 34.
191. Mahmood Mamdani, "What Was That Trip About?," *Washington Post*, April 5, 1998, Proquest.
192. Lara Santoro, "West Cheers Uganda's One-Man Show This Month, Clinton Will Visit a New Type of African Strongman, Yoweri Museveni," *Christian Science Monitor*, March 2, 1998, Proquest.
193. Ray Suarez, "Africa Policy," *NPR Talk of the Nation*, December 4, 1997; Okbazghi Yohannes, "The United States and Sub-Saharan Africa After the Cold War: Empty Promises and Retreat," *Black Scholar* 32, no. 1 (2002): 32; Oloka-Onyango, "'New-Breed' Leadership," 33.
194. Roessler and Verhoeven, *Why Comrades Go to War*, 415; Fisher, *East Africa After Liberation*, 273.
195. Levi Ochieng, "Uganda Out of US-Africa Peace Force," *Africa News*, September 15, 2000; Douglas Farah, "US Reviews Its Training of African Peacekeepers," *International Herald Tribune*, July 4, 2001.
196. Roger Tangri and Andrew M. Mwenda, "Military Corruption & Ugandan Politics Since the Late 1990s," *Review of African Political Economy* 30, no. 98 (2003): 543.
197. Gilbert M. Khadiagala, "Reflections on the Ethiopia-Eritrea Border Conflict," *Fletcher Forum World Affairs* 23 (1999): 42–43.
198. Tim Weiner and Steven Lee Meyers, "US Defends Missile Attack on Sudan Factory," *Patriot Ledger*, September 3, 1998; Adrian Michaels, "Khartoum to Recall Envoys from the US," *Financial Times*, September 3, 1998.
199. "Albright Urges Other Nations to Join Anti-Terrorism Fight," *Xinhua News Agency*, August 20, 1998; "Terrorism Upsurge US Warns," *Illawarra Mercury*, August 25, 1998.
200. Peter Rosenblum, "Irrational Exuberance: The Clinton Administration in Africa," *Current History* 101, no. 655 (2002): 196.
201. Jon Swain, "Back to Hell in the Horn of Africa," *Sunday Times*, June 7, 1998; David Anderson, "Death of the African Dream," *Independent*, August 27, 1998; Bill Berkeley, "It's Time to Be Candid About Africa's Leaders," *International Herald Tribune*, January 18, 2000.
202. US Department of State, "Rice Discusses US Africa Goals at Columbia University," *Africa News*, October 29, 1998; Thomas W. Lippman, "Africa's Unrest Shakes US Initiatives," *Washington Post*, December 13, 1998.
203. Rosenblum, "Irrational Exuberance," 196.

204. "Washington Steps Back a Bit," *Indian Ocean Newsletter*, May 29, 1999.
205. Rosenblum, "Irrational Exuberance," 200.
206. "Conflict-US: Inattention to Africa Deplored," *IPS-Inter Press Service*, May 27, 1999.
207. See essays by Bernard Makhosezwe Magubane, Mahmood Mamdani, N. Barney Pityana, and Thami Mazwai in *African Renaissance: The New Struggle*, ed. Malegapuru William Makgoba (Cape Town: Mafube Publishers, 1999).
208. Hon. Donald M. Payne, "Congressional Hearing-Ethiopia-Eritrea War: US Policy Options," US House of Representatives, Committee on International Relations, Subcommittee on Africa, May 25, 1999, Congressional.ProQuest.
209. Tillery Jr., *Between Homeland and Motherland*, 153–54; author interview, former senior US Diplomat to Uganda 1, August 2022; Charles P. Henry, "The Rise and Fall of Black Influence on US Foreign Policy," in *African Americans in Global Affairs: Contemporary Perspectives*, ed. Michael Clemons (Boston: Northeastern University Press, 2010), 199.
210. Nincic and Nincic, "Race, Gender, and War," 553; Rachel Allison, "Race, Gender, and Attitudes Toward War in Chicago: An Intersectional Analysis," *Sociological Forum* 26, no. 3 (August 2011): 687; Nosmot Gbadamosi, "How the West Lost Africa," *Foreign Policy*, May 25, 2022.
211. Ronald N. Jacobs, *Race, Media, and the Crisis of Civil Society: From Watts to Rodney King* (Cambridge: Cambridge University Press, 2000), 48; Michael C. Dawson, *Blacks In and Out of the Left* (Cambridge, MA: Harvard University Press, 2013), 114–15.
212. "Powell, Rumsfeld at Odds Over Continuation of African Peacekeepers' Training Program," *Bulletin's Frontrunner*, May 24, 2001; "US Moves to Reassess Pentagon Programs in Africa, *Bulletin's Frontrunner*, July 3, 2001; "PanAfrica; Bush Administration Reduces Africa Aid Bid," *Africa News*, October 25, 2001.
213. "Somalia May Be Next Terrorist Front," *Sunday Times*, December 2, 2001.
214. Tangri and Mwenda, "Military Corruption & Ugandan Politics," 543.
215. Roger Tangri and Andrew M. Mwenda, "President Museveni and the Politics of Presidential Tenure in Uganda," *Journal of Contemporary African Studies* 28, no. 1 (2010): 35.
216. "Is the Kampala Government's Last Meal Being Cooked? And When Besigye Met Colin Powell," *Monitor*, July 25, 2001.
217. James Lamont, "Africans and African Americans Split Over Slavery Reparations Issue," *Financial Times*, September 3, 2001.
218. "Uganda's Prez: Don't Blame US for Slavery," *Philadelphia Daily News*, March 23, 1998.
219. "Briefing by Jackson, Prendergast, Rice, Atwood, March 24 in Uganda 5 of 6," *US Newswire*, March 25, 1998.
220. "Bush Sidelining Museveni, Woos Bashir-US Group," *Monitor*, January 17, 2002.
221. "If Bin Laden Didn't Exist Moi, Bashir or Museveni Would Have Created Him," *Monitor*, October 10, 2001; Government of Uganda, "President Yoweri Museveni's Speech at the UN," *Africa News*, November 16, 2001.
222. Tim Reid, "Bush Goes on Safari to Hunt for Security and Oil," *Times* (London), July 7, 2003.

223. Ken Menkhaus "Terrorist Activities in Ungoverned Spaces: Evidence and Observations from the Horn of Africa," *Southern Africa and International Terrorism Workshop* (2007): 13; David Oakley and Pat Proctor, "Ten Years of GWOT, the Failure of Democratization, and the Fallacy of 'Ungoverned Spaces,'" *Journal of Strategic Security* 5, no. 1 (2012): 6; Yvan Guichaoua, "Mali: The Fallacy of Ungoverned Spaces," Matas Utas blog (2013); Promise Frank Ejiofor, "Beyond Ungoverned Spaces: Connecting the Dots Between Relative Deprivation, Banditry, and Violence in Nigeria," *African Security* (2022): 133.
224. David Stout, "Bush Joins Africa Allies in Vowing Terror Fight," *International Herald Tribune*, December 6, 2002.

5. AN ALLY TO BE RECKONED WITH

1. Felix Osike, "Uganda Talks to Islamic Courts Militia," *New Vision*, February 28, 2007, LexisNexis.
2. Alfred Wasike, "Uganda Winning Hearts in Somalia," *New Vision*, March 26, 2007, LexisNexis; "Pan-Africanist Obligations in Somalia," *Monitor*, April 7, 2007, LexisNexis; Charles Obbo, "Inside the Mind of President Museveni," *East African*, February 7, 2011, LexisNexis.
3. Edith M. Lederer, "UN Authorizes New AU Mission in Somalia to Combat Extremists," *Associated Press*, March 31, 2022, LexisNexis.
4. "Will America Fund South Sudan War?," *Independent (Kampala)*, January 18, 2014, LexisNexis; Darryl Li, "Migrant Workers and the US Military in the Middle East," *Middle East Report* 275 (2015): 4.
5. Frederic Musisi, "UPDF in Equatorial Guinea to Build Capacity-Museveni," *Daily Monitor*, April 28, 2017, LexisNexis; "Uganda and Somalia Sign New Deal on Military Training," *BBC Monitoring Africa-Political*, November 3, 2019, LexisNexis.
6. "Will America Fund South Sudan War?," *Independent (Kampala)*, January 18, 2014, LexisNexis; Paul Omach, "Uganda in the Great Lakes Region: Obstacles to Peace and Security," in *War and Peace in Africa's Great Lakes Region*, ed. Gilbert Khadiagala (London: Palgrave Macmillan, 2017), 78–80.
7. Paul Omach,"The African Crisis Response Initiative: Domestic Politics and Convergence of National Interests." *African Affairs* 99, no. 394 (2000): 90; "Senate Foreign Relations Subcommittee on Africa and Global Health Policy Hearing," *Congressional Documents and Publications*, June 4, 2015, LexisNexis.
8. Shannon Firth, "Can US Stop Museveni from Signing Uganda's Anti-Gay Bill?," *U.S. News & World Report*, February 20, 2014, LexisNexis.
9. Gorm Rye Olsen, "Fighting Terrorism in Africa by Proxy: The USA and the European Union in Somalia and Mali," *European Security* 23, no. 3 (2014): 296.
10. Helen Epstein, "Murder in Uganda," *New York Review of Books*, April 3, 2014; Helen Epstein, "Uganda: The General Challenges the Dictator," *New York Review of Books*, April 24, 2014; Roger Tangri and Andrew M. Mwenda, "President Museveni and the

Politics of Presidential Tenure in Uganda," *Journal of Contemporary African Studies* 28, no. 1 (2010): 35; Angelo Izama and Michael Wilkerson, "Uganda: Museveni's Triumph and Weaknesses," *Journal of Democracy* 22, no. 3 (2011): 69; Jonathan Fisher and David M. Anderson, "Authoritarianism and the Securitization of Development in Africa," *International Affairs* 91, no.1 (2015): 137; William Reno, "The Regionalization of African Security," *Current History*, 111, no. 175 (May 2012): 179.

11. Terry Mays, "The African Union's African Mission in Somalia: Why Did It Successfully Deploy Following the Failure of the IGAD Peace Support Mission to Somalia?," thesis, United Nations Peace Operations Training Institute, March 2009.
12. "AU Studying Ways of Funding Somalia Peacekeeping Force," *Ethiopian Herald*, January 7, 2007, LexisNexis.
13. "Second Batch of Burundi Peacekeepers in Somalia," *Agence France Presse*, December 24, 2007, LexisNexis.
14. Wikileaks Public Library of US Diplomacy, "US Embassy Addis Ababa to National Security Council, USAU Support for AMISOM Deployment," 07ADDISABABA263, January 30, 2007, https://wikileaks.org/; Jim Fisher-Thompson, "Somalia: US Official Immediate Help for Stabilization," US Department of State, February 7, 2007.
15. Michelle Gavin, "Jendayi Frazer on the Search for Multilateral Consensus," *Council on Foreign Relations Blog*, June 14, 2022, https://www.cfr.org/blog/jendayi-frazer-search-multilateral-consensus.
16. "We Should Never Have Gone to Somalia," *Observer (Kampala)*, July 20, 2016, LexisNexis.
17. Author interview, senior official 1, African Union Commision Peace and Security Department, July 10, 2018; author interview, senior official 2, African Union Commision Peace and Security Department, July 11, 2018.
18. Gilbert M. Khadiagala, "Pan-Africanism and Regional Integration," in *Routledge Handbook of African Politics*, ed. Nic Cheeseman, David M. Anderson, and Andrea Scheiber (London: Routledge, 2017), 382.
19. James C. McKinley Jr., "Clinton in Africa: A New Model for Africa: Good Leaders Above All," *New York Times*, March 25, 1998, LexisNexis.
20. Kwesi Aning, Thomas Jaye, and Samuel Atuob, "The Role of Private Military Companies in US-Africa Policy," *Review of African Political Economy* 35, no. 118 (2008): 622.
21. Lisa Vives, "President's Son Led Elite Force Linked to Rights Abuses," *Eurasia Review*, May 3, 2021, LexisNexis.
22. Wikileaks Public Library of US Diplomacy, "Counter-Terrorism: Cooperating with African Union," 02ADDISABABA2418_a, July 12, 2002, https://wikileaks.org/.
23. Wikileaks Public Library of US Diplomacy, "East Africa Regional Counter Terrorism Officers Meeting," 09NAIROBI2383_a, November 20, 2009, https://wikileaks.org/.
24. "Support East African Federation, President Tells UPDF," *Daily Monitor*, August 19, 2021, LexisNexis.
25. Yoweri Kaguta Museveni, *Sowing the Mustard Seed: The Struggle for Freedom and Democracy in Uganda* (Oxford: Macmillan, 1997), 26.

26. Museveni, 73.
27. "The Conflict Between Tanzania and Uganda," Tanzanian Government, November 20, 1979, African Union Archive-Folder Tanzania and Uganda 1971–1979, Addis Ababa, Ethiopia.
28. Yoweri Kaguta Museveni, "What Is Africa's Problem: Speeches and Writings on Africa by Yoweri Kaguta Museveni (Kampala: NRM Publications, 1992), 13.
29. Museveni, *Sowing the Mustard Seed*, 27.
30. Hakim Adi, *Pan-Africanism: A History* (London: Bloomsbury Academic, 2018), 3–4.
31. Kurt B. Young, "Towards An 8th Pan-African Congress: The Evolution of the Race–Class Debate," *Journal of Political Ideologies* 16, no. 2 (2011): 156.
32. Vukoni Lupa-Lasaga, "Africa Growled at Congress; Will It Bite," *Monitor*, May 23, 1994, LexisNexis; Young, "Towards an 8th Pan-African Congress," 162.
33. Philip Williams, "Ugandan President Criticizes Black Africa," *United Press International*, July 29, 1986, LexisNexis.
34. "South Sudan Leader Returns from Visits to Kenya, Uganda," *BBC Monitoring Africa-Political*, November 19, 2011, LexisNexis.
35. Daniel K. Kalinaki, "Forget the M23: Let's Deploy Bitature, Mukwano to Congo," *Daily Monitor*, November 18, 2013, LexisNexis.
36. Sam Mugumya, "Can Uganda Afford to Police the Region?," *Observer*, January 16, 2014, LexisNexis.
37. Author interview, veteran opposition Ugandan parliamentarian, March 2022, Kampala, Uganda.
38. Author interviews, Ugandan opposition leaders 1 and 2, March 2022, Kampala, Uganda.
39. Kasaija Phillip Apuuli, "Explaining the (Il) Legality of Uganda's Intervention in the Current South Sudan Conflict," *African Security Review* 23, no. 4 (2014): 362.
40. Kate Meagher, "Smuggling Ideologies: From Criminalization to Hybrid Governance in African Clandestine Economies," *African Affairs* 113, no. 453 (2014): 512.
41. "Somalia Mission Not Proxy for America," *Monitor*, March 28, 2007, LexisNexis; Charles Onyango-Obbo, "Museveni Enters Kenya Mediation Fray as Dark Horse—On Govt. Side?," *East African*, January 21, 2008, LexisNexis; "Do Donors Have a Right to Interfere in Our Affairs?," *New Vision*, April 11, 2009, LexisNexis; Andrew M. Mwenda, "Uganda's State Building in Somalia," *Independent* (Kampala), September 9, 2012, LexisNexis.
42. For discussions of statist Pan-Africanism or Pan-Africanism from above, see Horace Campbell, "Pan-Africanism in the Twenty-First Century," in *Pan-Africanism: Politics, Economy and Social Change in the Twenty-First Century*, ed. Tajudeen Abdul-Raheem (New York: New York University Press, 1996), 212; Abubakar Momoh, "Does Pan-Africanism Have a Future in Africa? In Search of the Ideational Basis of Afro-pessimism," *African Journal of Political Science* 8, no. 1 (2003): 32, 44; Horace Campbell, "Walter Rodney and Pan-Africanism Today," *Presentation at the Africana Studies Research Center Cornell University, Ithaca, New York, Africana Colloquium Series* (2005), 9; Issa G. Shivji, "Pan-Africanism or Imperialism? Unity and Struggle

Towards a New Democratic Africa," *African Sociological Review/Revue Africaine de Sociologie* 10, no. 1 (2006): 218.

43. Armed Activities on the Territory of the Congo (Democratic Republic of Congo v. Uganda), International Court of Justice, December 19, 2005, http://www.icj-cij.org/docket/files/116/10521.pdf.
44. "Uganda's Museveni Threatens to Deploy Troops in DR Congo if Rebels Attack," *Agence France Presse*, March 19, 2006, LexisNexis.
45. "We Fought Arabs Not Kony, Says Museveni," *New Vision*, April 29, 2008, LexisNexis.
46. Maxwell Wright, "Rhetorical Facades: Ugandan Counter-Terrorism Discourse in the Museveni Era" (PhD diss., Ohio State University, 2015), 27; Beth Elise Whitaker, "Exporting the Patriot Act? Democracy and the 'War on Terror' in the Third World," *Third World Quarterly* 28, no. 5 (2007): 1027.
47. "American Military Training to Resume," *Indian Ocean Newsletter*, April 15, 2006.
48. "Museveni's Obsession with the DRC," *Indian Ocean Newsletter*, October 15, 2005; "Country Warns Congo Again," *New Vision*, April 30, 2006; "Congo Targets UPDF," *New Vision*, May 30, 2006, LexisNexis.
49. Wikileaks Public Library of US Diplomacy, "US Embassy Kinshasa to Central Intelligence Agency, GDRC Terms Ugandan Threat to Intervene Unacceptable," 06KINSHASA488, March 24, 2016, https://wikileaks.org/.
50. Master Sgt. John Lasky, "Natural Fire Provides Assistance to African Nations," *Air Force Print News*, August 17, 2006, LexisNexis.
51. "Uganda; Army Happy With Khartoum Protocol on LRA," *UN Integrated Regional Networks*, March 19, 2002, LexisNexis.
52. Angelo Izama, "UPDF Outlives Mandate in Sudan," *Daily Monitor*, November 2, 2006, LexisNexis; Frank Mugabi, "UPDF to Remain in Southern Sudan," *New Vision*, November 5, 2006, LexisNexis.
53. "Talk to Kony, US Urges, but Kampala Doesn't Trust Machar Peace Deal," *East African*, July 26, 2006, LexisNexis.
54. "Time for Action Against Lord's Resistance Army," *New Vision*, March 30, 2008, LexisNexis.
55. Mareike Schomerus, "'They Forget What They Came for': Uganda's Army in Sudan," *Journal of East African Studies* 6, no. 1 (2012): 129.
56. Zach Vertin, "A Poisoned Well: Lessons in Mediation from South Sudan's Troubled Peace Process," International Peace Institute (April 2018), 19, https://www.ipinst.org/wp-content/uploads/2018/04/1804_Poisoned-Well.pdf.
57. "Talk to Kony, US Urges."
58. Anna Macdonald, "'In the Interests of Justice?' The International Criminal Court, Peace Talks and the Failed Quest for War Crimes Accountability in Northern Uganda," *Journal of Eastern African Studies* 11, no. 4 (2017): 632.
59. Schomerus, "'They Forget What They Came for,'" 129, 145.
60. "Sudan MPs Urge End to Uganda Army Presence," *Agence France Presse*, November 22, 2006, LexisNexis.

61. Wikileaks Public Library of US Diplomacy, "US Embassy Khartoum to Secretary of State, GOSS Vice President Tells Special Envoy That Distrust Pervades LRA Peace Talks," 06KHARTOUM2564, October 29, 2006, https://wikileaks.org/.
62. Abraham McLaughlin, "Africa After War: Paths to Forgiveness—Ugandans Welcome Terrorists Back," *Christian Science Monitor*, October 23, 2006, LexisNexis.
63. "US Urged to Salvage Uganda Peace Talks," *Agence France Presse*, September 29, 2006, LexisNexis.
64. Wikileaks Public Library of US Diplomacy, "US Embassy London to Secretary of State, Somalia: Museveni Tells A/S Frazer Ugandan Troops Can Guard Baidoa," 06LONDON8066, November 22, 2006, https://wikileaks.org/.
65. Editorial Board, "US Makes Errors, Enemies in Africa," *Philadelphia Inquirer*, December 4, 2006, LexisNexis (an anonymous US official, deriding the Bush Administration's sycophantic relationship with the Ugandan president, refers to Assistant Secretary Frazer as a "Museveniphile"); George Gedda, "Experts Say US Must Be More Active in Seeking Peace in Northern Uganda," *Associated Press International*, March 1, 2007, LexisNexis; "Make Peace or Face the Gun, US Tells Kony," *East African*, September 11, 2007, LexisNexis.
66. "US Wants Deadline for Talks," *New Vision*, September 5, 2007, LexisNexis.
67. "LRA Demands Hold Truce Ransom," *East African*, November 14, 2006, LexisNexis.
68. Macdonald, "In the Interests of Justice?," 634.
69. "Northern Leaders Still Want the Peace Process," *UN Integrated Regional Information Networks*, June 9, 2008, LexisNexis.
70. "South Sudan Army Pursues LRA Rebels," *Monitor*, September 21, 2008, LexisNexis.
71. Wikileaks Public Library of US Diplomacy, "Uganda/DRC/Sudan: Operation Lightening Thunder Rolling Along," 09KAMPLA279_a March 17, 2009, https://wikileaks.org/.
72. Ronald R. Atkinson, "From Uganda to the Congo and Beyond: Pursuing the Lord's Resistance Army," International Peace Institute, December 2009, 13, https://www.ipinst.org/wp-content/uploads/publications/e_pub_uganda_to_congo.pdf.
73. Wikileaks Public Library of US Diplomacy, "Uganda/DRC/Sudan: Operation Lightening Thunder."
74. "Army Captures Rebel Commander," *New Vision*, March 3, 2009, LexisNexis.
75. Atkinson, "From Uganda to the Congo and Beyond," 15.
76. "Museveni Asks US to Back Plan B Against LRA," *Monitor*, October 3, 2006, LexisNexis.
77. Wikileaks Public Library of US Diplomacy, "US Embassy Addis Ababa to Central Intelligence Agency, A/S Frazer Meeting with Ugandan President Museveni Focuses on Somalia, Darfur, and Chad," 07ADDISABABA312, February 1, 2007, https://wikileaks.org/.
78. "Ambassador Power Issues Remarks at a UN Security Council Briefing on Peacebuilding in Africa," *Targeted News Service*, July 28, 2016, LexisNexis.
79. Wikileaks Public Library of US Diplomacy, "US Embassy Addis Ababa to Central Intelligence Agency."

80. Author interviews, Ugandan opposition cadres 1 and 2, March 2022, Kampala, Uganda.
81. "Democratic Party Blames Corruption on Museveni," *Independent*, November 8, 2012, LexisNexis; Bernard Tabaire, "Waiting to Hear More Opposition Thinking on Uganda in the Region," *Daily Monitor*, May 11, 2014, LexisNexis; author interview, veteran Ugandan opposition leader 1, March 2022, Kampala, Uganda.
82. "We Are Not UN Employees, Museveni Tells AMISOM," *Daily Monitor*, September 23, 2017, LexisNexis.
83. "Uganda," *Congressional Research Service—In Focus*, August 6, 2019, https://www.congress.gov/crs-products.
84. US Military Aid to Uganda—Trends, Foreign Assistance Tracker, https://www.foreignassistance.gov/aid-trends.
85. "Uganda; Make Defence Spending Public-US Envoy," *Monitor*, March 22, 2005, LexisNexis; "Uganda, Neither Kony nor Museveni Wants War to End," *East African*, February 7, 2005, LexisNexis; "Uganda; Museveni on the Ropes, Instability Ahead," *New Times*, January 12, 2006, LexisNexis.
86. Charles Onyango-Obbo, "Somalia: It's Not Good for the Economy," *Nation Media Group*, March 2, 2007, LexisNexis.
87. "US Resumes Modest Military Aid to Uganda," *East African*, November 3, 2003, LexisNexis.
88. "Uganda; America Doubts Military Option to End LRA Rebellion," *Monitor*, April 27, 2005, LexisNexis.
89. William Brown and Sophie Harman, *African Agency in International Politics* (London: Routledge, 2013), 108.
90. Felix Osike, "Uganda Talks to Islamic Courts Militia," *New Vision*, February 28, 2007, LexisNexis.
91. Wikileaks Public Library of US Diplomacy, "US Embassy Kampala to Secretary of State, Uganda Action Items on Somalia from EUCOM Deputy Commander General Ward's Visit," 07KAMPALA342, February 28, 2007, https://wikileaks.org/.
92. Wikileaks Public Library of US Diplomacy, "US Embassy Kampala to Secretary of State, Uganda Action Items on Somalia."
93. "US Official Pledges Immediate Help for Somalia Stabilization; State's Frazer Says US Is Prepared to Help Ugandan Troops Deploy," *State Department Documents and Publications*, February 7, 2007, LexisNexis.
94. "US Assistance to the African Union—Fact Sheet," US Department of State, http://photos.state.gov/libraries/usau/231771/PDFs/us_assistance_to_the_au_fact_sheet.pdf.
95. Nina M. Serafino, "The Global Peace Operations Initiative: Background and Issues for Congress," *Congressional Research Service*, June 11, 2009, https://www.congress.gov/crs-products.
96. "Foreign Military Training and DoD Engagement Activities of Interest," Bureau of Political-Military Affairs, US Department of State, https://www.state.gov/reports/foreign-military-training-and-dod-engagement-activities-of-interest-2020-2021/.

97. Felix Osike, "Allowances Due to Ugandan Peacekeepers in Somalia Delayed," *New Vision*, May 8, 2007, LexisNexis.
98. Paul D. Williams, "Paying for AMISOM: Are Politics and Bureaucracy Undermining the AU's Largest Peace Operation?," International Peace Institute Global Observatory, January 11, 2017, https://theglobalobservatory.org/2017/01/amisom-african-union-peacekeeping-financing/.
99. Risdel Kasasira, "Who Is Who? List of UPDF Brass and What They Do," *Daily Monitor*, November 27, 2014, LexisNexis.
100. "UPDF Suspends 15 for Selling AMSIOM Slots," *Observer (Kampala)*, November 4, 2014, LexisNexis.
101. "General Aronda Explains UPDF Promotions, Reshuffle," *New Vision*, October 30, 2005, LexisNexis.
102. Epstein, "Murder in Uganda."
103. Julia Gallagher, *Images of Africa: Creation, Negotiation, and Subversion* (Manchester: Manchester University Press, 2015), 74.
104. "Foreign Military Training and DoD Engagement Activities of Interest," https://www.state.gov/reports/foreign-military-training-and-dod-engagement-activities-of-interest-2020-2021/ and https://2009-2017.state.gov/t/pm/rls/rpt/fmtrpt/index.htm.
105. "Kitgum's Ten Days of Natural Fire," *New Vision*, October 30, 2009, LexisNexis; Rich Bartell, "Ugandans Train for Future AMISOM Mission," US Army Public Affairs, October 24, 2013, LexisNexis.
106. Ty McCormick, "Is the US Military Propping Up Uganda's Elected Autocrat?," *Foreign Policy*, February 18, 2016, LexisNexis.
107. "US Queries Gaps in Military Budget," *Monitor*, April 24, 2004, LexisNexis.
108. Wikileaks Public Library of US Diplomacy, "US Embassy Kampala to Department of Defense, Uganda May Be Open to MANPADS Strategy," 07KAMPALA1848, December 6, 2007, https://wikileaks.org/.
109. "Arms Race Could Turn Region Into Tinderbox," *Daily Monitor*, May 20, 2019, LexisNexis.
110. "Will America Fund South Sudan War?," *Independent (Kampala)*, January 18, 2014, LexisNexis.
111. "Mbabazi Responds to Opposition M23 Concerns," *New Vision*, April 12, 2013, LexisNexis.
112. Mary Beth Sheridan, "US Has Sent 40 Tons of Munitions to Aid the Somali Government," *Washington Post*, June 27, 2009, Proquest.
113. "UPDF Stops Training AMISOM Somalians," *Indian Ocean Newsletter*, October 23, 2015.
114. Wikileaks Public Library of US Diplomacy, "US Embassy Kampala to Central Intelligence Agency, Uganda: Assistant Secretary Carson's Meeting with President Museveni," 09KAMPALA1276, November 4, 2009, https://wikileaks.org/.
115. "First Peacekeepers Are in Somalia," *British Broadcasting Company*, March 1, 2007, http://news.bbc.co.uk/2/hi/africa/6406877.stm; "Uganda: Government Gunmen

Storm High Court Again," *Human Rights Watch*, March 5, 2007, https://www.hrw.org/news/2007/03/05/uganda-government-gunmen-storm-high-court-again.

116. "Profile of Western Uganda Rebel Groups," *BBC Monitoring Africa*, June 21, 2007, LexisNexis.

117. "Ugandan Judiciary on Strike After Police Storm Courthouse," *Agence France Presse*, March 5, 2007, LexisNexis.

118. "Court Siege, Donors Look the Other Way," *Monitor*, March 14, 2007, LexisNexis.

119. Solomon Muyita, "US Envoy Says Uganda 'Eaten Up By High Levels of Corruption,'" *Daily Monitor*, April 9, 2006, LexisNexis.

120. Wikileaks Public Library of US Diplomacy, "US Embassy Kampala to Secretary of State, Scenesetter for AND NSC Deputy Advisor David McCormick and Assistant Secretary of State Dina Powell," 07KAMPALA345, March 1, 2007, https://wikileaks.org/.

121. "Why Museveni Letter on Corruption Can't Be Taken Seriously," *Monitor*, May 26, 2008, LexisNexis; "Media Crackdown: Bye-Bye to Democracy," *Monitor*, May 27, 2008, LexisNexis; "Who Cares If Barack Obama Wins or Loses on Tuesday," *Monitor*, November 1, 2008, LexisNexis.

122. Wikileaks Public Library of US Diplomacy, "US Embassy Kampala to Secretary of State, Uganda: If a Tree Falls in Mabira Forest, Who Will Hear It?," 07KAMPALA744, May 2, 2007, https://wikileaks.org/.

123. "US Envoy Defends Bush's Behind the Scenes Diplomacy," *New Vision*, January 14, 2009, LexisNexis.

124. "Uganda Appoints New Commander for its Forces in Somalia," *BBC Monitoring Africa*, March 23, 2009, LexisNexis.

125. John Njoroge, "US Hopes 2011 Elections Will Be Better than Before," *Independent*, February 4, 2010, LexisNexis.

126. Tabu Butagira, "Government Tells US Envoy to Steer Clear of Local Politics," *Monitor*, February 5, 2010, LexisNexis.

127. "Obama Condemns Uganda Anti-Gay Bill as 'Odious,'" *Mail & Guardian*, February 5, 2010, LexisNexis.

128. Wikileaks Public Library of US Diplomacy, "US Embassy Addis Ababa to Secretary of State, AU Summit: Museveni's Musings on African Conflicts and Family Values," 10ADDISABABA280, February 11, 2010, https://wikileaks.org/.

129. "Hillary Clinton's Mission Is an Intricate Chore," *Monitor*, February 11, 2010, LexisNexis; "What Next After Clinton's Damning Report," *Independent*, May 10, 2010, LexisNexis.

130. "Donors Warn EC Over Vote Rigging," *Monitor*, March 12, 2010, LexisNexis.

131. Wikileaks Public Library of US Diplomacy, "US Embassy Kampala to Central Intelligence Agency, Uganda: Assistant Secretary Carson's Meeting with President Museveni," 09KAMPALA1276, November 4, 2009, https://wikileaks.org/; Wikileaks Public Library of US Diplomacy, "US Embassy Kampala to Secretary of State, the International Component of President Museveni's Inbox," 07KAMPALA1595, October 16, 2010, https://wikileaks.org/.

132. Wikileaks Public Library of US Diplomacy, "US Embassy Kampala to Central Intelligence Agency, Scenesetter for Assistant Secretary Carson," 09KAMPALA1197, October 19, 2009, https://wikileaks.org/.
133. "Skepticism Over Uganda's Vow to Crush Somali Insurgents," *Deutsche Presse-Agentur*, July 16, 2010, LexisNexis.
134. Tabu Butagira, "Clinton's New Report Praises and Attacks Electoral Commission," *Monitor*, September 24, 2010, LexisNexis.
135. "FBI Reportedly Supervising Investigations to Uganda Bomb Attack," *BBC Monitoring Africa*, October 4, 2010, LexisNexis.
136. "Assistant Secretary of State for Public Affairs Phillip PJ Crowley Holds State Department Regular News Briefing," *Congressional Quarterly—Roll Call*, February 22, 2011, LexisNexis.
137. Helen Epstein, "What the US Is Ignoring in Uganda," *New York Review of Books*, July 19, 2011.
138. Epstein, "What the US Is Ignoring in Uganda."
139. Adbi Shiekh, "Ethiopian Troops Move Into Somalia, Kenya Began Attack Five Weeks Ago on Islamists It Blames for Kidnappings," *Ottawa Citizen*, November 20, 2011, LexisNexis.
140. "Kenya; UN Approves Nation's Bid to Join African Force in Somalia," *Nation*, January 12, 2012, LexisNexis.
141. Paul D. Williams, "AMISOM in Transition: The Future of the African Union Mission in Somalia," *Rift Valley Institute Briefing Paper*, February 13, 2013.
142. "Clinton Threatens Sanctions, Increased Presence in Somalia," *Antiwar.com News Articles*, February 24, 2012, LexisNexis.
143. Horace Campbell, "Kenya Terror Attack: Putting the Westgate Siege in Context," *Pambazuka News*, September 26, 2013, https://allafrica.com/stories/201309271530.html; Gorm Rye Olsen, "The October 2011 Kenyan Invasion of Somalia: Fighting Al-Shabaab or Defending Institutional Interests?," *Journal of Contemporary African Studies* 36, no. 1 (2018): 48.
144. John Njoroge, "US Warns E.A. African Armies Against Threatening Democracy," *Daily Monitor*, January 29, 2013, LexisNexis.
145. Stephen Kafeero, "If Uganda Doesn't Want Our Aid, We'll Give It to Another Country—US Envoy," *Daily Monitor*, March 16, 2014, LexisNexis.
146. US Military Aid to Uganda—Trends, Foreign Assistance Tracker, https://www.foreignassistance.gov/aid-trends.
147. Barbara Among, "Government to US: We Will Not Leave S. Sudan," *Daily Monitor*, February 10, 2014, LexisNexis.
148. "US Reiterates Call for Uganda to Withdraw Troops from South Sudan," *BBC Monitoring Africa*, February 13, 2014, LexisNexis.
149. Peter Baker and Jacey Fortin, "Obama Urges South Sudan Truce; Regional Leaders Meet with President to Discuss How to Stop Civil War," *International New York Times*, July 28, 2015, LexisNexis; "Museveni Plays Both Sides of the Street," *Indian Ocean Newsletter*, September 11, 2015.

150. Zach Vertin, *A Rope from The Sky: The Making and Unmaking of the World's Newest State* (New York: Pegasus Books, 2019), 356.
151. "Nobody Can Order Me on Sudan—Museveni," *Daily Monitor*, May 8, 2014, LexisNexis.
152. Julius Barigaba, "Behind Museveni's Defiance of US, Igad Orders," *East African*, February 15, 2014, LexisNexis.
153. Colum Lynch, "Inside the White House Fight Over the Slaughter in South Sudan," *Foreign Policy*, January 26, 2015, LexisNexis.
154. Duop Chak Wuol, "How Uganda Outsmarts the United States in South Sudan," *Sudan Tribune*, December 31, 2016, LexisNexis.
155. Darlene Superville, "Obama: Anti-Gay Bill a Step Back for Ugandans," *Associated Press*, February 16, 2014, LexisNexis.
156. Kafeero, "If Uganda Doesn't Want Our Aid."
157. Liesl Louw-Vaudran, "American Aid as a Political Tool—If Uganda, Why Not Egypt?" *Defence Web*, June 26, 2014, LexisNexis.
158. Jason Patinkin, "US Sanctions Tread Lightly on Uganda's 'Odious' Anti-Gay Law," *Christian Science Monitor*, July 1, 2014, LexisNexis.
159. "Background Gaggle Aboard Air Force One en Route to Ethiopia," *White House Documents and Publications*, July 26, 2015, LexisNexis.
160. Capt. Christine Guthrie, "Uganda Troops Support US Airlift Missions," *US Air Forces in Europe and US Air Forces Africa Public Affairs*, January 22, 2014.
161. "Obama to Send Up to 200 US Troops to Respond to South Sudan," *Channel NewsAsia*, July 15, 2006, LexisNexis .
162. Wafula Wamunyinyi, "The World Must Assist AMISOM to Complete the Task of Bringing Peace to Nation," *East African*, December 2011, LexisNexis.
163. "Somalia Country Profile," British Broadcasting Corporation, February 2, 2016, http://www.bbc.com/news/world-africa-14094503.
164. Charles Onyango-Obbo, "Big Rush to Cash in on Somalia, Protect Uganda, Save Sudan," *East African*, December 2011, LexisNexis; "AMISOM Force Commander: 'Al Shabab Will Be Out in 2012,'" *Shabelle Media Network*, January 9, 2012, LexisNexis.
165. "Q and A with Nicholas Kay," *East African*, January 13, 2015, LexisNexis.
166. "Death in the Morning: Why AMISOM Soldiers Had Little Fighting Chance in Janaale," *East African*, September 26, 2016, theeastafrican.co.ke/tea.
167. Paul D. Williams, "Why Kenya's Defence Force Fell at the Battle of El Adde," *The Conversation—Africa*, October 29, 2020, https://theconversation.com/why-kenyas-defence-forces-fell-at-the-battle-of-el-adde-149001.
168. Chris Suckling, "Kenyan Military Likely to Remain in Somalia Despite Calls for AMISOM reforms, Following Mass Casualty Attacks by Al-Shabaab," *IHS Global Insight*, February 12, 2016.
169. Paul D. Williams, "AMISOM Under Review," *RUSI Journal* 161, no. 1 (2016): 47.
170. Patricia Daley and Rowan Popplewell, "The Appeal of Third Termism and Militarism in Burundi," *Review of African Political Economy* 43, no. 150 (2016): 648.

171. Edmund Blair, "EU Takes Aim Where It Hurts Burundi: Peacekeeper Funding," *Reuters*, March 28, 2016, https://www.reuters.com/article/world/exclusive-eu-takes-aim-where-it-hurts-burundi-peacekeeper-funding-idUSKCN0WV0BD/.
172. "US Suspends Burundi Peacekeeping Training Over Protests," *Reuters*, May 22, 2015, https://www.reuters.com/article/us-burundi-unrest-usa-training/u-s-suspends-burundi-peacekeeping-training-over-protests-idUSKBN0O72I820150522/.
173. "On the Results of Uganda's Presidential Elections," US Embassy in Uganda, press statement, February 20, 2016, LexisNexis.
174. "Kerry in Call to Uganda's Museveni Expresses Election Concerns," *Reuters*, February 19, 2016, https://www.reuters.com/article/world/kerry-in-call-to-ugandas-museveni-expresses-election-concerns-idUSKCN0VT09U/.
175. "Ugandan Opposition Leaders Arrested," *Times* (London), July 10, 2015, LexisNexis.
176. Ole Tangen Jr., "Arrest of Key Opposition Candidate Capped Off Ugandan Polls," *Deutsche Welle*, February 18, 2016, LexisNexis.
177. "Museveni Talks to Monitor After Kerry Call on Polls," *Daily Monitor*, February 20, 2016, LexisNexis.
178. "US Accuses Uganda of Rights Violations After Presidential Vote," *Reuters*, March 12, 2016, https://www.reuters.com/article/world/u-s-accuses-uganda-of-rights-violations-after-presidential-vote-idUSKCN0WE0D9/.
179. "Ugandan President Holds Talks with US Envoy," *BBC Monitoring Africa—Political*, May 6, 2016, LexisNexis.
180. Mohammed Ibrahim, "Somalia Raid Aided by US Kills Fighters from Shabab," *New York Times*, March 10, 2016, LexisNexis.
181. Author interview, former senior US diplomat to Uganda, April 14, 2022.
182. "AFRICOM Campaign Plan Targets Terror Groups," *State News Service*, January 5, 2016, LexisNexis.
183. "General Rodriguez Testifies at Hearing on U.S. Africa Command 2016 Posture," *Targeted News Service*, March 8, 2016, LexisNexis.
184. "Ugandan Army to End Mission in Somalia, CAR-Report," *BBC Monitoring Africa—Political*, May 6, 2016, LexisNexis.
185. Eriasa Mukiibi Sserunjogi, "Stop Political Arrests or Lose US Trade—Obama," *Daily Monitor*, July 24, 2016, LexisNexis.
186. Gaaki Kigambo, "US Reportedly in Dilemma Over What Action to Take Against Ugandan President," *East African*, May 23, 2016, LexisNexis.
187. "Sen. John McCain Holds a Hearing to Consider the Nominations of Thomas D. Waldhauser and Joseph Lengyel," *CQ Transcriptions*, June 21, 2016, LexisNexis.
188. Mark Mazzetti, Jeffrey Gettleman, and Eric Schmitt, "In Somalia, US Escalates a Shadow War," *New York Times*, October 16, 2016, LexisNexis.
189. Nick Turse, "The US Military and the Unraveling of Africa," *Antiwar.com Original Articles*, June 19, 2013, LexisNexis; "American Firms Keen to Invest in Kenya as Ties with US Improve," *Financial Services Monitor Worldwide*, October 8, 2016, LexisNexis.

190. "Full Committee Hearing on the United States Central Command, United States Africa Command, and the United States Special Operations Command," *Federal News Service*, March 8, 2016, LexisNexis.
191. "Security Cooperation—Delivering Bell Huey II Helicopters," *Targeted News Service*, December 2, 2016, LexisNexis; "Uganda Receives 5 Helicopters for Enhanced War Against Al-Shabaab," *Defence Monitor Worldwide*, July 10, 2017, LexisNexis.
192. "Uganda Provides Support to Mission in Somalia," *US Fed News*, April 26, 2016, LexisNexis.
193. "We Should Never Have Gone to Somalia," *Observer (Kampala)*, July 20, 2016, LexisNexis.
194. "UN Approves $600mn Budget Cut to Peacekeeping," *Digital Journal*, June 30, 2017, LexisNexis.
195. "Security Fears in EA as AMISOM Starts Withdrawing from Somalia," *East African*, December 23, 2017, LexisNexis.
196. J. Weston Phippen, "The First US Casualty in Somalia Since 'Black Hawk Down,'" *Atlantic Online*, May 5, 2017, LexisNexis.
197. Tabu Butagira and Risdel Kasasira, "Museveni Ready to Send 5,000 Troops to Somalia," *Daily Monitor*, October 26, 2017, LexisNexis.
198. "US Army Africa Commander Meets with Uganda Chief of Defense," *DefenceWeb*, August 8, 2017, LexisNexis.
199. Aggrey Mutambo, "Somalia Remembers Its '9/11' Amid Renewed Terror Attacks, *Daily Nation (Kenya)*, October 15, 2021, LexisNexis.
200. "How Museveni Is Using AMISOM to Pursue His Own Agenda," *Africa Intelligence—Indian Ocean Newsletter*, December 1, 2007.
201. "EACJ to Rule in Suit Against Museveni's Bid to Extend Leadership," *Daily Monitor*, February 2, 2020, LexisNexis.
202. Tabu Butagira, "US Condemns Raids, Arrests Ahead of Tabling of Age Limit Motion," *Daily Monitor*, September 21, 2017, LexisNexis.
203. Helen Epstein, "The US Turns a Blind Eye to Uganda's Assault on Democracy," *Nation Blogs*, July 20, 2018, LexisNexis.
204. "Don't Intimidate Age Limit Opponents—US," *Daily Monitor*, December 10, 2017, LexisNexis.
205. Author interview, senior Ugandan diplomat 1, March 2022, Kampala, Uganda.
206. "We Are Not UN Employees, Museveni Tells AMISOM," *Daily Monitor*, September 23, 2017, LexisNexis.
207. Eric Schmitt and Charlie Savage, "Trump Administration Steps Up Air War in Somalia," *New York Times*, March 10, 2019, LexisNexis; "US Military Carries Out a Fresh Airstrike in Southern Somalia," *Shabelle Media Network*, April 11, 2019, LexisNexis.
208. "President Sends Letter to Congress on Military Counterterrorism Operations," *Targeted News Service*, June 6, 2017, LexisNexis.
209. Daniel Flatley, "Africa Terror Fight to Suffer as China, Russia Take US Focus," *Bloomberg*, July 10, 2018, Bloomberg.com.
210. Faith Karimi and Briana Duggan, "Uganda's President Says He Loves Donald Trump Because He's Frank About Africa," *CNN Wire*, January 24, 2018, LexisNexis.

211. "Treasonable for Kayihura to Own Assets in USA-Museveni," *Observer*, September 23, 2019, LexisNexis.
212. US Military Aid to Uganda—Trends, *Foreign Assistance Tracker*, https://www.foreignassistance.gov/aid-trends.
213. Alex Horton, "Trump Orders Departure of Majority of 700 US Troops in Somalia," *Washington Post*, December 4, 2020, Proquest.
214. "How US Steers Uganda's AMISOM Activities," *Africa Intelligence*, August 31, 2020.
215. Samuel Okiror and Jason Burke, "Bobi Wine Charged with COVID Rule Breach After Uganda Protests," *Guardian (London)*, November 20, 2020, LexisNexis; Oryem Nyeko, "One Year Later, No Justice for Victims of Uganda's Lethal Clampdown," *Human Rights Watch—Dispatches*, November 18, 2021, https://www.hrw.org/news/2021/11/18/one-year-later-no-justice-victims-ugandas-lethal-clampdown.
216. "Bobi Wine's Injuries 'Fake News'—Museveni," *Observer*, August 20, 2018, LexisNexis.
217. "US Warns of Consequences for Hindering Uganda Election," *Agence France Presse*, December 10, 2020, LexisNexis.
218. "US Withdraws Observer Mission in Uganda Polls," *BBC Monitoring Africa-Political*, January 13, 2021, LexisNexis.
219. "Opondo Slams US Envoy Over Attempted Visit to Bobi Wine," *Daily Monitor*, January 19, 2021, LexisNexis.
220. Ian Katusiime, "Museveni's American Dilemma," *Independent (Kampala)*, March 8, 2021, LexisNexis.
221. Mohamed Olad Hassan, "Ugandan Airstrike in Somalia Kills 189 Al-Shabab Fighters," *Voice of America News*, January 23, 2021, https://www.voanews.com/a/africa_ugandan-airstrikes-somalia-kill-189-al-shabab-fighters/6201121.html.
222. Rashid Abdi, "Ugandan Claims Its AMISOM Contingent Killed 189 Al-Shabaab Is False," Twitter.com, January 26, 2021, https://mobile.twitter.com/adoniaayebare/status/1354132177324273665.
223. "Uganda Denies Claim UPDF Killed 189 Militants in Somalia Attack," *Garowe Online*, January 1, 2021, https://www.garoweonline.com/en/world/africa/uganda-denies-claims-updf-killed-189-al-shabaab-militants-in-somalia.
224. "Bullish in Public, Museveni Charms Diplomats in Private," *East African*, February 1, 2021, LexisNexis.
225. "US Sanctions CMI Boss Abel Kandiho," *Daily Monitor*, December 7, 2021, LexisNexis.
226. Author interview, senior Ugandan military official 1, Kampala, Uganda, March 2022.
227. "House Appropriations Subcommittee Issues Statement from US Africa Command," *Targeted News Service*, April 13, 2022, LexisNexis.
228. "State Department Terrorist Designation of ISIS Affiliates and Leaders in the Democratic Republic of the Congo and Mozambique," *US Embassy in Mozambique*, March 11, 2021, https://mz.usembassy.gov/state-department-terrorist-designations-of-isis-affiliates-and-leaders-in-the-democratic-republic-of-the-congo-and-mozambique/.
229. Kristof Titeca and Daniel Fahey, "The Many Faces of a Rebel Group: The Allied Democratic Forces in the Democratic Republic of Congo," *International Affairs* 92, no. 5

(2016): 1194; Helen C. Epstein, "The Bewildering Search for the Islamic State in Congo," *Nation*, April 20, 2021, LexisNexis.

230. Lindsay Scorgie-Porter, "Militant Islamists or Borderland Dissidents? An Exploration Into the Allied Democratic Forces' Recruitment Practices and Constitution," *Journal of Modern African Studies* 53, no. 1 (2015): 9.
231. Tabu Butagira, "Inside ADF Terror Threat Over Uganda, Neighbors," *Daily Monitor*, October 26, 2021, LexisNexis.
232. "Texas Investment Firm Bridgeway Plays Humanitarian Privateer for the State Department in DRC," *Africa Intelligence*, July 5, 2021.
233. "US Army Passes Baton to Private Sector in Somalia," *Africa Intelligence*, December 10, 2020.
234. "Tracing Uganda's Oil Journey," *Daily Monitor*, June 16, 2022, LexisNexis.
235. Edward Wong, "Competing Against Chinese Loans, US Companies Face Long Odds in Africa," *New York Times*, January 13, 2019, LexisNexis.
236. Rodney Muhumuza, "US: Africa Can Buy Russian Grain But Risks Actions on Oil," *Associated Press*, August 4, 2022, LexisNexis.
237. "Remarks by Ambassador Thomas-Greenfield at a Press Conference Announcing $20M in Development Assistance in Uganda Amid a Global Food Crisis," *Thai News Service*, August 8, 2022, LexisNexis.
238. Ruth Maclean, "As Blinken Visits Africa, the Revival of Cold War–Style Politics Is in Full Swing," *New York Times*, August 7, 2022, LexisNexis.
239. "Uganda: Lavrov Visit to Museveni Creates Headache for Washington," *Africa Report*, July 29, 2022, LexisNexis.
240. Maclean, "As Blinken Visits Africa."
241. Thandie Chadzandiyani, "Yoweri Museveni's Son Gen. Muhoozi Kainerugaba Backs Russia on Ukraine Invasion," *Maravi Post*, March 1, 2022, LexisNexis.

CONCLUSION

1. US Central Intelligence Agency, Senior Interagency Group No. 27, *The Base Negotiations Study*, January 14, 1983, National Archive and Records Agency, College Park, MD.
2. UC CIA, *The Base Negotiations Study.*
3. Moses K. Tesi, "Economic Relations and Political Behavior: A Study of the Political Economy of Cameroon's Relations with France Since 1960" (PhD diss., Vanderbilt University, 1985), 57.
4. Princeton N. Lyman and J. Stephen Morrison, "The Terrorist Threat in Africa," *Foreign Affairs* 83, no. 1 (February 2004), 85, https://doi.org/10.2307/20033830; Phillippa Atkinson, "Liberal Interventionism in Liberia: Towards a Tentatively Just Approach?," *Conflict, Security, and Development* 8, no. 1 (2008): 26, https://doi.org/10.1080/14678800801977062.
5. Mike Westphal, Secretary of Defense for African American Affairs, "Mike Westphal Holds Defense Department Briefing," *FDCH Political Transcripts*, April 2, 2002, Lexis/Nexis.

6. "Directing the President, Pursuant to Section 5(C) of the War Powers Resolution, to Remove All United States Armed Forces, Other than United States Armed Forces Assigned to Protect the United States Embassy, from Somalia . . .; Congressional Record, vol. 169, no. 71 (House—April 27, 2023)," *Impact News Service*," May 1, 2023.
7. "UPDF Soldiers Abroad Surge Beyond 12,000," *Daily Monitor*, April 11, 2023, Lexis/Nexis.
8. "U.S. Rep. Kendrick B. Meek Leads Congressional Delegation to Africa Fact Finding Mission Examined U.S. Political, Security and Economic Commitment to Africa and Ongoing Genocide in Darfur," *States News Service*, December 7, 2007, Lexis/Nexis.
9. Jennifer Brass, "Djibouti's Unusual Resource Curse," *Journal of Modern African Studies* 46, no. 4 (2008): 526, 531; "President Obama Announces Presidential Delegation to the Republic of Niger to Attend the Inauguration of His Excellency Mahamadou Issoufou, President of the Republic of Niger," White House Office of the Press Secretary, March 31, 2016; "Cameroon's Safe Boats Patrol Vessels End Up in Djibouti," *Africa Intelligence*, January 1, 2020, https://www.africaintelligence.com/eastern-and-southern-africa_politics/2020/01/17/cameroon-s-safe-boats-patrol-vessels-end-up-in-djibouti,108389951-art; "Niger: Post-election Period Marred by Violence, Mass Arrests, and Internet Disruption," Amnesty International, March 4, 2021, https://www.amnesty.org/en/latest/news/2021/03/niger-post-election-period-marred-by-violence/.
10. Michael A. Allen, Michael E. Flynn, and Carla Martinez Machain, "US Global Military Deployments, 1950–2020," *Conflict Management and Peace Science* 39, no. 3 (2022): 361–62.
11. Oliver Kearns, "Beyond Enclosure: Military Bases and the Spatial Dynamics of Secrecy," *Geoforum* 127 (December 2021): 17.
12. "Exclusive: Inside the Secret World of US Commandos in Africa," Pulitzer Center, accessed August 22, 2022, https://pulitzercenter.org/stories/exclusive-inside-secret-world-us-commandos-africa.
13. Eren Ersozoglu, "Camp Lemonnier: Line in the Sand," *Grey Dynamics* (blog), January 10, 2022, https://greydynamics.com/africom-part-ii-djibouti-camp-lemonnier-line-in-the-sand/.
14. Neta C. Crawford, "The US Budgetary Costs of the Post 9–11 Wars," Report: Costs of War Research Series, Watson Institute, Brown University, September 1, 2021.
15. "African Militant Islamist Groups Set Record for Violent Activity," Africa Center for Strategic Studies, July 2020; "East Africa and North and West Africa Counterterrorism Operations," Lead Inspector General Report to the United States Congress, US Department of Defense, February 11, 2020.
16. "Audit of the DoD's Management of Global Train and Equip Program Resources Provided to U.S. Africa Command Partner Nations," Inspector General, US Department of Defense, July 21, 2021.
17. "Evaluation of the US Africa Command's Response to the Coronavirus Disease-2019," Inspector General, US Department of Defense, September 30, 2020 (accessed through FOIA).

18. "US Central Command and US Africa Command's Oversight of Counternarcotic Activities," Inspector General, US Department of Defense, December 26, 2017.
19. "Audit of the Department of State Bureau of African Affairs Monitoring and Coordination of the Trans-Sahara Counterterrorism Partnership Program," Office of the Inspector General, United States State Department, September 2020.
20. Rich Bartell, "Professional Partnership Focus of Medical Exercise in Congo," US Army Africa Public Affairs, July 18, 2013, https://www.army.mil/article/107636/professional_partnership_focus_of_medical_exercise_in_congo; "Rekindling the Flame," *African Defense Forum Magazine*, US Africa Command, September 30, 2014, https://adf-magazine.com/2014/09/rekindling-the-flame/; John Vandiver, "Trainees Try to Be a Force That Can Overcome Child-Abducting Rebels—and Their Own Horrific Past," *Stars and Stripes*, May 23, 2011, https://www.stripes.com/trainees-try-to-be-a-force-that-can-overcome-child-abducting-rebels-and-their-own-horrific-past-1.144366; Craig Whitlock, "US-Trained Congolese Troops Committed Rapes and Other Atrocities, U.N. Says," *Washington Post*, May 13, 2013, https://www.washingtonpost.com/world/national-security/us-trained-congolese-troops-committed-rapes-and-other-atrocities-un-says/2013/05/13/9781dd88-bbfe-11e2-a31d-a41b2414d001_story.html.
21. "UN Accuses Multiple Countries of Quietly Sending Arms to DR Congo," *Defense Post*, June 19, 2020, https://www.thedefensepost.com/2020/06/19/un-arms-dr-congo/.
22. "DR Congo Accepts US Military Help Against ADF Militia," *Voice of America*, August 15, 2021.
23. Rukmini Callimachi, "ISIS, After Laying Groundwork, Gains Toehold in Congo," *New York Times*, April 20, 2019.
24. Author interviews, senior official 1, African Union Commision Peace and Security Department, July 10, 2018, and senior official 2, African Union Commision Peace and Security Department, July 11, 2018.
25. Senate Committee on Foreign Relations, "Senate Foreign Relations Committee Holds Hearing on US Security Cooperation and Assistance," March 10, 2022, Congressional.ProQuest.
26. "Pompeo Takes Dig at China on Africa Trip to 'Counter Chinese Influence,'" *Mercury*, February 20, 2020, Lexis/Nexis; House Committee on Foreign Affairs, "House Foreign Affairs Subcommittee on Africa, Global Health, Global Human Rights and International Organizations Holds Hearing on Sub-Saharan Africa Democratic Backsliding," September 30, 2020, Congressional.ProQuest; House Committee on Armed Services, "House Armed Services Committee Holds Hearing on US Security Challenges and Military Activities in the Greater Middle East and Africa," March 17, 2022, Congressional.ProQuest.

INDEX

GPSR Authorized Representative: Easy Access System Europe, Mustamäe tee 50, 10621 Tallinn, Estonia, gpsr.requests@easproject.com

www.ingramcontent.com/pod-product-compliance
Lightning Source LLC
Chambersburg PA
CBHW032119020426
42334CB00016B/1006

* 9 7 8 0 2 3 1 2 0 2 6 9 5 *